A New Steinbeck Bibliography 1929-1971

by

Tetsumaro Hayashi

Ball State University

The Scarecrow Press, Inc.
Metuchen, N.J.   1973

Library of Congress Cataloging in Publication Data

Hayashi, Tetsumaro.
 A new Steinbeck bibliography (1929-1971).

 (Author bibliographies series, no. 1)
 Based on the author's John Steinbeck: a concise
bibliography, 1930-65.
 1. Steinbeck, John, 1902-1968--Bibliography.
I. Hayashi, Tetsumaro. John Steinbeck: a concise
bibliography, 1930-65. II. Title.
Z8839.4.H314   016.813'5'2   73-9982
ISBN 0-8108-0647-9

DEDICATED TO
PETER LISCA AND JOSEPH FONTENROSE
WHO HAVE TAUGHT ME HOW TO APPRECIATE
STEINBECK'S LITERATURE

OTHER BOOKS BY TETSUMARO HAYASHI

1. Sketches of American Culture (1960)

*2. John Steinbeck: A Concise Bibliography (1930-65)
     (1967)

*3. Arthur Miller Criticism   (1969)

*4. A Looking Glasse for London and England, An
     Elizabethan Text, ed.   (1970)

*5. Robert Greene Criticism   (1971)

6. Steinbeck: The Man and His Work, ed. with Richard
    Astro (1971)

*7. Shakespeare's Sonnets: A Record of 20th Century
     Criticism (1972)

*8. Steinbeck's Literary Dimension; A Guide to Compara-
     tive Studies, ed.   (1973)

MONOGRAPHS BY TETSUMARO HAYASHI

1. A Textual Study of A Looking Glasse for London and
    England by Thomas Lodge and Robert Greene, ed.
    (1969)

2. John Steinbeck: A Guide to the Doctoral Dissertations,
    ed.   (1971)

3. The Special Steinbeck Collection of the Ball State Uni-
    versity Library, A Bibliographical Handbook, com-
    piled with Donald L. Siefker (1972)

SERIALS EDITED BY TETSUMARO HAYASHI

1. Steinbeck Quarterly (1968-)

2. Steinbeck Monograph Series (1971-)

* (Published by Scarecrow Press)

iv

CONTENTS

APPENDICES

PREFACE

I. PURPOSE

No serious student of Steinbeck can be unaware of one of the frustrating paradoxes of contemporary criticism: while the uninterrupted flow of scholarship attests both to Steinbeck's personal appeal and to his richness, this same criticism serves to set back the student and scholar alike; so vast, so dazzling, and so chaotic does it sometimes seem to be. Consequently, scholars and students have long felt the need for a clear and functional bibliography for Steinbeck's works, a guide which might provide a sense of order and coherence to this fascinating aspect of Steinbeck criticism. For although many of the materials herein have been recorded, indexed, reviewed, and catalogued before, they have never had the shelter of a single roof. My objectives are first to save the serious students of Steinbeck time, energy, and frustration as much as possible, and then to bring about a more up-to-date and more functional guide than my John Steinbeck: A Concise Bibliography (1930-65), published by Scarecrow Press in 1967.

II. SCOPE AND LIMITATIONS

This bibliography, while comprehensive, is not exhaustive; it is more American than international; and it is English-language material oriented. My controlling principle was to include all known primary and secondary sources written in English since 1929, when Steinbeck published his first novel, Cup of Gold. My sincere hope is that I have successfully wedded a close and informed selection with a broad enough scope, so that no significant item has been omitted.

III. SPECIAL FEATURES OF THIS BOOK

Every bibliography is defined by its bibliographical intent and informed by the identity of its author, genre, or

vii

topic. Yet, I feel this book has several distinctive features. First, it attempts to update my own John Steinbeck: A Concise Bibliography (1930-65) by adding all known materials published especially since 1966. Secondly, my work attempts not only to give a clear and comprehensive picture of Steinbeck's works and critical output about them, but also by its arrangement to map out directions that future criticism might take. Thirdly, it attempts to simplify the organization by integrating critical articles, essays included in book-length studies, biographies, and book reviews (all under Part II, G), and thus to avoid unnecessary repetitions found in my 1967 bibliography. Lastly, it provides a handy general index (author, subject, and title) so that the book may be used efficiently and eclectically. It also includes "A List of Annuals, Newspapers, and Periodicals Indexed," which provides the means by which the user of this bibliography can piece together and update his own criticism long after the publication of this book.

IV. RESEARCH METHODS AND ACKNOWLEDGMENTS

To complete my work I have entered the debt of many individuals and institutions. I have had access to some of the finest libraries in the United States either by direct visit, by interlibrary loan, or by correspondence. Especially cooperative and helpful have been the Ball State University Library, the Indiana University Library, the Library of Congress, Princeton University Library, Humanities Research Center of the University of Texas at Austin, Texas, the University of California (Berkeley) Library, the University of Virginia Library, and the Beinecke Rare Book and Manuscript Library at Yale University. The following people were extremely generous in providing me with a number of unknown sources and were helpful in revising some inaccuracies and repetitions found in my 1967 bibliography: Professor Richard Astro of Oregon State University; Mr. Preston Beyer of Columbus, Ohio; Professor Robert DeMott of Ohio University; Professor Warren French, President of the John Steinbeck Society of America; Reloy Garcia of Creighton University; the late Professor Lawrence W. Jones of Canada; Mr. Fred Koloc; Miss Joanne Reed, Miss Joey Nelson, and Miss Monica Hilton, my secretaries; Mrs. Clare P. Romero of California; Mr. Donald L. Siefker and Mr. George H. Spies III, both of Ball State University.

Professor Peter Lisca, the eminent Steinbeck scholar and author of The Wide World of John Steinbeck in 1958, a

book which is still a major influence today, was kind enough
to advise me on the reorganization of this book in its initial
stage. If this new bibliography is substantially improved in
its organization, I owe that to Dr. Lisca's meticulous and
splendid advice.

Mr. Roy S. Simmonds, a leading Steinbeck scholar
and a Steinbeck Quarterly correspondent from England, gen-
erously allowed me to include in this work many of his
British bibliographical findings.

Mr. Dean Keller, Editor of the Serif at Kent State
University, allowed me to reprint, with minor revisions,
my "Steinbeck: Movie Reviews," which I originally published in the Serif, 7 (June 1970), 18-22.

To these scholars, students, librarians, institutions,
and friends, and to many other generous people like them,
I owe my sincere and grateful thanks.

V. CONCLUSION

Should this book achieve its primary objectives--to
save students, scholars, and teachers time, energy and
frustration by helping them find Steinbeck's many works
and the equally prolific literature about them, and to bring
about a more efficient dissemination and use of scholarly
and journalistic materials--then the expenditure of my own
time and effort will have been worthwhile. In the final
analysis, my larger hope was to discover a sense of historical perspective in the work of scholars, who, working
independently in many lands, find a community of purpose
in elucidating Steinbeck's fascinating but controversial works.

In principle I have followed the MLA Style Sheet
(2nd edition), but I have simplified or modified this bibliographical system whenever I thought it beneficial to the user
of this book.

Tetsumaro Hayashi
Muncie, Indiana

September 1, 1972

CHRONOLOGY OF JOHN STEINBECK (1902-1968)

1902   John Ernst Steinbeck born February 27, in Salinas,
        California, the third of four children, the only son.

1919   Graduated from Salinas High School, a good student
        and athlete.

1920   Began intermittent attendance at Stanford University.

1924   First publication, "Fingers of Cloud" and "Adventures
        in Arcademy," two stories in The Stanford Spectator
        (February and June).

1925   Left Stanford permanently without a degree.   Went to
        New York City and worked as a construction laborer
        and reporter for The American (newspaper).

1926   Returned to California.   Humorous verses published
        in Stanford Lit: 1. "If Eddie Guest Had Written the
        Book of Job: Happy Birthday," 2. "If John A.
        Weaver Had Written Keats's Sonnet in the American
        Language: On Looking at a New Book by Harold
        Bell Wright," 3. "Atropos: Study of a Very Femi-
        nine Obituary Editor."

1929   First novel, Cup of Gold, published by Robert M.
        McBride, New York.

1930   Married Carol Henning and began residence in
        Pacific Grove.   First met Edward F. Ricketts,
        marine biologist and Steinbeck's "artistic conscience";
        began permanent association with McIntosh & Otis,
        his literary agent.

1932   Moved to Los Angeles in summer.   The Pastures of
        Heaven published by Brewer, Warren & Putnam,
        New York.

1933   Returned to Pacific Grove early in the year.   To a

God Unknown published by Robert O. Ballou, New York. Two stories, the first two parts of The Red Pony ("The Gift" and "The Great Mountains") published in North American Review in November and December (later included in LV).

1934 Olive Hamilton Steinbeck, John's mother, died in February. "The Murder" selected as an O. Henry Prize Story and published in O. Henry Prize Stories. "The Raid" published in North American Review (both in LV). Ben Abramson brought The Pastures of Heaven and To a God Unknown to the attention of Pascal Covici.

1935 Tortilla Flat published by Covici-Friede, New York, bringing immediate fame and financial success. Won the Commonwealth Club of California Gold Medal. Cited as the "Year's Best by a Californian." Verses "Mammy," "Baubles," "To a Carmel," "The Visitor," "Four Shades of Navy Blue," "The Genius," "Ivanhoe," "Thoughts on Seeing a Stevedore" published in Monterey Beacon. "The White Quail" published in North American Review (later in LV). "The Snake" published in Monterey Beacon (LV).

1936 In Dubious Battle and "Saint Katy the Virgin" published. The California Novel of 1936 Prize for the novel. Moved to Los Gatos, California. His father, John Ernst Steinbeck, died in May. A series of 8 articles, "The Harvest Gypsies," published in San Francisco News in October (5-12). Trip to Mexico.

1937 A novel, Of Mice and Men, published in February, chosen by the Book-of-the-Month Club. Went to New York and Pennsylvania to work on stage version, which was produced at Music Box Theatre in New York in November and won Drama Critics' Circle Silver Plaque for that season. Chosen one of the ten outstanding young men of the year. The Red Pony in three parts, published. First trip to Europe. Later in year, went to California from Oklahoma with migrants. "The Promise" and "The Ears of Johnny Bear" published in Esquire (September 3) (later in LV). "The Chrysanthemums" published in Harper's (October, 1937).

1938 The Long Valley (Viking Press, N.Y.), including

fourth part of The Red Pony, and Their Blood Is
Strong, pamphlet reprint of "The Harvest Gypsies"
plus an epilogue, published. "The Harness" published in Atlantic Monthly (LV).

1939 The Grapes of Wrath published. National Institute
of Arts and Letters membership given.

1940 The Grapes of Wrath won 1) Pulitzer Prize; 2) Amer-
can Booksellers Association Award; and 3) Social
Work Today Award. With Edward F. Ricketts went
to Gulf of California on "Western Flyer" to collect
marine invertebrates, March-April. Filmed The
Forgotten Village in Mexico (the book published in
1941). The Grapes of Wrath (1939) filmed. Of
Mice and Men (1937) filmed.

1941 The Forgotten Village and Sea of Cortez (with Ed
Ricketts) published. "How Edith McGillicuddy Met
Robert Louis Stevenson" published in Harper's Maga-
zine (later in Portable Steinbeck).

1942 Separation and interlocutory divorce from Carol
Henning. The Moon Is Down (novel and play) pub-
lished. Bombs Away written for Army Air Corps.
Tortilla Flat filmed.

1943 Married Gwyndolen Conger (Verdon) in March and
began residence in New York. Spent several months
in European war zone as correspondent for New York
Herald Tribune. The Moon Is Down filmed. The
Moon Is Down (play) published. Lifeboat published.
The Portable Steinbeck with a foreword by Pascal
Covici published.

1944 His first son, Thomas, born. Wrote film story
(unpublished) for Lifeboat, 20th Century Fox.

1945 Cannery Row published. The Red Pony republished
with fourth chapter, "The Leader of the People."
"The Pearl of the World" (same as The Pearl) appeared in Woman's Home Companion in December.
A Medal for Benny (Paramount) filmed. Bought
home in New York.

1946 Won the King Haakon (Norway) Liberty Cross for
The Moon Is Down. A filmscript, "A Medal for
Benny," published. John IV born, his second son.

1947   Trip to Russia with Robert Capa, August-September.
        The Wayward Bus published. The Pearl published
        and filmed. Norwegian Award for The Moon Is
        Down. The Wayward Bus selected as The-Book-of-
        the-Month Club book.

1948   Elected to American Academy of Arts and Letters.
        Divorced from Gwyn Conger. A Russian Journal
        with Robert Capa, an account of his trip to Russia,
        published. Edward F. Ricketts died. A short
        story, "Miracle of Tepayac" published in Collier's.

1949   The Red Pony filmed. A short story, "His Father,"
        published in Reader's Digest.

1950   Burning Bright (play and novel) published. Married
        to Elaine Scott in December. Viva Zapata! (20th
        Century Fox) filmed.

1951   The Log from the Sea of Cortez published, contain-
        ing introduction and narrative from Sea of Cortez and
        biography of Edward F. Ricketts. Burning Bright
        (play) published.

1952   East of Eden published. Sent reports to Collier's
        from Europe (May-September).

1954   Sweet Thursday published.

1955   Pipe Dream (Richard Rodgers and Oscar Hammer-
        stein II musical comedy based on Sweet Thursday)
        produced. Editorials for Saturday Review. East of
        Eden (1952) filmed. Bought house in Sag Harbor,
        Long Island, for summers.

1956   The O. Henry Award for "Affair at 7, Rue de M.----."

1957   The Short Reign of Pippin IV published. The Way-
        ward Bus (1947) filmed. Trip to Europe with sister
        Mary Dekker and wife. Beginning of serious research
        into Malory and the Morte d'Arthur, including first
        trip into "Malory country."

1958   Once There Was a War, a collection of wartime dis-
        patches, published. June in England; more Malory
        explorations; involved with Malory scholarship and
        Dr. Eugene Vinaver.

1959   Eleven months in England, living in Discove Cottage near Bruton, Somerset, working on modernization of Morte.

1960   A three-month trip by truck around U. S. A. Work on Morte put off till "later."

1961   The Winter of Our Discontent, his last novel, published. The Book-of-the-Month Club selected The Winter of Our Discontent. "Flight" (a short story) filmed in San Francisco and independently produced. Traveled 10 months in Europe. In November, had first heart attack.

1962   Travels With Charley published. Received Nobel Prize for Literature in December.

1963   Cultural Exchange trip behind Iron Curtain: Steinbeck and Edward Albee.

1964   An Annual Paperback of the Year Award, a plaque for his Travels with Charley (Bantam), and the John F. Kennedy Memorial Library Trusteeship given. Won a Press Medal of Freedom and a United States (Presidential) Medal of Freedom. Death of Pascal Covici in October.

1965   Travel in London and Paris at first of year. Death of sister, Mary Dekker.

1966   America and Americans published. Articles ("Letters to Alicia") for Newsday (1966-67). Trips to Israel and South Asia writing for Newsday. [The John Steinbeck Society of America was founded in January at Kent State University by Tetsumaro Hayashi and Preston Beyer in honor of Steinbeck.]

1967   Home from Asia, May 1. Autumn: back operation and spinal fusion.

1968   Suffered from coronary disease and died of a heart attack in New York City on December 20. [The Steinbeck Quarterly began to be published in February under T. Hayashi's editorship at Kent State University (originally entitled the Steinbeck Newsletter).]

*   *   *   *   *

1969   The Journal of a Novel posthumously published (Decem-
        ber). [The Steinbeck Conference held in May at the
        University of Connecticut under the direction of John
        Seelye.]

1970   [The Steinbeck Conference held in May at Oregon
        State University under the direction of Richard
        Astro.]

1971   [The Steinbeck Monograph Series began to be pub-
        lished under T. Hayashi's General Editorship at
        Ball State University. The Steinbeck Conference and
        Film Festival held in February at California State
        University at San Jose with Martha Cox as Director
        and Peter Lisca as Consultant.]

1972   [The Steinbeck Society Meeting at the Modern Lan-
        guage Association Convention in New York City,
        December, held under the co-sponsorship of the John
        Steinbeck Society, Ball State University and The
        University of Windsor. John Ditsky as Discussion
        Leader; Daryl Adrian as Program Chairman; Peter
        Lisca as Keynote Speaker; and Hayashi as Consultant.]

[Cf. the chronologies of Covici (1971), Davis (1972),
Fontenrose (1963), French (1961), Hayashi (1967) (1971),
Lisca (1958) (1972), and others.]

KEY TO ABBREVIATIONS

A.	Annual.
AL	American Literature.
ALS	Autograph letter, signed.
AMS	Autograph manuscript, signed.
ANS	Autograph note, signed.
APS	Autograph postcard, signed.
ASTC Bulletin	Appalachian State Teachers College Bulletin (Later ASTC Faculty Publications).
Astro and Hayashi (eds.)	Steinbeck: The Man and His Work ed. by Richard Astro and Tetsumaro Hayashi (1971).
(B)	Bantam edition.
CLAJ	College Language Association Journal.
CTA Journal	California Teachers' Association Journal.
DA	Dissertation Abstracts.
DAI	Dissertation Abstracts International.
Davis (ed.)	Steinbeck: A Collection of Critical Essays ed. by Robert Murray Davis (1972).
Donohue (ed.)	A Casebook on The Grapes of Wrath ed. by Agnes McNeill Donohue (1968).
d.w.	dust wrappers.

ed.	edited or editor(s).
French (ed.)	A Companion to The Grapes of Wrath ed. by Warren French (1963).
G. of W.	The Grapes of Wrath.
HLQ	Huntington Library Quarterly.
HLR	Harvard Law Review.
J	Journal.
JEGP	Journal of English and Germanic Philology.
J. E. S.	John Ernst Steinbeck.
J. S.	John Steinbeck.
KAL	Kyushu American Literature.
l.	line(s).
Lisca (ed.)	John Steinbeck: The Grapes of Wrath, Text and Criticism ed. by Peter Lisca (1972).
LV	The Long Valley.
MFS	Modern Fiction Studies.
Mi MS	Mimeographed manuscript.
MS or MSS	Manuscript(s).
n. d.	no date.
NEA Journal	National Education Association Journal.
n. p.	no page number.
n. v.	no volume number.
8vo	octavo.
p.	page(s).

PH	The Pastures of Heaven.
PM or " "	Postmarked.
P. R.	Play Review.
PS	Postcard, signed.
PS	Portable Steinbeck (Viking).
Q.	Quarterly.
4to	quarto.
(R)	Book Review.
R	Review.
(RH)	Random House edition in the Primary Sources Section.
SHC	Steinbeck and His Critics ed. by Ernest W. Tedlock, Jr. and C. V. Wicker (1957).
SN	Steinbeck Newsletter.
SQ	Steinbeck Quarterly (formerly SN).
SR	Saturday Review.
SRP	The Short Reign of Pippin IV: A Fabrication.
TCL	Twentieth Century Literature.
TCS	Typed card, signed.
TLS	Typed letter, signed (manuscript).
TLS	Times Literary Supplement (London, England).
TMS or TMSS	Typed manuscript(s).
TPS	Typed postcard, signed
TSS	Typed script, signed.

(V)	Viking edition.
WAL	Western American Literature.
w. e.	with original envelope.

PART I. PRIMARY MATERIAL (1-379)

A. FICTION (NOVELS) (1-18)

1. Burning Bright. New York: Viking Press, 1950 (B)
(V).

2. Cannery Row. New York: Viking Press, 1945 (B)
(V).

3. Cup of Gold: A Life of Henry Morgan, Buccaneer,
with Occasional References to History. New York:
Robert M. McBride, 1929 (B).

4. East of Eden. New York: Viking Press, 1952 (B)
(V).

5. The Grapes of Wrath. New York: Viking Press,
1939 (B) (V).

6. In Dubious Battle. New York: Covici-Friede, 1936.
[99 deluxe copies, numbered and signed by the
author] (B) (RH) (V).

7. The Long Valley. New York: Viking Press, 1938.
Including the following short stories:
"The Chrysanthemums"
"The White Quail"
"Flight"
"The Snake"
"The Breakfast"
"The Raid"
"The Harness"
"The Vigilante"
"Johnny Bear"
"The Murder"
"St. Katy the Virgin"
The Red Pony:
"The Gift"

1

"The Great Mountains"
"The Promise"
"The Leader of the People" (B) (V), [See The Red
Pony.]

8. The Moon Is Down. New York: Viking Press, 1942.
    [700 copies bound in paper for distribution exclu-
    sively to booksellers] (B) (V).

9. Of Mice and Men. New York: Covici-Friede, 1937.
    [2,500 copies were printed. Page 9, lines 2-3
    from the bottom of the page, read "and only moved
    because the heavy hands were/pendula." This was
    removed in later printings. Text of the Book-of-
    the-Month Club copies is identical to the second
    printing] (B) (RH) (V).

10. The Pastures of Heaven. New York: Brewer, Warren
    and Putnam, 1932 (B) (V).

11. The Pearl. New York: Viking Press, 1947 (B) (V).

12. The Red Pony. New York: Covici-Friede, 1937.
    Set in monotype Italian Oldstyle and printed on hand-
    made La Garde paper; 699 numbered copies were
    printed by the Pynson Printers of New York under
    the supervision of Elmer Adler, each copy signed
    by the author, September, 1937.
    I.   "The Gift"
    II. "The Great Mountains"
    III. "The Promise" (The 1945 ed. includes IV.
    "The Leader of the People."
    Included in LV in 1938 (B) (V).

13. The Short Reign of Pippin IV: A Fabrication. New
    York: Viking Press, 1957 (B) (V).

14. Sweet Thursday. New York: Viking Press, 1954
    (B) (V).

15. To a God Unknown. New York: Robert O. Ballou,
    1933 (B) (V).

16. Tortilla Flat. Illustrated by Ruth Gannett. New
    York: Covici-Friede, 1935
    [500 copies were printed as prepublication copies.
    Later editions so indicated on copyright page] (B)
    (RH) (V).

17. The Wayward Bus. New York: Viking Press, 1947
    (B) (V).

18. The Winter of Our Discontent. New York: Viking
    Press, 1961 (B) (V).

N. B. For current editions check the latest Books in Print
(New York: Bowker).

B. FICTION (SHORT STORIES) (19-69)

19. "Adventures in Arcademy: A Journey into the Ridicu-
    lous, " Stanford Spectator, 2 (June, 1924), 279, 291.

20. "Affair at 7, Rue de M. " (tr. into Japanese by Kat-
    suhiko Jogo), Gekkan Pen (Monthly Pen), (n. v.)
    (November, 1969), 290-97.

20. "Affair at 7, Rue de M. ....," Prize Stories
    1956: The O. Henry Awards, ed. Paul Engle and
    Hansford Martin. Garden City, N. Y.: Doubleday,
    1956. Reprinted from Harper's Bazaar. pp. 258-65.
    Also in Knight, 5 (September, 1966), 26-29.

21. "Breakfast," Progressive Weekly, (n. v.) (May 6, 1939),
    [n. p.]. Also in LV and PS as well as in Pacific
    Weekly, 15 (November 9, 1936), [n. p.]. Also in
    Turning Point: Fourteen Great Tales of Daring and
    Decision, ed. George Bennett. New York: Dell, 1965.
    pp. 174-77.

22. "The Chrysanthemums," American Literature, ed.
    Richard Poirier and William L. Vance. Boston:
    Little, Brown, 1970. II, 840-48.

22. "The Chrysanthemums," The Best Short Stories 1938,
    ed. Edward O'Brien. London: Jonathan Cape, 1938.
    pp. 433-45.

22. "The Chrysanthemums," Fiction for Composition by
    Bert C. Bach and Gordon Browning. Chicago: Scott,
    Foresman, 1968. pp. 262, 276-86.

22. "The Chrysanthemums," 50 Best American Short
    Stories: 1915-65, ed. Martha Foley. London: Mac-
    Gibbon & Kee, 1966. pp. 203-13.

22.   "The Chrysanthemums, " Harper's, 175 (October, 1937),
       513-19. Also in LV, PS, 1938.

23.   "Cutting Loose, " in collaboration with Michael Rat-
       cliffe. Encore, ed. Leonard Russell. London: Michael
       Joseph, 1963.

24.   "Danny and His Friends, " PS and A Treasury of Friend-
       ship, Comp. and ed. Ralph L. Woods. New York:
       David McKay, 1957.

25.   "Death of Grampa, " Taken at the Flood: The Human
       Drama as Seen by Modern American Novelists, ed.
       Ann Watkins. New York: Harper, 1946.

26.   "Death Shall Be Paid, " PS.

27.   "Dust, " Reading I've Liked, ed. C. Fadiman. New York:
       Simon and Schuster, 1945.

28.   "The Ears of Johnny Bear, " Best of the Bedside Es-
       quire. pp. 205-23.

28.   "The Ears of Johnny Bear, " The Bedside Esquire,
       pp. 379-93.

28.   "The Ears of Johnny Bear, " Esquire, 8 (September,
       1937), 35, 195-200. Also in LV as "Johnny Bear."
       Also in The Bedside Esquire, ed. A. Gingrich. New
       York: Tudor, 1937.

29.   "Edith McGillicuddy, " Lilliput, 12 (April, 1943), 285-
       90.

29.   "Edith McGillicuddy, " The 1943 Saturday Book, ed.
       Leonard Russell. London: Hutchinson, 1942. pp.
       189-99.

30.   "Elf in Algiers, " Pause to Wonder, ed. Marjorie
       Fischer and Rolfe Humphries. Garden City, N. Y.:
       Sun Dial Press, 1947; also New York: Julian Mess-
       ner, Inc. , 1944. pp. 401-403.

31.   "Fingers of Cloud: A Satire on College Protervity, "
       Stanford Spectator, 2 (February, 1924), 149,161-64.
       (Author's name printed John E. Steinback.) Also in
       Stanford Writers, 1891-1941, ed. Violet L. Shue.
       pp. 103-108.

Dramatists Alliance, Stanford University. Limited to
300 copies.

32.   "Flight, " Fiction Form and Experience: 30 Stories with
       Essays, ed. William M. Jones. Lexington, Mass.:
       Heath, 1969. pp. 147-61.

32.   "Flight, " An Introduction to Short Fiction and Criticism,
       ed. Emil Hurtik and Robert Yarber. Waltham, Mass.:
       Xerox College Publishing, 1971. pp. 96-107.

32.   "Flight, " LV and PS. Also in Adventures in American
       Literature, ed. R. B. Inglis, et al. New York: Har-
       court, Brace, 1951. Also in Introduction to the Short
       Story: Study Materials, ed. W. Boynton and Maynard
       Mack. New York: Hayden Book Co., 1965.

32.   "Flight, " The Narrative Impulse: Short Stories for
       Analysis, ed. Mary Purcell and Robert C. Wylder.
       New York: Odyssey Press, 1963. pp. 166-87.

32.   "Flight, " Short Story Masterpieces, ed. Robert Penn
       Warren and Albert Erskine. New York: Dell, 1954.
       pp. 454-74.

33.   "Free Ride to Monterey, " Argosy, 4 (March, 1943),
       69-76.

34.   "The Gift, " American Literature: A Representative
       Anthology of American Writing from Colonial Times
       to the Present, selected and introduced by Geoffrey
       Moore. London: Faber & Faber, 1964. pp. 1283-
       1302.

34.   "The Gift, " LV, PS, and The Red Pony. Also in The
       Pocket Reader. New York: Pocket Books, 1941.

35.   "The Great Mountains, " North American Review, 236
       (December, 1933), 492-500. Also in LV and PS and
       Two and Twenty, A Collection of Short Stories, ed.
       R. H. Singleton. New York: St. Martin's, 1962.
       pp. 236-38; 236-38 contain some biobibliographical
       information about Steinbeck. Also in Accents, ed.
       Robert C. Pooley, et al. (eds.). Chicago: Scott,
       Foresman, 1965. pp. 584-91.

36.   "The Hanging at San Quentin, " Avon, No. 20. 1945

[Modern Age Books, Short Story Monthly].

37.   "The Harness," Argosy, 6 (June, 1945), 15-25.

37.   "The Harness," Atlantic, 161 (June, 1938), 741-49.
      Also in LV and PS.

37.   "The Harness," 50 Great American Short Stories, ed.
      Milton Crane. New York: Bantam, 1966 (1971).

38.   "His Father," Reader's Digest, 55 (October, 1949),
      10-12 (British Version).

38.   "His Father," Reader's Digest, 55 (September, 1949),
      19-21.

39.   "How Edith McGillicuddy Met Robert Louis Stevenson,"
      Harper's, 183 (August, 1941), 252-58. Also in PS and
      Scholastic, 44 (April 24, 1944), 21-22. Also in The
      Best American Short Stories of 1942, ed. Martha
      Foley. Boston: Houghton Mifflin, 1952; and The Best
      Short Stories of 1942, O. Henry Memorial Stories, ed.
      H. Brickell. New York: Literary Guild, 1942.

39.   "How Edith McGillicuddy Met R. L. Stevenson," Strand
      Magazine, 103 (June, 1942), 16-23.

40.   "How Mr. Hogan Robbed a Bank," Atlantic, 197 (March,
      1956), 58-61. Also in Working With Prose, ed. Otto
      Reinert. New York: Harcourt, Brace, 1959. pp.
      20-30.

41.   "Johnny Bear," Argosy, 1 (New Series) (January, 1941),
      97-111.

41.   "Johnny Bear," LV [See "The Ears of Johnny Bear"].
      Also in Great Tales of the Far West, No. 88. New
      York: Lion Library, 1956.

41.   "Johnny Bear," (from The LV), Pulitzer Prize Reader
      (The Popular Living Classics Library), ed. Leo
      Hamalian and E. L. Volpe. (Introduction by Leon
      Edel) (No. 95-172) New York: Popular Library, 1961.

42.   "The King Snake and the Rattles," Brief, 66 (April,
      1953), 22-27.

43. "The Leader of the People," American Literature.
     Boston: Heath, 1969. II, 3231-50.

43. "The Leader of the People," American Literature Sur-
     vey, ed. Milton R. Stern and Seymour L. Gross. New
     York: Viking, 1962 (1972). IV, 152-67.

43. "The Leader of the People," Argosy, 20 (August, 1936),
     99-106.

43. "The Leader of the People," Insight I: Analyses of
     American Literature, ed. John V. Hagopian and Mar-
     tin Dolch. Frankfurt: Hirschgroben, 1962. pp. 231-
     35.

43. "The Leader of the People," LV and PS. Also in
     The Golden Argosy. New York: The Dial Press,
     1955. Also in The Pocket Book of Modern American
     Short Stories, ed. Philip Van Doren Stern. New
     York: Pocket Books, 1943. Also in This is My Best
     Edition, ed. Whit Burnett. New York: Dial Press,
     1942. Also in The United States in Literature, ed.
     Walter Blair, et al. (eds.). Chicago: Scott, Fores-
     man, 1963. pp. 417-86.

43. "The Leader of the People," Youth and Maturity: 20
     Short Stories, ed. James Coulos. New York: Mac-
     millan, 1970. pp. 319-30.

44. "Lilli Marlene," The Best of the Diners' Club Maga-
     zine. New York: Regent American Pub., 1962.
     p. 322.

45. "The Lonesome Vigilante," The Bedside Esquire.
     pp. 307-12.

45. "The Lonesome Vigilante," Best of the Bedside Es-
     quire, ed. Arnold Gingrich. London: Strato Publi-
     cations Ltd., 1954. pp. 189-95.

45. "The Lonesome Vigilante," Esquire, 6 (October,
     1936), 35; 186A-186B. Also in LV as "The Vigilante";
     [See "Vigilante"].

45. "The Lonesome Vigilante," The Esquire Treasury, ed.
     Arnold Gingrich. London: Heinemann, 1954. pp.
     99-103.

46.   "The Miracle," Argosy, 10 (April, 1949), 97-103.

47.   "Miracle of Tepayac," Collier's, 122 (December 25, 1948), 22-23.

48.   "Molly Morgan," in PS. Also in Avon, No. 31, 1946.

49.   "The Murder," The American Tradition in Literature, ed. Sculley Bradley, et al. New York: Norton, 1967. II, 1506-26.

49.   "The Murder," Argosy, 2 (New Series) (March, 1941), 31-40.

49.   "The Murder," North American Review, 237 (April, 1934), 305-12. Also in LV and O. Henry Prize Stories of 1934. New York: Doubleday, Doran, 1934. Also in The Bedside Tales, introduced by Peter Arno. New York: William Penn Pub., 1945. Also in Lovat Dickson's Magazine (England) 3 (October, 1934), 442-56.

50.   "Nothing for Himself," Continent's End; A Collection of California Writing, ed. Joseph Henry Jackson, et al. New York: McGraw-Hill, 1944.

51.   Nothing So Monstrous, New York: Pynson Printers, 1936.
   [A reprint of the Junius Maltby story from The Pastures of Heaven with illustration by Donald McKay and an epilogue by the author written for this edition of 370 un-numbered copies. Also in Modern Age Books. Avon (Short Story Monthly), No. 20, 1945].

52.   "Over the Hill," Half-a-Hundred: Tales by Great American Writers, ed. Charles Grayson. Toronto: Blakiston, 1945. Also in Philadelphia: Blakiston, 1945, 450-52.

53.   "The Pearl of the World," Woman's Home Companion, 72 (December, 1945), 177ff [See The Pearl].

54.   "The Promise," Harper's, 175 (August, 1937), 243-52. Also in LV and PS. Part III of The Red Pony: O. Henry Prize Stories of 1938. New York: Doubleday, Doran, 1938.

55.   "The Raid," Modern American Short Stories, ed. Alan
      Steele and Joan Hancock.   Penguin Books, No. 116
      (Forces Book Club Edition), 1942.   pp. 65-75.

55.   "The Raid," North American Review, 238 (October,
      1934), 299-305.   Also in LV.

55.   "The Raid," Stories of Our Time, ed. Douglas R.
      Barnes.   London: Harrap, 1963.   pp. 120-33.

56.   "The Red Pony," North American Review, 236 (No-
      vember, 1933), 421-38.   Also in LV as "The Gift"
      and PS.

56.   "The Red Pony," Reading I've Liked, ed. Clifton
      Fadiman.   London: Hamish Hamilton, 1946.   pp.
      437-95.   (NB.   "The Leader of the People" is omit-
      ted.)

56.   "The Red Pony--Part I: 'The Gift'," Stories From The
      Quarto, ed. Leonard Brown, New York: Scribner's,
      1963.   pp. 142-53.

57.   "Reunion at the Quiet Hotel," Evening Standard, Janu-
      ary 25, 1958.   p. 9.

58.   Saint Katy the Virgin.   New York: Convici-Friede,
      1936.
      [199 numbered copies, signed by the author.   Also
      in LV].

59.   "The Short-Short Story of Mankind," Penguin Science
      Fiction, ed. Brian Aldiss.   Harmondsworth: Penguin
      Books, 1961.   pp. 51-57.

59.   "The Short-Short Story of Mankind," The Permanent
      Playboy, ed. Ray Russell.   New York: Crown, 1959.
      p. 325.

59.   "The Short-Short Story of Mankind," The Twelfth
      Anniversary Playboy Reader, ed Hugh M. Hefner.
      London: Souvenir Press, 1966.   pp. 539-44.

60.   "A Snake of One's Own," The Bedside Esquire, ed.
      Arnold Gingrich.   New York: Tudor Pub., 1954;
      London: Heinemann, 1941.   pp. 530-38.   Also in
      The Best, a Quarterly Magazine, "a continuing

anthology of the world's greatest writing, " New York:
Macfadden-Bartell Corp. (Winter, 1965).

60. "A Snake of One's Own, " The Girls from Esquire, ed.
     Frederic A. Birmingham. London: Arthur Barker,
     1953. pp. 18-27.

61. "The Snake, " Monterey Beacon, 1 (June 22, 1935), 10-
     14. Also in LV. Also in Great American Short
     Stories, ed. Wallace and Mary Stegner. New York:
     Dell, 1957.

62. "Sons of Cyrus Trask, " Collier's, 130 (July 12, 1952),
     14-15.

63. "The Summer Before, " Punch, 128 (May 25, 1955),
     647-51.

64. "The Time the Wolves Ate the Vice Principal, " '47 The
     Magazine of the Year, 1 (March, 1947), 26-27.
     [An interchapter omitted from Cannery Row].

65. "Tractored Off, " Literature for Our Time: An An-
     thology for College Freshmen, ed. Leonard Stanley
     Brown, et al. New York: H. Holt and Co., 1947.
     Also in America in Literature, ed. Tremaine McDowell.
     Madison, Wis.: F. S. Crofts and Co., for the U.S.
     Armed Forces Institute, 1944.

66. "The Tractors, " Our Lives: American Labor Stories,
     ed. Joseph Gaer. New York: Boni and Gaer, 1948.

67. "The Turtle, " PS. Also in Reading I've Liked, ed.
     Clifton Fadiman. New York: Simon and Schuster,
     1945.

68. "The Vigilante, " LV. See "The Lonesome Vigilante. "

69. "The White Quail, " American Short Stories, ed. Eugene
     Current-Garcia & Walton R. Patrick. Chicago: Scott,
     Foresman, 1964. [n. p.].

69. "The White Quail, " North American Review, 239
     (March, 1935), 204-211. Also in LV and American
     Short Stories. Chicago: Scott, Foresman and Co.,
     1952.

C. PLAYS (70-72)

70. Burning Bright (Acting Edition). New York: Drama-
    tists Play Service, 1951 (B) (V).

71. The Moon Is Down: A Play in Two Parts. New York:
    Viking Press, 1943 (V).

72. Of Mice and Men: A Play in Two Parts. New York:
    Covici-Friede, 1937. Also in Famous American Plays
    of the 1930s, ed. Harold Clurman. New York: Dell,
    1959. pp. 297-384 and Twenty Best Plays of the
    Modern American Theatre, ed. John Gassner. New
    York: Crown, 1941. pp. 643-80.

D. FILM STORIES AND SCRIPTS (73-77)

73. The Forgotten Village. New York: Viking Press, 1941.

74. Lifeboat. Unpublished story. (20th Century Film Corp.,
    1944).

75. The Pearl (from his novel). Unpublished script (RKO,
    1947).

76. The Red Pony (from his stories). Unpublished script
    (Feldman Group Productions & Lewis Milestone Pro-
    duction, 1949).

77. Viva Zapata! Screen play abridged in Argosy, 33
    (February, 1952). Based on the Steinbeck-Elia Kazan
    movie. The pictures were taken on location along the
    Mexican border.
    [The Viking Press is publishing the play].

E. NON-FICTION (BOOKS AND BOOKLETS)(78-88)

78. America and Americans. New York: Viking, 1966.
    Photos by the staff of Viking Photo Studio (B) (V).

79. Bombs Away: The Story of a Bomber Team. Written
    for the U.S. Army Air Forces with 60 photographs by
    John Swope. New York: Viking Press, 1942.

80.   Journal of a Novel: The East of Eden Letters.   New
      York: Viking, 1969 (B) (V).

81.   The Log from the Sea of Cortez.   New York: Viking
      Press, 1951.   The narrative portion of Sea of Cortez:
      A Leisurely Journal of Travel and Research, 1941,
      with a profile "About Ed Ricketts."   See Sea of Cortez.

82.   Once There Was a War.   New York: Viking Press,
      1958.
      [A collection of Steinbeck's wartime dispatches to
      the New York Herald Tribune] (B) (V).

83.   A Russian Journal.   New York: Viking Press, 1948
      (B).   Robert Capa as photographer.

84.   Sea of Cortez: A Leisurely Journal of Travel and Re-
      search, with Edward F. Ricketts.   New York: Viking
      Press, 1941.
      [See The Log from the Sea of Cortez].

85.   Their Blood Is Strong (Booklet).   San Francisco:
      Simon J. Lubin Society of California, 1938.
      [Pamphlet of articles published in San Francisco
      News, October 5-12, 1936 as "The Harvest Gyp-
      sies"].

86.   Their Blood Is Strong (Booklet).   San Francisco: The
      Simon J. Lubin Society of California, 1938.   Reprint-
      ed in A Companion to the Grapes of Wrath, ed. War-
      ren French.   New York: Viking Press, 1963. pp.
      53-92.

87.   Travels with Charley in Search of America.   New
      York: Viking Press, 1962 (B) (V).

88.   Vanderbilt Clinic (Booklet).   New York: Presbyterian
      Hospital, 1947.
      [An illustrated brochure, with commentary by
      Steinbeck on the services of the Medical Center
      and its clinics, with Victor Kepler as photographer].

F. NON-FICTION (ARTICLES, ESSAYS INTERVIEWS, AND REPORTS) (89-237)

89. "About Ed Ricketts," Preface to The Log from the
    Sea of Cortez. New York: Viking Press, 1951. pp.
    vii-lxvii.

90. "The Alien They Couldn't Intern," Daily Express,
    July 10, 1943. p. 2.

91. "Alliance by Gum," Daily Express, September 13,
    1943. p. 2.

92. Allsop, Kenneth. "The Wrath Hasn't Left Steinbeck,"
    Daily Mail, September 18, 1961. p. 8 (Interview).

93. "Always Something to Do in Salinas," Holiday, 17
    (June, 1955), 58ff.

94. "... And Some Cars of Yesterday," Reader's Digest,
    65 (November, 1954), 53-54, 56-57.

95. An article by S. in Pascal Covici 1888-1964.
    [Series of articles in tribute to Pascal Covici].
    Privately printed. Limited to 500 copies. Not for
    sale. p. 19.

96. "Atque Vale," Saturday Review, 43 (July 23, 1960), 13.
    See also "Blackman's Ironic Burden" (98).

97. Atticus, "Steinbeck's Critics--Natural Enemies,"
    Sunday Times, September 24, 1961. p. 15 (Interview).

98. "Black Man's Ironic Burden; Reprint," Negro History
    Bulletin, 24 (April, 1961), 146ff (reprint of "Atque
    Vale").

99. "Bomber, Our Best Weapon," Science Digest, 14 (July,
    1943), 61-63.

100. "Bricklaying Piece," Punch, 229 (July 27, 1955), 92.

101. "The Cab Driver Doesn't Give a Hoot," Daily Mail,
     August 14, 1956.

102. "Camping Is for the Birds" (The Great Camping Debate
     with Stanley Gardner), Popular Science, 190 (May, 1961),
     160-161+.

103.   "The Case of Arthur Miller," The Armchair Esquire,
        ed. Arnold Gingrich. London: Heinemann, 1959.
        pp. 239-42.

104.   "Commander Goat, D. S. O.," Daily Express, July 15,
        1943. p. 2.

105.   "The Common Man at War," Daily Express, June 28,
        1943. p. 2.

105.   "The Common Man at War 2: When the Saints Go In,"
        Daily Express, June 29, 1943. p. 2.

105.   "The Common Man at War 3: This Is Your Target;
        Knock It Out," Daily Express, June 30, 1943. p. 2.

106.   "Contribution to Symposium Entitled 'California:
        the Exploding State'," Sunday Times Colour Section,
        December 16, 1962. p. 2.

107.   "Conversation at Sag Harbor," Holiday, 29 (March,
        1961), 60-61, 129-131, 133.

108.   "Critics, Critics Burning Bright," SR, 33 (November
        11, 1950), 20-21. Also as "My Short Novels," in
        SHC. pp. 43-47. Also in Bantam edition (913), 1951.
        pp. 106-11.
        [A statement of Steinbeck's intention in Burning
        Bright and in other writings].

109.   "Critics from a Writer's Point of View," SR, 38
        (August 27, 1955), 20. Also in SHC as "Critics
        ... from a Writer's Viewpoint." pp. 48-51.

110.   "Cutting Loose at 60" (Interview), Sunday (London)
        Times, December 16, 1962.

111.   "D for Dangerous," McCalls, 85 (October, 1957),
        57ff.

112.   "A Day, a Mood, a Faith in a Spirited Collection of
        Classic Holiday Messages You Will Long Remember,"
        Good Housekeeping, 165 (1967), 82-83.

113.   "The Death of a Racket," SR, 38 (April 2, 1955), 26.

113.   "The Death of a Racket," Spectator, 6615 (April 8,
        1955), 430-31.

114.   "Dedication, " Journal of American Medical Associa-
        tion, 167 (July 12, 1958), 1388-89.   See "Spivacks
        Beat the Odds" condensed in Reader's Digest.

115.   Del Monte Recipes. Del Monte, California, 1937.
        Issued by the Del Monte Properties Co. as a promo-
        tion piece for the Hotel Del Monte. S's favorite
        recipe is included among those of other people.
        [S's article included].

116.   "Dichos: the Way of Wisdom, " SR, 40 (November 9,
        1957), 13.

117.   "Discovering the People of Paris, " Holiday, 20
        (August, 1956), 36.

118.   Dispatches from the European War Theater appearing
        in The New York Herald Tribune, June 21 to Decem-
        ber 10, 1943.

        June 21 (p. 1); 22 (p. 1); 23 (p. 1); 24 (p. 1); 25
        (p. 1); 26 (p. 1); 27 (p. 1); 28 (p. 1); 29 (p. 23); 30
        (p. 23)

        July 1 (p. 21); 2(p.17); 3 (p. 13); 4 (p. 7); 5 (pp. 1,
        9); 6 (p. 17); 7 (p. 23); 8 (p. 21); 9 (p. 15); 10 (p.
        7); 11 (p. 14); 12 (p. 15); 13 (p. 21); 14 (p. 21);
        15 (p. 21); 16 (p. 13); 17 (p. 7); 18 (p. 18); 19 (p.
        13); 25 (p. 12); 26 (p. 17); 27 (p. 17); 28 (p. 17);
        29 (p. 17); 30 (p. 13)

        August 3 (p. 15); 4 (p. 17); 5 (p. 17); 6 (p. 13); 9
        (p. 11); 10 (p. 21); 12 (p. 17); 26 (p. 15); 27 (p. 13);
        28 (p. 7); 29 (p. 10); 31 (p. 17)

        September 1 (p. 21); 2 (p. 21); 3 (p. 17); 5 (p. 5);
        17 (p. 2); 29 (p. 21)

        October 1 (p. 21); 3 (p. 35); 4 (p. 13); 6 (p. 25); 8
        (p. 17); 11 (p. 17); 12 (p. 21); 13 (p. 25); 14 (p. 25);
        15 (p. 1); 18 (p. 17); 19 (p. 21); 20 (p. 1); 21 (p. 1);
        29 (p. 17)

        November 1 (p. 17); 3 (p. 23); 5 (p. 15); 8 (p.17);
        15 (p. 17); 17 (p. 25); 19 (p. 21); 22 (p. 17); 24 (p.
        17); 26 (p. 21)

        December 1 (p. 23); 3 (p. 21); 6 (p. 21); 8 (p. 25);

10 (p. 25)

[Cf. Peter Lisca's dissertation].

119. "Dover--It Will Bloom Again, Prettier Than Ever,"
      Daily Express, July 9, 1943. p. 2.

120. "Dubious Battle in California," Nation, 143 (Septem-
      ber 13, 1936), 302-304.

121. "Duel without Pistols," Collier's, 130 (August 23,
      1952), 13-15, 26ff.

122. "The Easiest Way to Die," SR, 41 (August 23, 1958),
      12ff.

122. "The Easiest Way to Die," The S.R. Sampler of Wit
      and Wisdom, ed. Martin Levin. New York: Simon
      and Schuster, 1967.

123. "The Family Who Beat the Odds," Reader's Digest,
      73 (June, 1957), 39-42.

124. Famous Recipes by Famous People, ed. Herbert
      Cerivin. Illustrated by Sinclair Ross. Published by
      Sunset Magazine in cooperation with Hotel Del Monte,
      San Francisco, California. "Of Beef and Men," p. 11.

125. "Fishing in Paris," Punch, 227 (August 25, 1954),
      248-49.
          [This article is reprinted in translation under the
          title "Sur les Bords de l'Oise" as the 8th edition of
          Un Americain à New York et à Paris. Paris:
          Julliard, 1956].

126. Foreword to Between Pacific Tides. Stanford Univ.
      Press, 1948.
          [An offprint from the revised edition, issued
          August, 1948, of a work by Edward F. Ricketts
          and Jack Calvin. Privately printed at the Stanford
          Univ. Press by Nathan Van Patten].

127. Foreword to Burning Bright (a Play in Story Form).
      New York: Viking Press, 1950. pp. 9-13.

128. "Foreword" to Hard-Hitting Songs for Hard-Hit Peo-
      ple. New York: Oak Publications, 1967. [n. p.].

129.   "Foreword" to Much Ado about Me, by Fred Allen.
        Boston: Little, Brown, 1956.

130.   Foreword to Speeches of Adlai Stevenson, ed. Richard
        Harrity. New York: Random House, 1952. pp. 5-8.

131.   "For Those Who Have Forgotten What It Was Like--
        For Those Too Young to Know," Esquire, [n.v.], June,
        n.d.), 85-93 [G. of W].

132.   "A Game of Hospitality," SR, 40 (April 20, 1957), 24.

133.   "Gathering Knowledge," The Treasure Chest, ed. J.
        Donald Adams. New York: Dutton, 1946. p. 373.

134.   "The GI's War.......," New York Herald Tribune
        Weekly Book Review, May 18, 1947. p. 1.

135.   "Golden Handcuff: J. S. Writes about San Francisco,"
        San Francisco Examiner, November 23, 1958.

136.   "Good Guy--Bad Guy," Punch, 227 (September 22,
        1954), 375-78.

137.   "Green Paradise," Argosy 17 (May, 1956), 41-47.

138.   Grosvenor, Peter. "You Don't Have to Be Angry to
        Write Good Books," Daily Express, December 13, 1962
        (Interview).

138(a). "The Harvest Gypsies," San Francisco News, October
        5-12, 1936. A series of articles on migrant labor
        in California.
        Chapter I.   October 5, 1936 (p. 3)
                II.   "   6,   "   (p. 3)
                III.   "   7,   "   (p. 6)
                IV.   "   8,   "   (p. 16)
                V.   "   9,   "   (p. 14)
                VI.   "   10,   "   (p. 14)
                VII.   "   11,   "   (p. 8)

        [I am indebted to Peter Lisca's dissertation.]

139.   "He Knew What He Wanted," Daily Express, July 24,
        1943. p. 2.

140.   "Henry Fonda," Harper's Bazaar, [n.v.] (November,

1966), 215. Also reprinted in The Fondas: The Films
and Careers of Henry, Jane, and Peter (New York:
Citadel Press, 1970). pp. 22-25 [S's tribute].

141.   "High Drama of Bold Thrust Through Ocean Floor,"
        Life, 50 (April 14, 1961), 110-18.

142.   Holloway, David. "J. S. Is Still a Rebel," News
        Chronicle, June 15, 1957, p. 4 (Interview).

143.   "Hostess with the Mostest in the Hall," Daily Mail,
        August 17, 1956. p. 4.

144.   "How to Fish in French," Reader's Digest, 66
        (January, 1955), 59-61.

145.   "How to Recognize a Candidate," Punch, 229 (August
        10, 1955), 146-48.

146.   "How to Tell Good Guys from Bad Guys," Reach Out
        by Marsha Jeffer and Nancy Rayl. Boston: Little,
        Brown, 1972. pp. 126-28.

146.   "How to Tell Good Guys from Bad Guys," Reporter,
        12 (March 10, 1955), 42-44. Also in The Art of
        the Essays, ed. Joseph Henry Satin. New York:
        Crowell, 1958. pp. 357-62. Also in Punch, 22
        (September 22, 1954), 375-78.

147.   "I Go Back to Ireland," Collier's, 131 (January 31,
        1953), 48-50.

148.   "I Remember the Thirties," The Thirties: A Time
        to Remember, ed. Don Congdon. New York: Simon
        & Schuster, 1962. pp. 23-36. Edited from Esquire,
        103 (June, 1960), 85-93.

149.   "If You See Me on the Hoe with a PUMA," Daily
        Mail, September 30, 1959. p. 6.

150.   "In Passing, Then My Arm Glassed Up," Weekend
        Telegraph (England), September 16, 1966.

151.   "In a Radio Broadcast Beamed....," SR, 38 (No-
        vember 26, 1955), 8-9.

152.   "The Inside," The Iron Gate of Jack and Charlie's

"21". New York: The Jack Kriendler Memorial Foundation, 1950. p. 27.
[In memory of John Carl Kriendler for the benefit of the New York Heart Association].

153. Introduction to The World of Li'l Abner by Al Capp. New York: Farrar, Straus and Young, 1953.

154. "It Was Dark As Hell," They Were There: The Story of World War II and How It Came About, ed. C. Riess. New York: Putnam's, 1944. pp. 584-85.

155. "Jalopies I Cursed and Love," Holiday, 16 (July, 1954), 44-45; 89-90. Also in Ten Years of Holiday, ed. the Holiday editors. New York: Simon & Schuster, 1956. pp. 439-44.

156. "The Joan in All of Us," SR, 39 (January 14, 1956), 17.

157. "J. S.: The Art of Fiction XLV," Paris Review, 12 (1969), 169-88 [Interview].

158. "J. S. to a Russian Friend," Reader's Digest, 91 (August, 1967), 41.

159. Kretzmer, Herbert. "Steinbeck's New Mood: I Am Scared, Boastful But Also Humble," Daily Express, January 15, 1965 (Interview).

160. "Let's Go After the Neglected: A Plea for Equal Effort on Treasure Beneath the Seas 'Inner Space' Exploration," Popular Science, [n.v.] (September, 1966), 189.

161. "The Light That Still Shines," Daily Express, July 17, 1943. p. 2.

162. "....... Like Captured Fireflies" (J. S. Says a Great Teacher Is One of the Great Artists), CTA Journal, 51 (November, 1955), 6-8.

163. Lowrie, Henry. "Nobel John," Daily Express, October 26, 1962. p. 4 (Interview).

164. "Madison Avenue and the Election," SR, 39 (March

31, 1956), 11.

165. "The Mail I've Seen," SR, 39 (August 4, 1956), 16,
      34.

166. "Making of a New Yorker," New York Times Maga-
      zine. February 1, 1953. VI, Pt. 3, p. 26.
      February 22, 1953. VI, 4. Also in The Empire
      City: A Treasury of New York, ed. Alexander Klein.
      New York: Rinehart, 1955. pp. 469-75.

167. "Man with a Ski Nose," This Was Your War, ed.
      Frank Bookhauser. New York: Dell, 1963.

168. "Merry Christmas, All Authorized Personnel?" House
      and Garden, 136 (December, 1969), 68-69.

169. "Miracle Island of Paris," Holiday, 19 (February,
      1956), 43.

170. "Mixed Battery--Can You See These Girls Going
      Back to the Old Jobs," Daily Express, July 8, 1943.
      p. 2.

171. "A Model T Named 'It'," Ford Times, 45 (July,
      1953), 34-39.

171. "A Model T Named 'It'," reprinted from the Ford
      Times in High Gear, ed. Evan Jones. New York:
      Bantam Books, 1955. pp. 64-66.

172. "More About Aristocracy: Why Not a World Peer-
      age?" SR, 38 (December 10, 1955), 11.

173. "Mulligan Had a Lucky Comrade," Daily Express,
      August 21, 1943. p. 2.

174. "Mulligan Knows What He Wants...and Gets It,"
      Daily Express, August 14, 1943. p. 2.

175. "Mulligan Won't Take a Stripe," Daily Express,
      August 7, 1943. p. 2.

176. "My Short Novels," Wings, 26 (October, 1953), 1-8
      (Literary Guild Review). Also in English Journal,
      43 (March, 1954), 147.
          [Excerpt from Wings]; SHC, pp. 38-40.

177. "Mystery of Life," The Treasure Chest, ed. James
      Donald Adams. New York: Dutton, 1946. pp. 371-
      72.
      [From Sea of Cortez].

178. "My War with the Ospreys," Holiday, 21 (March,
      1957), 72-73; 163-65. Also in Essays Today 3, ed.
      M. Ludwig. New York: Harcourt, Brace, 1958.
      Also in Reader's Digest, 70 (June, 1957), 39-42.

179. "Nobody Ever Gets Killed in a War," Daily Express,
      October 7, 1943. p. 2.

180. "The Novel Might Benefit By the Discipline and
      Terseness of the Drama," Stage, 15 (January, 1938),
      50-51.

181. "Of Beef and Men" (recipe), Famous Recipes by
      Famous People, ed. Herbert Cerivin. San Francisco:
      Lane, 1940.

182. "On Learning Writing," Writer's Yearbook, No. 34,
      1963. Cincinnati: F. and W. Publishing, 1963.
      p. 10.

183. "One American in Paris (A Plea for Tourists),"
      Punch, 228 (January 26, 1955), 148-49.

183. "One American in Paris (Reality and Illusion),"
      Punch, 227 (November 17, 1954), 616-17.

183. "One American in Paris," Holiday in France, select-
      ed and decorated by L. Bemelmans. Boston:
      Houghton Mifflin, 1957. p. 141.
      [This consists of the 4 Holiday articles: "Miracle
      Island of Paris," "What Is the Real Paris?,"
      "The Yank in Europe," and "Discontinuing the
      People of Paris," reprinted in that order as a
      single essay].

184. "One More for Lady Luck," Star Reporters and 34 of
      Their Stories, ed. Ward Greene. New York: Ran-
      dom House, 1948. pp. 320-24.
      [Dispatch to New York Herald Tribune from Lon-
      don, 1943].

185. "Our Best, Our Fliers," New York Times Magazine,
      November 22, 1942. pp. 16-17.

186. "Our Rigged Morality," Coronet, 47 (March, 1960),
      144-47. Also in Fabulous Yesterdays, ed. Lewis W.
      Gellenson. New York: Harper, [n.d.]
      [S. and Adlai Stevenson, an exchange of letters].

187. "Over There," Ladies' Home Journal, 61 (February,
      1944), 20-21. Also in The Ladies' Home Treasury,
      ed. John Mason Brown and the editors of The Ladies'
      Home Journal. New York: Simon & Schuster, 1956.

188. Perrick, Eve. "John Steinbeck Seeks a Wayward
      London Bus," Daily Express, August 6, 1952, p. 4
      (Interview).

189. Perrick, Eve. "Session with S.," Daily Express,
      June 15, 1957. p. 7 (Interview).

190. "A Plea for Tourists," Punch, 228 (January 26,
      1955), 148-49.

191. "A Plea to Teachers," NEA Journal, 44 (September,
      1955), 359. Also in SR, 38 (April 30, 1955), 24.

192. "Poker for Keeps," Masterpieces of War Reporting,
      ed. Louis L. Snyder. New York: Julius Messner,
      1962. p. 314.

193. "Positano," Harper's Bazaar, [n.v.] (May, 1953),
      158, 185, 187, 188, 194.

193. "Positano," Harper's Bazaar, [n.v.] (August, 1953),
      41, 68, 70.

194. Preface to Story Writing by Edith Ronald Mirrielees.
      New York: Viking Press, 1962.

195. "A President....Not a Candidate," Washington,
      D.C.: Democratic Convention Program Book Com-
      mittee, 1964.

196. "A Primer on the 30's," Esquire, 103 (June, 1960),
      85-93.

197. "Ragged Crew," True, 44 (February, 1963), 33-35;
      79-82.

198. "Random Thoughts on Random Dogs," Cold Noses and

Warm Hearts, ed. Corey Ford. Englewood Cliffs,
N.J.: Prentice-Hall, 1958. p. 1.

198. "Random Thoughts on Random Dogs," SR, 38 (October
8, 1955), 11. Also in SR Treasury, ed. Saturday
Review. New York: Simon & Schuster, 1957. pp.
529-31.

199. Ratcliffe, Michael. "Cutting Loose at Sixty by J. S.,"
Sunday Times, December 16, 1962. p. 20 (Interview).

200. Ratcliffe, Michael and J. S. "Cutting Loose," The
Sunday Times Book: Encore (Second Year), ed. Leon
Russell. London: Michael Joseph, 1963. pp. 151-
54 (Interview).

201. "Rationale," SHC. pp. 308-309.

202. "Reality and Illusion," Punch, 227 (November 17, 1954),
616-17.

203. "Report on America," Punch, 228 (June 22, 1955),
754-55.

204. "Robert Capa: An Appreciation by J. S.," Images of
War by Robert Capa. New York: Grossman, 1964.
p. 7.
[This is a special edition assembled by his brother
Cornell, also a photograph] [Introduction to the
book].

205. "Robert Capa," Photography, 35 (September, 1954),
48-53.

206. "The Routine at a Bomber Station," This Was Your
War, ed. Frank Bookhauser. New York: Dell,
1963.

207. "The Secret Weapon We Were Afraid to Use,"
Collier's, 131 (January 10, 1953), 9-13.

208. "Some Random and Randy Thoughts on Books," The
Author Looks at Format, ed. Ray Fliman. New
York: The American Institute of Graphic Arts, 1951.
pp. 31-32.

209. "Some Thoughts on Juvenile Delinquency," SR, 38
(May 28, 1955), 22.

210.   "Song of the Disgusted Modern, " Monterey Beacon, 1 (February 1, 1935), 7.

211.   "The Soul and Guts of France, " Collier's, 130 (August 30, 1952), 26 ff.

212.   "The Spivacks Beat the Odds"; Condensed from The Journal of American Medical Association in Reader's Digest, 73 (October, 1958), 153-54. See "Dedication."

213.   "The Stars Point To Shafter, " Progressive Weekly, December 24, 1938. [n. p.].

214.   "S. in Vietnam, " Daily Sketch, January 6, 1967. p. 6.

215.   "S's Voices of America, " Scholastic, 65 (November 3, 1954), 15f.

216.   "The Stevenson Spirit, " The Faces of Five Decades, Selected from Fifty Years of the New Republic, 1914-1964. Introduced by A. M. Schlesinger, Jr. New York: Simon & Schuster, 1964. p. 332.

217.   "The Summer Before, " Punch, 228 (May 25, 1955), 647-51.

218.   "A Teddy Bear Called Miz Hicks, " News Chronicle, January 18, 1960. [n. p.].

219.   "Then My Arm Glassed Up, " Weekend Telegraph, 103 (September 16, 1966), 46.

220.   "They Don't Talk about Anything Else When Bob Hope's Coming, " Daily Express, July 31, 1943. p. 2.

221.   "A Thing Is Bigger Than a Scramble, " Daily Express. July 23, 1943.   p. 2.

222.   "Tommy Gets Well, " Daily Express, January 30, 1943.   p. 2.

223.   "Trade Wind: Predictions of Reviews East of Eden Would Receive, " SR, 37 (February 27, 1954), 8.

224.   "Troopship: Condensed from New York Herald

Tribune, " Reader's Digest, 44 (March, 1944), 67-70.

225. "Trust Your Luck, " SR, 40 (January 12, 1957), 42-44.

225. "Trust Your Luck, " From Paragraph to Essay Readings for Progress in Writing by Woodrow Ohlson and Frank L. Hammond. New York: Scribner's, 1963. pp. 192-96.

226. "The Vegetable War," SR, 39 (July 21, 1956), 34-35.

227. Weatherby, W. J. "Big Man from Monterey, " Manchester Guardian, October 13, 1959. p. 7 (Interview).

228. "What Is The Real Paris?" Holiday, 18 (December, 1955), 94.

229. "What Sort of Letter Do You Write to Your Soldier, " Daily Express, August 6, 1943. p. 2.

230. "Who Said the Old Lady was Dying?" (Article on London theater). Evening Standard (England), August 1, 1952. [n. p.].

231. Williams, Alan Moray. "I'll Have a Row in London: S. , " Sunday Citizen, December 9, 1962. p. 2. (Interview).

232. Williams, Gordon. "J. S. 's Press Conference, " Scene, 15 (December 27, 1962), 22 (Interview).

233. "Women and Children in the U.S.S.R. , " Ladies' Home Journal, 65 (February, 1948), 44-59.

234. "The Women Watch Their Men, " The Treasure Chest, ed. J. Donald Adams. New York: Dutton, 1946. pp. 374-75.

235. "Writer's Mail, " The Pick of Punch, ed. Nicholas Bentley. Foreword by Malcolm Muggeridge. London: Andre Deutsch, 1956.

235. "Writer's Mail, " Punch, 229 (November 2, 1955), 512-13.

236. "The Yank in Europe, " Holiday, 19 (January, 1956), 25.

237.   "Your Audiences Are Wonderful, " Sunday Times,
        August 10, 1952. p. 5.

        G. PUBLISHED LETTERS AND POSTCARDS (238-267)

238.   "The Americans Embark for War, " PS (1943). pp.
        575-578.

239.   "Battle Scene, " PS (1943).   pp. 585-88.

240.   Bradley, Berton.   "A Letter of J. S. , " Morgan Sails
        the Caribbean.   New York: Macmillan, 1934. pp.
        vii-viii.
            [Steinbeck gives his permission to the author to use
            certain incidents from Cup of Gold.].

241.   "A Day, a Mood, a Faith, " Good Housekeeping,
        [n. v.] (December   1967), 82-83
            [An excerpt from a letter by S. to Adlai Stevenson].

242.   Dreiser, Theodore.   The Letters of Theodore Dreis-
        er, ed. Robert H. Elias.   Philadelphia: University
        of Pennsylvania Press, 1959.   pp. 800, 845, and
        passim.

243.   The First Watch.   Los Angeles: Ward Ritchie Press,
        1947.   S's humorous letter of thanks for the gift of
        a watch.   6 pp.   (Limited to 60 copies; 10 for the
        use of the author and 50 copies for presentation by
        Marguerite and Louis Henry Cohn).

244.   Fitzgerald, F. Scott.   The Letters of F. Scott Fitz-
        gerald, ed. Andrew Turnbull.   London: Bodley Head,
        1964.   pp. 73, 280, and passim.

245.   "Izvestia published S. letter apologizing to Soviet
        writers who were his hosts during 1963 visit for mix-
        up over copies of his 1962 Nobel Prize speech and
        mimeographing thank-you notes he sent to them and
        accidentally to others he had never met, " New York
        Times, August 30, 1964. p. 24.

246.   John Steinbeck--A Letter Written in Reply to a Re-
        quest for a Statement about His Ancestry, together
        with the letter originally submitted by the Friends of

Democracy. Stanford, Conn.: Overbrook Press, 1940.
13 pp. [350 copies].

247. John Steinbeck Replies. New York: Friends of
Democracy, Inc., 1940. A letter written in reply to
a request for a statement about his ancestry, together
with the letter originally submitted by the Friends of
Democracy. A printed leaflet containing an exchange
of letters between the author and Rev. L. M. Birk-
head, national director of the Friends of Democracy.
Stanford, Conn.: The Overbrook Press, 1940. 2 pp.
[350 copies only].

248. A Letter from J. S. [n.p.p.]: Roxburghe & Zamor-
ano Clubs, 1944.
[S's letter to Professor Carrutu]. 6 pp. [150
copies, printed by Sherwood and Katharine
Grover].

249. Letter from S. on page following title, as well as
dust jacket, of Greek edition of East of Eden and re-
produced in the catalog of An Exhibition of American
and Foreign Editions. Austin, Texas: Humanities
Research Center, University of Texas, 1963. p. 27.

250. Letters from John Steinbeck. St. Louis, Missouri:
National Student Committee for Victory in Vietnam,
1967.

251. "A Letter from S.," The Thinking Dog's Man. By
Ted Patrick. New York: Random House, 1964.
Contains Steinbeck's letter explaining why he could
not write an introduction for this book.

252. Letter from S. to Jacqueline Kennedy after the as-
sassination of President Kennedy is quoted in The
Death of a President by William Manchester. New
York: Harper & Row, 1967. p. 563.

253. "A Letter on Criticism," Colorado Quarterly, 4
(Autumn, 1955), 218-219. Also in SHC. pp. 52-53.

254. "Letters to Alicia," a series of letters addressed to
Alicia (Patterson Guggenheim), published in Newsday,
starting November 20, 1965. Alicia is the late wife
of the editor and publisher of Newsday.
[Also in Sunday Bulletin, News and Views Section,
Philadelphia].

255.   "A Letter to His Editor," Lisca (ed.), pp. 857-59.

256.   "A Letter to Inmates of the Connecticut State Prison,"
       Monthly Record, a monthly journal devoted to the in-
       terests of the inmates [n. v.] (June, 1938), [n. p.].

257.   Lowry, Malcolm. Selected Letters of Malcolm Lowry,
       ed. Harvey Breit and Marjorie Bonner Lowry. Lon-
       don: Jonathan Cape, 1965. p. 145.

258.   "More of Pvt. Big Train Mulligan," PS (1943), pp.
       582-85.

259.   No entry.

260.   "Postscript from S.," SHC. pp. 307-308.

261.   "Pvt. Big Train Mulligan," PS (1943), pp. 578-82.

262.   Sandburg, Carl. The Letters of Carl Sandburg, ed.
       Herbert Mitgang. New York: Harcourt, Brace, &
       World. p. 460.
       [Letter dated April 14, 1949 to Kenneth Dodson].

263.   "S's Letter," Writers Take Sides. New York: The
       League of American Writers, 1938.
       [Letters about the war in Spain from 418 American
       authors].

264.   "S's Suggestion for an Interview with Joseph Henry
       Jackson," Lisca (ed.), pp. 859-62.

265.   "The Way It Seems to J. S.," Occident (Fall, 1936),
       [n. p.].

266.   "Why Soldiers Won't Talk," PS (1943), pp. 588-90.

267.   Writers Take Sides: Letters about the War in Spain
       from 418 American Authors. New York: League of
       American Writers, 1938. 82 pp.
       [S's answer, pp. 56-57].

       H. PUBLISHED SPEECHES (268-277)

268.   His Nobel Prize Acceptance Speech on December 10,
       1962 quoted in Contemporary Authors, 2. Michigan:

Gale Research, 1963. p. 184.

269. "His Nobel Prize Acceptance Speech," Story, Issue 2, 36 (March-April, 1963). New York: Story Magazine, 1962.

270. "J. S.'s Acceptance Speech for the Nobel Prize for Literature in 1962," Vogue, 141 (March 1, 1963), 16. Also in Donohue (ed.), pp. 293-95.

271. "J. S's (Nobel Prize) Acceptance Speech," Vogue, 141 (March 1, 1963), 16.

272. "Man's Hope: S. in Stockholm; Excerpt from His Address," Newsweek, 60 (December 24, 1962), 67.

273. "Nobel Prize Acceptance Speech and the Presentation by Anders Osterling," Nobel Prize Lectures (1901-1967), ed. Horst Frentz. New York: American Elsevier Publishing Co., 1969. pp. 575-77.

274. "Nobel Prize Acceptance Speech," A Supplement to the Book-of-the-Month Club News. New York: Book-of-the-Month Club, 1962 (4 pp.).

275. O. Henry's Full House (1952).
[Copyrighted in 1952 by 20th Century Fox Film Corporation, consisting of 5 O. Henry stories].
Narrated by J. S.

276. "Speech Accepting the Nobel Prize for Literature, Stockholm, December 10, 1962." New York: Viking Press, 1962.
[3,200 copies have been printed].

277. "To the Swedish Academy; Nobel Prize Acceptance Speech," Story, 139 (1963), 6-8.

I. VERSE (278-289)

278. "Atropos: Study of a Very Feminine Obituary Editor," Stanford Lit, 1 (March, 1926), 95.
[Stanford Lit is not an abbreviation of Stanford Literature].

279.   "Baubles," Monterey Beacon, 1 (January 5, 1935), 7
        [Amnesia Glasscock as pseudonym].

280.   "Four Shades of Navy Blue," Monterey Beacon, 1
        (January 26, 1935), 12.
        [Amnesia Glasscock as pseudonym].

281.   "The Genius," Monterey Beacon, 1 (January 26, 1935),
        12.
        [Amnesia Glasscock as pseudonym].

282.   "If Eddie Guest Had Written the Book of Job: Happy
        Birthday," Stanford Lit, 1 (March, 1926), 94.

283.   "If John A. Weaver Had Written Keats' Sonnet in the
        American Language: On Looking at a New Book by
        Harold Bell Wright," Stanford Lit, 1 (March, 1926),
        94.

284.   "Ivanhoe," Monterey Beacon, 1 (January 26, 1935), 12.
        [Amnesia Glasscock as pseudonym].

285.   "Mammy," Monterey Beacon, 1 (January 5, 1935), 7.
        [Amnesia Glasscock as pseudonym].

286.   "Song of the Disgusted Modern," Monterey Beacon, 1
        (February 2, 1935), 7.

287.   "Thoughts on Seeing a Stevedore," Monterey Beacon, 1
        (January 26, 1935), 11.
        [Amnesia Glasscock as pseudonym].

288.   "To Carmel," Monterey Beacon, 1 (January 5, 1935),
        7.

289.   "The Visitor," Monterey Beacon, 1 (January 5, 1935),
        7.
        [Amnesia Glasscock as pseudonym].

                    J. ADAPTATIONS (290-295)

290.   The Leader of the People. Chicago: Dramatic,
        1952. A dramatization by Luella E. McMahon of S's
        short story.

291.   A Medal for Benny, a screen play by Frank Butler,
       based on J. S. and Jack Wagner's short story, in
       Best Film Plays, 1945, ed. John Gassner and Dudley
       Nichols. New York: Crown, 1946. pp. 586-648.

292.   Molly Morgan, based on story from The Pastures of
       Heaven, dramatized by Reginald Lawrence. New
       York: Dramatic, 1961.
       [Chicago: Dramatic, 1951].

293.   Osborn, Paul (ed.), "Dialogue Script: East of Eden, "
       Study of Current English (Tokyo), 10 (September,
       1955), 16-32.
       [Screen play of S's novel in English with Japanese
       translation, continued from August issue].

294.   Pipe Dream (Musical comedy by Richard Rogers and
       Oscar Hammerstein II; the script of the Broadway
       musical play by Oscar Hammerstein II. (Based on
       Sweet Thursday). New York: Viking Press, 1954.

295.   A Screen play by Nunnally Johnson, based on G. of W.
       in Twenty Best Film Plays 1941-42, ed. John Gass-
       ner and Dudley Nichols. New York: Crown, 1943.
       pp. 333-77.

                 K. EXCERPTS FROM S. (296-351)

       From America and Americans (1966)

296.   "I Rediscover America, " The Sacramento Union Family
       Weekly, April 21, 1963.

297.   "March Hare Mother, " Library Journal, 91 (December
       15, 1966), 6169.

298.   "What's Happening to America?" Reader's Digest, 89
       (1966), 175-76.

       From Bombs Away (1942)

299.   "The Aerial Engineer, " Scholastic, 43 (December 6,
       1943), 17-18.

300.   Bombs Away, PS (1943).

301.   "We're Off to Berlin," PS (1963).

        From Cannery Row (1945)

302.   "Cannery Row," Argosy, 6 (September, 1945), 17-34.

303.   "Frog Hunt," PS.

304.   "Life in the Great Tide Pool," Book of the Sea, ed.
        A. C. Spectorsky. New York: Appleton-Century
        Crofts, 1954. pp. 450-51.

        From East of Eden (1952)

305.   "Adam & His Sons," "Choice and Responsibility,"
        "Technology & a Technocrat," "Timshel," PS (1971),
        pp. 553-618.

306.   "Afterglow," Argosy, 14 (January, 1953), 29-48.

307.   "East of Eden," Reader's Digest Condensed Books, 8
        (Summer, 1956), pp. 34-254 (Illustrations by Stevan
        Dohanos).

308.   "The Sons of Cyrus Trask," (Chapter 3 of E of E),
        Lilliput (November-December, 1952), 89-102.

309.   "Writer's Credo," Reader's Digest, 62 (March, 1953),
        130.

        From The Grapes of Wrath (1939)

310.   Chapters 13, 14, and 15 from The Grapes of Wrath
        in The Literature of the United States, ed. W. Blair,
        et al. Chicago: Scott, Foresman, 1949.

311.   "Empty House" and "The Turtle," The Craft of Prose,
        ed. Robert H. Woodward. Belmont, California:
        Wadsworth, 1963 (1968). pp. 52-53; 290-92.

312.   "The Grapes of Wrath," The American Writer and the
        Great Depression, ed. Harvey Swados. Indianapolis:
        Bobbs Merrill, 1966. pp. 119-29.

312.   "The Grapes of Wrath," Composition: An Approach
        Through Reading by Lucille Clifton and Alexander
        MacGibbon. New York: Harcourt, Brace and World,

1968. pp. 51-54.

312. "From The Grapes of Wrath," Currents by Delores
      Minor. New York: Harcourt, Brace and Jovanovich,
      1971. pp. 93-96.

312. "The G. of W.," PS (1943).

313. "No Riders," SR, 19 (April, 1939), 13-14.

314. "The Okies," The Great Depression, ed. David A.
      Shannon. Englewood Cliffs, N. J.: Prentice-Hall,
      1964. pp. 68-71.

315. "Social 'World' of the Transients' Camp," Outside
      Readings in Sociology, ed. E. A. Schuler, et al.
      New York: Crowell, 1952. pp. 170-74.

316. "The Turtle," Reading I've Liked, ed. Clifton Fadi-
      man. London: Hamish Hamilton, 1946. pp. 500-502.

317. "The Turtle," "The Last Clear Definite Function of
      Man," "Migrant People," "Life and Death," "Break-
      fast and Work," "Ma and Tom," "The Flood," PS.
      pp. 423-80.

318. "Two for a Penny," Reader's Digest, 37 (August, 1940),
      9-12. Also in Reader's Digest Omnibus. London:
      Andre Deutsch, 1952. pp. 297-301.

319. (Two quotations from The Grapes of Wrath) The
      Penguin Dictionary of Modern Quotations, ed. J. M.
      and M. J. Cohen. Harmondsworth: Penguin Books,
      1971. p. 218.

320. "The Women Watch Their Men," The Treasure Chest:
      An Anthology of Contemplative Prose, ed. J. Donald
      Adams. New York: Dutton, 1946. pp. 374-75.

      From In Dubious Battle (1936)

321. "A Future We Can't Foresee," PS.

322. "A Truce in the Battle," The Social Rebel in American
      Literature, ed. Robert H. Woodward and James J.
      Clark. New York: Odyssey Press, 1968. pp. 270-
      75.

From Journal of a Novel (1969)

323.   "Journal of a Novel," Daily Telegraph Magazine, No.
        292 (May 22, 1970), 40-41, 43, 46.

323.   "Journal of a Novel," Writer, 83 (1970), 13-15.

From "Letters to Alicia"

324.   "My Dear Friend Genga," Reader's Digest, 89 (1966),
        128.
        [Condensed from Newsday].

From The Log from the Sea of Cortez (1951)

325.   "The Log from the Sea of Cortez," A Treasury of the
        World's Great Diaries, ed. Phillip Dunaway.   Garden
        City, N.Y.: Doubleday, 1957.

326.   "Out of the Two Approaches," Writing From Experi-
        ence, ed. Richard A. Condon and B. O. Kurth.   New
        York: Harper, 1960. pp. 119-22.

327.   "Sea Cow," Argosy, 12 (December, 1951), 49-51.

From The Long Valley (1938)

328.   "The Chrysanthemums," "Flight," "The Harness,"
        "The Snake," PS. pp. 3-71, 417-22.

329.   "The Promise," The Young Man in American Litera-
        ture: The Initiation Theme, ed. William Coyle.   New
        York: Odyssey, 1969. pp. 58-72, passim.

From The Moon Is Down (1942, 1943)

330.   "The Debt Shall Be Paid," PS (1963).

331.   "The Moon Is Down," Argosy, 3 (New Series) (Sep-
        tember, 1942), 91-124, (October, 1942), 89-124.

331.   "The Moon Is Down" (Play), The Best Plays in 1941-
        42, ed. Robert B. Mantle. New York: Dodd, Mead,
        1942. pp. 72-108.

331.   "The Moon Is Down," Reader's Digest, 40 (June,
        1942), 115-52.

331. "The Moon Is Down," Reader's Digest, 90 (June, 1967), 151-56, 159-60, 162, 164-66, 168, 171-72, 174-77, 179, 181-85, 187-89, 191, 194-96, 199-200, 203-204 (British).

From Of Mice and Men (1937)

332. "Of Mice and Men," Argosy, 2 (New Series), (April, 1941), 115-157.

332. "Of Mice and Men," Daily Express, June 28, 1937, p. 8; June 29, 1937, p. 4; June 30, 1937, p. 18; July 1, 1937, p. 8; July 2, 1937, p. 4; July 3, 1937, p. 4.

332. "Of Mice and Men" (Play), The Best Plays of 1937-1938, ed. Robert B. Mantle. New York: Dodd, Mead, 1938. pp. 31-66.

From Once There Was a War (1958)

333. "Lilli Marlene," Diner's Delight: The Best of the Diner's Club Magazine, ed. Matty Simmons and Sam Boal. London: Souvenir Press, 1963. pp. 322-24.

334. "Man with a Ski Nose," This Was Your War, ed. F. Bookhauser. Garden City, N.Y.: Doubleday, 1960. pp. 431-33.

335. "A Night on Ventotone," Argosy, 20 (September, 1959), 56-66.

336. "The Routine at a Bomber Station; Excerpt from Once There Was a War," This Was Your War. pp. 256-58.

337. "Troopship," Reader's Digest, 44 (April, 1944), 54-57.

From The Pastures of Heaven (1932)

338. "Molly Morgan," "Pat Humbert's," "Tularecito," PS. pp. 73-1, 329.

From The Red Pony (1937)

339. "The Red Pony," The Great Horse Omnibus, ed.

Thurston Macauley.   London: Eyre and Spottiswoode,
1957.   pp. 21-26.

339(a). "The Red Pony," Great Horse Stories of the World,
ed. Thurston Macauley.   London: New English Library, 1968.   pp. 15-20.

From A Russian Journal (1948)

340.   "We Can Only Think of Augustus Caesar," Treasury
of Great Reporting: Literature Under Pressure from
the 16th Century to our Own Time, ed. L. L. Snyder
and R. B. Morris.   New York: Simon & Schuster,
1949.   pp. 711-13.

From The Sea of Cortez (1941)

341.   "Easter Sunday," The World's Best: 105 Greatest Living Authors, ed. Whit Burnett.   New York: Dial
Press, 1950.   pp. 61-76.
        [Chapter 14 of The Log.   "March 24, Easter Sun-
day"].

342.   "Gathering Knowledge," The Treasure Chest, ed.
James D. Adams, New York: Dutton, 1946.   p. 373.

343.   "Homing," "Old Man of the Sea," PS (1963), pp. 532-
34.

343(a). " 'Is' Thinking and 'Living Into'," "The Pearl of La
Paz," "Parable of Laziness," "Differences," " 'It
Might Be So'," PS (1971), pp. 481-520.

From Sweet Thursday (1954)

344.   "Sweet Thursday," Argosy, 15 (October, 1954), 67-
82.   (November, 1954), 31-46, (December, 1954),
85-100.

From Tortilla Flat (1935)

345.   "Danny," "Pilon," "The Pirate," "The Treasure
Hunt," "Tortillas and Beans," PS. pp. 133-91.

From Travels with Charley (1962)

346.   "The Cheerleaders," The Outnumbered, ed. Charlotte
Brooks. New York: Dell, 1967.

347. "Forests," Daily Telegraph Magazine, No. 270.
December 12, 1969. pp. 36-42, 44.

348. "J. S's Travels with Charley," Americana (American
Motors Magazine), 1 (November-December, 1965), 21-
22.

349. "People," "Texan Ostentation," "Southern Troubles,"
"Last Leg," PS (1971).

350. "Travels with Charley," Argosy, 23 (December, 1962),
38-41.

350. "Travels with Charley," Reader's Digest, 84 (June,
1964), 275-78f.

350. "Travels with Charley," Reader's Digest, 85 (July,
1964), 175-78, 181-84, 187-88, 191-92, 197-200, 203.

350. "Travels with Charley," The Whole Wide World, A
Treasure of Great Travel Writings of our Time, ed.
William Clifford. New York: Crown, 1965, pp. 53-
7.

From The Winter of Our Discontent (1961)

351. "The Winter of Our Discontent," Reader's Digest Condensed Books. Vol. 32 (Summer, 1962), 135-297.
(Illustrations by Stevan Dohanos).

L. ANTHOLOGIZED WORK (352-356)

352. Nobel Prize Library. William Faulkner, Eugene
O'Neill, J. S. New York: Alexis Gregory; Del Mar,
California: CRM Publishing, 1971. pp. 201-375.
Contents:
John Steinbeck:
Presentation Address
Acceptance Address
Acceptance Speech
In Dubious Battle
The Life and Works of John Steinbeck
The 1962 prize

353. The Portable Steinbeck, ed. Pascal Covici. New York:

Viking Press, 1943. Enlarged editions, 1946 and
1958.
Contents:
   I.   Introduction by Lewis Gannett
  II. Excerpts from: The Long Valley; The Pas-
      tures of Heaven; Tortilla Flat; In Dubious
      Battle; The Grapes of Wrath; The Sea of
      Cortez; The Moon Is Down; Bombs Away;
      Cannery Row
 III. Complete Works: Of Mice and Men; The
      Red Pony; A Fragment ("Breakfast"),
      An uncollected story: "How Edith Mc-
      Gillicuddy Met R. L. S." The Red Pony.
      New York: Covici-Friede, 1937.
        I.   "The Gift"
        II. "The Great Mountains"
       III. "The Promise" (The 1945 ed. includes
          IV. "The Leader of the People.")

354.   The Portable Steinbeck revised and selected by Pascal
      Covici, Jr. New York: Viking, 1971.
      Contents:
      Introduction by Pascal Covici, Jr.; Biographical and
      Bibliographical Notes
      From The Long Valley
        "Flight"; "The Snake"; "The Harness"; "The
        Chrysanthemums"
      From The Pastures of Heaven
        "Tularecito"; "Molly Morgan"; "Pat Humbert's"
      From Tortilla Flat
        "Danny"; "Pilon"; "The Pirate"; "The Treasure
        Hunt"; "Tortillas and Beans"
      From In Dubious Battle
        "A Future We Can't Foresee"
      Of Mice and Men (Complete novel)
      The Red Pony
      From The Long Valley
        "The Turtle"; "The Last Clear Definite Function
        of Man"; "Migrant People"; "Life and Death";
        "Breakfast and Work"; "Ma and Tom"; "The
        Flood"
      From Sea of Cortez
        " 'Is' Thinking and 'Living Into' "; "The Pearl
        of La Paz"; "Parable of Laziness"; "Differ-
        ences"; " 'It Might Be So' "
      From "About Ed Ricketts"
        "Knowing Ed Ricketts..."; "Speculative Meta-
        physics"

From Cannery Row
"Frog Hunt"
From East of Eden
"Adam and His Sons"; "Choice and Responsibili-
ty"; Technology and a Technocrat"; "Timshel"
Two Uncollected Stories
"The Affair at 7, rue de M..."; "How Mr.
Hogan Robbed a Bank"
From Travels with Charley in Search of America
"People"; "Texan Ostentation"; "Southern Trou-
bles"; "Last Leg"
The Language of Awareness
From East of Eden
Nobel Prize Acceptance Speech

355.   The Short Novels. Introduced by Joseph Henry Jack-
son. New York: Viking Press, 1953. Book Club
Edition, 1963. This includes:
Cannery Row; The Moon is Down; Of Mice and Men;
The Pearl; The Red Pony; and Tortilla Flat
London: Heinemann, 1954. New edition: Completely
reset in 1963, with Tortilla Flat newly copyrighted
1962 and The Red Pony in 1961.

356.   The Steinbeck Omnibus, ed. Pascal Covici. London:
William Heinemann, 1950. Includes long and representative passages or complete stories from:
The LV; The Pastures of Heaven; Tortilla Flat; In
Dubious Battle; The Grapes of Wrath; Sea of Cortez; The Moon Is Down; and Bombs Away. In addition Of Mice and Men and The Red Pony are given
complete, the latter including the 4th part, not published in the original volume.

M. UNPUBLISHED MANUSCRIPTS (357-379)

A List of Steinbeck Manuscripts, Unpublished Letters by and
to the Author, Documents and Special Collections Relating to
Him (Materials are arranged by institution in which they are
currently held.   See the Key to Abbreviations if necessary.)
The descriptions are varied, for each library catalogs unique-
ly.

357.   American Academy of Arts and Letters
633 West 155th Street
New York, N.Y. 10032

One-page handwritten critical appraisal of John O'Hara.

Seven letters to Miss Felicia Geffen, Assistant to
the President of the Academy.

Thirteen letters to the author.

Two documents relating to the author: his nomination to the National Institute of Arts and Letters, and
his nomination to the American Academy of Arts and
Letters.

358.   Ball State University Library
        The Elizabeth R. Otis Steinbeckiana Collection
        Muncie, Indiana 47306

        "A Postcard to Mr. Harry W. Zollars" (AS), Los
        Gatos, California, postmarked October 25, 1937 (182).

        "A Postcard to Mr. Harry W. Zollars" (TS unsigned),
        Postmarked Los Gatos, California, November 7,
        1937 (183).

        Steinbeck: Handwritten Letter. One-page (184).

        "A Letter to Mr. Harry W. Zollars from Carol
        Steinbeck" (TLS). postmarked January 11, 1939 [on
        the stationery of "Carol Steinbeck, Greenwood Road,
        Los Gatos, California"]. Mailing envelope is hand
        addressed (185).

        ALS. October 21, 1937. 1p., 4to. To "Mr. Fol-
        som." Declines to a manuscript for a limited edition
        to be published by the Booksellers' Guild.

        ALS. October 21, 1937. 1p., 4to. To "Mr. Fol-
        som." Declines to furnish a ms. for a limited ed.
        to be published by the Bookseller's Guild. (Ibid.,
        1965, 2, 976).

        ALS. April 25, (n.d.). To a Mr. Decker. States
        he has no ms. (From American Book Prices Current,
        1964, 1, 872). ·

        ALS. April 25, (n.d.) 1p. To a Mr. Decker.
        States he has no manuscripts.

A Letter from Steinbeck about the Greek edition of
East of Eden (1953) in An Exhibition of American and
Foreign Editions (May, 1963), p. 27.

359.   The California State Library
       Sacramento, California 95809

       Two author cards filled out by the author in June,
       1935.

360.   Cornell University Library
       Ithaca, N.Y. 14850

       Three ALS to Franklin Folsom, October 2, 1938?, 1p.;
       to George Jean Nathan, April 19, 1938, 1p.; and to
       George Jean Nathan, May 23, 19??, 1p.

       One letter from Theodore Dreiser, January 24, 1940,
       4p.

361.   Harvard University
       The Houghton Library
       Cambridge, Mass.   02138

       Twenty-one letters by the author:
           ALS to William Needham, September 9, 1936.
           Seven ALS and APS to Lawrence Clark Powell,
               October, 1936-April 5, 1939 and n.d.
           TLS to Roger W. Watkins, May 13, 1938.
           Three ALS to Alexander Woolcott, May 7, 1937-
               August 29, 1937.

       Miscellaneous newspaper clippings, offprints, bib-
       liographical notes, etc., collected by Lawrence Clark
       Powell.

362.   Indiana University Library
       Bloomington, Indiana 47401

       One ALS to Upton Sinclair from Los Gatos, California,
       n.d.

       ALS from Los Gatos, California, April 3, 1934 (car-
       bon copy).

363.   The Library of Congress
       Manuscript Division
       Washington, D.C.   20540

The Grapes of Wrath, TL with MS corrections. 751 p.

The Grapes of Wrath, corrected proof sheets.
(Both were presented to the Library by the late
Frank J. Hogan in 1941).

Sea of Cortez in collaboration with Edward R. Ricketts,
TS with MS corrections. 447 p., September 5, 1941.

Sea of Cortez, corrected proof sheets and a type-
written bibliography, with related correspondence.
(Sea of Cortez presented to the Library by Viking
Press, March 18, 1943).

2 letters to James A. Michener, February 28 and
March 18, 1957. In The James A. Michener Papers.

364.   Louisiana State University
        Department of Archives and Manuscripts
        Baton Rouge, La. 70803

        Two letters which mention the author: TLS by Lyle
        Saxon to Judith Hyamas Douglas, 1943, 2 p., March
        24, 1943 and June 1, 1943 (Three letters are in the
        Judith Hyamas Douglas Papers, a collection of 578
        items of the late Mrs. Douglas (1875-1955).

365.   Mills College Library
        Oakland, California 94613

        ALS to Albert Bender, n.d., about 5 lines, in which
        the author declines an invitation to see Mr. Bates.

366.   Museum of the City of New York
        5th Avenue at 104th Street
        New York, New York 10029

        "The Moon Is Down" Mi MS, 102 p. (the play at the
        Martin Beck Theatre on April 7, 1942).

367.   New York Public Library
        5th Avenue and 42nd Street
        New York, New York 10018

        "Tortilla Flat" MS foreword, 1937.   5p. (MS and
        letters in the Berg Collection).

ALS to Whitfield Kane, February, 1950. 1p., w.e.
(in the Whitfield Kane Papers).

ALS to (John Mackenzie) Cory, September 14, 1953.
1p. (in Miscellaneous Papers).

368.   The Pierpont Morgan Library
        33 East Thirty-sixth Street
        New York, New York 10016

One ALS by the author.

"Address before the Swedish Academy on Receiving
the Nobel Prize for Literature":

Eight MS pages in pencil: p. 1, outline of address;
pp. 2-8, includes first and second draft of the
proposed speech.

TS of early drafts of speech with MS corrections,
3p. With three carbon copies, uncorrected.

Three MS pages of part of third draft, with three
TS pages slightly corrected, with two carbon copies,
uncorrected.

Three four-page TS after the above.

Five MS and corrected TS pages of the fifth draft.

Final MS draft headed "Freeze it now." 4p.

TS of speech with MS slips added.

Final TS of speech with MS slips added and TS
much corrected.

TS of radio announcement made on the 25th of
October, 1962 by Dr. Anders Osterling, et al.
Printed two leaf pamphlets issued by the Book-of-
the-Month Club, "Nobel Prize Acceptance Speech
by John Steinbeck."

"Short Reign of Pippin IV": The author's MS consisting of thirty autograph pages, 196 typewritten pages
with autograph corrections and additions, and sixty-
four uncorrected typewritten pages (c. 1957).

"The Winter of Our Discontent," MS in pen and pencil on sheets of yellow pad paper. 1960-61. 356p. (This item is in addition to the later typewritten MS with autograph corrections which was presented to the Library by Steinbeck in 1961).

"The Winter of Our Discontent," MS.

"Travels with Charley in Search of America," MS. The last two items were presented by the author in 1961).

368(a). Princeton University Library
Princeton, New Jersey 08540

S. letters to Adlai E. Stevenson (unspecified).

369.   Stanford University Libraries
Stanford, California 94305

TLS to Anne Hadden, February 8, 1935, 2p.

ALS to Leon Gelber, August 15, 1940, 1p.

370.   Steinbeck Research Center Library
California State University at San Jose
San Jose, California 95114

Special Collection.

371.   Tulane University Libraries
Howard-Tilton Memorial Library
New Orleans, Louisiana 70118

ALS to Lyle Saxon, "New Orleans, January 6, 1964," 2p., Gwyn Steinbeck to Saxon, "June 22, 1943," 1p., "New York, October 1, 1943," 1p., and "Mexico (City), March 8, 1944," 1p.

372.   University of California at Berkeley Libraries
The Bancroft Library
Berkeley, California 94720

Four folders containing:
    A letter from the Cerveceria Cuanhtemoc in Monterey, Mexico, December 22, 1944; and a carbon of a release of rights, October 12, 1944.

ALS to Joseph Fontenrose, February 2, 1949, 2p., w. e. and 1-leaf TS; Also copy of prospectus of essay by the latter, 2-leaves.

TS of unpublished essay, with explanatory note. Carbon, 2-leaves, TS, 1-leaf.

In addition the Bancroft Library has the following:

Fifty-one letters from the author during the period 1930-50 (in the George S. Albee Papers), with a letter, October 11, (1935) from Carol H. Steinbeck and a postcard, c. September 20 (1951) from Elaine S. Steinbeck.

Thirty-five letters from the author during 1936-1948 (in the Joseph Henry Jackson papers).

ALS from the author, March 23, 1959 (in the Gertrude Albertson Papers).

ALS from the author, February 19, 1959 (in the Mark Schorer Papers).

ALS from the author to Benjamin H. Lehman, c. 1932, TSS, 1-leaf (in the Rafe Book Room of the General Library).

Additions since 1965 (August, 1972):

Correspondence with A. Grove Day, 1925-50. 1 portfolio.

Fragment of a journal, 1943. Photocopy.

Galley proofs of The Wayward Bus.

Letters to Gwendolyn C. S. and other papers, ca. 1941-61. 1 box.

Letter to Joseph Fontenrose, August 26, 1958, from Sag Harbor.

Letters and Mss., 1938-63. 1 box.

Letters to Mr. and Mrs. Ritchie Lovejoy.

Letter to S. from John Roy Carlson.

Letters to the Steinbecks from Hector Bolitho,
Paul de Kruif, Gene Fowler, Howard O. Hunter,
Charles Jackson, Ed. Ricketts, Barnie Stavis,
Annie Laurie Williams, Stanley Young, and others.

MS. of "The Red Pony."

Nathaniel Benchley's theme on Of Mice and Men.

Notebook containing draft of scenario for the film,
The Forgotten Village.

Photographs.

Preface for an unpublished handbook on common
marine invertebrates of the California coast.

Scenario for the film, The Red Pony.

373.   University of Colorado Library
       Boulder, Colorado 80304

       ALS to Paul Carter, February 2, 1955, 2p., 48 lines
       on legal size paper.

374.   University of Pennsylvania Libraries
       The Charles Patterson Van Pelt Library
       Philadelphia, Pennsylvania 19104

       Four letters from the author:
          To Theodore Dreiser, January 28, 1940, 1p.
          To Burton Rascoe, January 25, 1935?, 1p.
          September 9, 1935, 1p., and January 12,
          1936, 1p.

375.   University of Southern California Library
       Los Angeles, California 90007

       ALS by the author to Karl Zamboni, a Los Angeles
       book dealer, January 2, 1935.

376.   The University of Texas
       Academic Center Library
       Austin, Texas 78712

       Five ALS to Ben Abramson, n.d., 1p.; n.d., 1p.;
       n.d., 1p.; n.d., 1 and 1/2p.; and n.d., 1p.

ANS to Ben Abramson, July 22, 1941, 1p.

Two APS to Ben, "March 4, 1935"; and "October 1, 1935"

TLS to Ben, July 14, 1935, 1p.

List of names headed "Of Mice and Men", 3p., with signed note to Ben on p. 3, n.d.

ANS to Mrs. (John Stuart) Groves, "February 27, 1956."

TLS to Mabs (Gertrude Anderson), February 19, 1947, 1p.

TL to Mabs and Max, December 1, 1947, 1p.

TLS to Max, a note saying "Answered November 29, 1946," 1p.

Three ALS to Max and Mabs, January 3, 1946, 1p.; January 25, 19??, 1p. ("January 28, 1950"); and n.d. ("April 21, 1946").

Telegram from the author to Gwyn Conger and Maxwell Anderson, June 22, 1949.

Telegram to Maxwell Anderson, January 7, 19??.

ALS to Mrs. (Francis Warren) Roberts, February 8, 1960, 1p.

376(a). The University of Texas
Humanities Research Center
Box 7219
Austin, Texas 78712

Additions since 1966:

Nineteen letters from Steinbeck.   Date received: 25 March 1969.

Steinbeck, John.   L.S. 1 full page, 4to, Pacific Grove, California, April 13, 1932.   To Mr. Ballou, accompanied by a carbon of his reply.   Two pieces.

Two LsS, each almost 1 full page, 4to, Salinas, California, June 1 and August 8, 1933. To "Dear Ballou."

Two LsS, each 1 full page, 4to, Salinas, County of Monterey (California), June 12 and September 11, 1933. To "Dear Ballou."

ALS, "John." 1p. folio, Los Gatos (California), Thursday. To "Dear Bob."

LS, 2 and 1/4p., 4to (on three separate leaves), Election Day, Eagle Rock, California. With an AL (unsigned), 1 and 1/4p., 4to, and an original, holograph postmarked envelope. To Robert Ballou. In all, three pieces.

ALS, "John," almost 1 and 1/2p., 8vo (on two different leaves), Pacific Grove, February 27. With an LS, "John," almost 1 full page, 4to, Wednesday. To Mr. Ballou. Two pieces.

ALS, 2p., 8vo (penned on different leaves), Salinas, California, August 13. With a typewritten letter (signed "js" by typewriter), 1p., 4to, Pacific Grove, California. To "Dear Ballou." Two pieces.

LS, 3/4 p., 4to, County of Monterey, Salinas, California, July 18 (probably 1933). To "Dear Ballou."

LS and brief ALS. To Robert Ballou. Two pieces. Comprises: STEINBECK LS, 1 and 1/4p. (on two separate 4to pages), Montrose, California, January 13. Steinbeck, ALS, "John," five lines on a small sheet, commenting on a book.

Group of four LsS (two with initials, one "John," the other by typewriter), each about 3/4p., 4to to 8vo, Pacific Grove and Salinas, California, November 6 to 20, 1933. To Robert Ballou.

"The Wayward Bus." Corrected typescript and galley proofs. Published 1947. Date received: April 8, 1969.

Steinbeck Manuscript of "The Wayward Bus." Date

received: May 1, 1969.

Pascal Covici Collection--(John Steinbeck Collection)
including more than 5,000 pages of holograph manuscript or original typescript by John Steinbeck, a
unique journal by J. S. in the form of a letter to
Pascal Covici, and letters from J. S. to Pascal
Covici.   Date received: May 13, 1969.

Gift of Pascal Covici, Jr. (March 21, 1972) Letter
from Mrs. John Steinbeck to Pascal Covici, Jr.,
Date received: May 13, 1969.

TMS of "America and the Americans." Date received: March 8, 1971.

377.   University of Virginia
       The Clifton Waller Barrett Library
       Charlottesville, Virginia 22901

"The Grapes of Wrath"; AMS for "The Grapes of
Wrath" in ink on 165 pages of blue-lined paper re-
moved from a bound ledger (10" x 16").

The MS is untitled and is headed, "New Start/Big
Writing" (referring to the size of the handwriting).

Acquired for the Clifton Waller Barrett Library by
Mr. Barrett from John Howell Books of San Francisco in 1954.   John Howell Books had acquired it
from Steinbeck's former wife, Carol.)

"The Grapes of Wrath":   Photocopy of TPS, December 17, 1960 to Warren R. Howell.

ALS to Henry Moore, February or March, 1936.

AMS, n.d., bearing note in hand of (Gene Salow)
"added scene for picture version of Of Mice and Men
. . . . . cut out of picture," 3p.

Letters:
    Fifteen ALS to Gene Salow, "August 19, 1949,"
       2p., w.e.;
    October 11, 1949, 1p., w.e.;
    December 30, 1949, 1p., w.e.;
    January 25, [1950], w.e.;

February 8, 1950, 2p., w.e.;
February 20, 1950, 1p., w.e.;
March 30, 1950, 1p., w.e.;
April 11, 1950, 1p., w.e.;
August 15, [1950], 2p., w.e.;
August 22, [1950], 1p., w.e.;
September 14, [1950], 1p., w.e.;
October 21, 1950, 1p., w.e.;
November 2, [1950], 1p., w.e.;
November 5, 1950 and November 17; (written in
   two parts about a week apart), 4p., w.e.;
January 27, [1951], 1p., w.e.

PS to Gene Salow, February 10, 1954.

TLS to Gene Salow, November 9, 1962, 1p., w.e.

Photograph of post card, December 17, 1960 to John
Howell.

Newspaper picture of the author and his wife, Elaine,
inscribed and initialed by the author, n.d.

PS to Wilbur Needham, August 6, 1936, 2p.

ALS to W. N., April 4, (1934), 1p., w.e.

TLS to W. N., "February 7, 1935," 2p., w.e.

Two APS to W. N., "January 3, 1936 and October 4,
1938."

TL to W. N., "June 6, 1939," 1p., w.e.

ALS to Merle Armitage, February 17, 1939.

ALS to W. N., "September 29, 1940," 2p.

TLS to M. A., December 31, 1946, 1p.

TLS to H. Kauti, February 16, 1953, 1p.

TLS to M. A., December 1, 1958, 1p.

Two APS to W. N., "n.d., 1935?"; February 12,
19??.

Two ALS to W. N. from Manchester S., Mexico

D. F., n.d., 4p., w.e.; and n.d., written from Los
Gatos, 1p.

ALS to Docker, April 25, 19?? (Purchased on January 13, 1966).

Additions since 1965 (August, 1972):
    Map made by S. for Louis Paul of Los Gatos,
        California. [1936].
    Notes made by [Mary Paul] re. S. and his works.
        n.d.
    Photograph. S. seated. n.d.
    ALS to Merle Armitage. February 17, 1939. 1p.
    ALS to Merle Armitage. May 10, 1940. 1p.
    TLS to Merle Armitage. December 31, 1946. 1p.
    TLS to Merle Armitage. December 1, 1958. 1p.
    APS to Bob Crosby. [?].
    ALS to [?] Docker. April 25, [?]. 1p.
    TLS to H. Kauti. February 16, 1953. 1p.
    ALS to Lola L. Kovener. May 27, 1939. 1p.
    ALS to Wilbur Needham. April 4, [1934]. 1p.
    L to Wilbur Needham. [February 7, 1935]. 2p.
    APS to Wilbur Needham. [January 3, 1936].
    APS to Wilbur Needham. [May 26, 1936].
    APS to Wilbur Needham. [October 4, 1938].
    TL to Wilbur Needham. [June 6, 1939]. 1p.
    ALS to Wilbur Needham. n.d. [from Los Gatos].
        1p.
    ALS to Wilbur Needham. [from Manchester 8,
        Mexico D. F., Mexico]. [n.d. 4p.
    APS to Wilbur Needham. [February 12, 1936].
    ALS to Wilbur Needham. [September 29, 1940].
        2p.
    ALS to Clifford Odets. December 8, [1950]. 1p.
    ALS to Clifford Odets. December 13, [1950]. 1p.
    APS to Clifford Odets. [1951]. 1p.
    ALS to Louis Paul. [September, 1935]. 2p.
    APS to Louis Paul. [August 22, 1935].
    ALS to Louis Paul. [1935]. 11 1.
    ALS to Louis Paul. [February, 1936]. 2p.
    ALS to Louis Paul. [February, 1936]. 11 1.
    APS to Louis Paul. [April 6, 1936].
    APS to Louis Paul. [June 11, 1936].
    APS to Louis Paul. [June 22, 1936].
    APS to Louis Paul. [December, 1936].
    APS to Louis Paul. [January 6, 1937].
    APS to Louis Paul. [January 27, 1937].

APS to Louis Paul. [March 7, 1937].
APS to Louis Paul. [May 4, 1937].
APS to Louis Paul. [August 15, 1937].
APS to Louis Paul. [November 12, 1937].
TL [S.] to Louis and Mary Paul. [Fall, 1937].
    11 1.
APS to Louis Paul. [December 28, 1937].
TL to Paul. [December, 1937]. 11 1.
ALS to Louis Paul. [1937]. 11 1.
TP, [S.] to Louis Paul. [January 3, 1938].
APS to Louis and Mary Paul. [March 22, 1938].
APS to Louis Paul. [August 3, 1938].
APS to Louis and Mary Paul. [September 6, 1938].
APS to Louis Paul. [October 18, 1938].
APS to Louis Paul. [July 6, 1939]. [Notes on
    front of card].
APS to Louis Paul. [July 15, 1939].
TL to Louis Paul. [May, 1940]. TL, [xerozed
    copy]. 11 1.
TL to Louis Paul. [December, 1940]. [xeroxed
    copy]. 11 1.
ALS to Louis Paul. [1940]. 11 1.
APS to Louis Paul. [July 15, 1941].
ALS to Louis Paul. [July, 1941]. 11 1.
TLS to Louis Paul. [1941]. [xeroxed copy]. 11 1.
ALS to Louis Paul. [December, 1943]. 11 1.
ALS to Louis Paul. [December, 1945]. 11 1.
ALS to Louis Paul. [1949]. 11 1.
TLS (Carbon), Louis Paul to S. October 29,
    [1961]. 11 1.
ALS to Louis Paul. November 1, 1962. 21 1.

378. Viking Press
    625 Madison Avenue
    New York, N.Y. 10022

    Letters to Pascal Covici, 1937-1964.

379. Yale University Libraries
    New Haven, Connecticut 06520

    Two ALS and one TLS to Ben Abramson, one dated
    September 29 and others undated, from Los Gatos,
    3p.

    TLS from a secretary to Fred B. Millet, April 28,
    1937, from New York, N.Y., 1-leaf, w.e.

Additions:
18 letters and cards to Ben Abramson (Argus Book Shop), 20 pages.
44 retained carbons of typed letters from Abramson to Steinbeck, 71 pages.
Letter to Lawrence Langner (Theatre Guild), January 26, [1950]. 1 page.

PART II.   SECONDARY MATERIAL (380-2184)

A. BOOKS (380-394)

380.   Astro, Richard and Hayashi, Tetsumaro (eds.).
S.: The Man and His Work.   Corvallis: Oregon
State University Press, 1971.
Contents: T. Hayashi, "J. S. Society"; R.
Astro, "Introduction"; J. Ditsky, "Faulkner Land
and S. Country"; C. Shively, "J. S.: From the
Tide Pool to the Loyal Community"; W. Street,
"J. S.: A Reminiscence"; R. E. Morsberger,
"S's Zapata"; J. P. Degnan, "In Definite Battle";
P. Lisca, "Escape and Commitment: Two Poles
of the S. Hero"; J. W. Hedgpeth, "Philosophy on
Cannery Row"; R. M. Benton, "The Ecological
Nature of Cannery Row"; C. R. Metzger, "S's
Mexican-Americans"; R. DeMott, "S. and The
Creative Process (Sweet Thursday)."

381.   Davis, Robert Murray (ed.).   S.:   A Collection of
Critical Essays.   Englewood Cliffs, N.J.:   Prentice-
Hall, 1972.
Contents: Introduction by R. M. Davis; "J. S.
Californian" by Freeman Champney; "The Arthuri-
an Cycle in Tortilla Flat" by André Gide; "The
Unity of In Dubious Battle: Violence and Dehu-
manization" by Howard Levant; "End of a Dream"
by Warren French; "Thematic Rhythm in The Red
Pony" by Arnold L. Goldsmith; "The Grapes of
Wrath" by Peter Lisca; "The Grapes of Wrath" by
George Bluestone; "Sea of Cortez" by Joseph
Fontenrose; "Cannery Row: S's Pastoral Poem"
by Stanley Alexander; "The Pearl: Realism and
Allegory" by Harry Morris; "J. S.:   The Fitful
Daemon" by R. W. B. Lewis.

382.   Donohue, Agnes McNeill (ed.).   A Casebook on The
Grapes of Wrath. New York: Thomas Y. Crowell,
1968.

Books   55

Contents: Lyle H. Doren, "The Grapes of Wrath";
Edwin T. Bowden, "The Commonplace and the Gro-
tesque"; Gerald Cannon, "The Pauline Apostleship
of Tom Joad"; Eric W. Carlson, "Symbolism in
The G. of W."; Frederic I. Carpenter, "The
Philosophic Joads"; Jules Chametzky, "The Ambi-
valent Endings of The G. of W."; Commonweal,
"Red Meat and Red Herrings"; Malcolm Cowley,
"A Farewell to the 1930's"; H. Kelly Crockett,
"The Bible and The G. of W."; George DeSchwein-
itz, "S. and Christianity"; Agnes McNeill Donohue
"The Endless Journey to No End: Journey and
Eden Symbolism in Hawthorne and S."; Charles T.
Dougherty, "The Christ-Figure in The G. of W.";
Thomas F. Dunn, "The G. of W."; Chester E.
Eisinger, "Jeffersonian Agrarianism in The G. of
W."; Warren French, "The Education of the
Heart"; Maxwell Geismer, "J. S.: Of Wrath or
Joy"; Robert J. Griffin and William A. Freedman,
"Machines and Animals: Pervasive Motifs in The
G. of W."; Leo Gurko, "From The Angry Decade";
Harvard Law Review, "Depression Migrants and
The States"; Christopher Isherwood, "The Tragedy
of Eldorado"; Peter Lisca, "The G. of W. as Fic-
tion"; B. R. McElderry, Jr., "The G. of W.: In
the Light of Modern Critical Theory"; Carey Mc-
Williams, "California Pastoral"; Arthur Mizener,
"Does a Moral Vision of the Thirties Deserve a
Nobel Prize?"; Edwin M. Moseley, "Christ as the
Brother of Man; S's G. of W."; The New Yorker,
"Our Man in Helsinki"; Theodore Pollock, "On the
Ending of The G. of W."; Martin Shockley,
"Christian Symbolism in The Grapes of Wrath";
Martin Shockley, "The Reception of The Grapes of
Wrath in Oklahoma"; Samuel Sillen, "Censoring
G. of W."; John Steinbeck, "J. S's Acceptance
Speech for the Nobel Prize for Literature in 1962";
Frank J. Taylor, "California's Grapes of Wrath";
Walter Fuller Taylor, "The G. of W. Recon-
sidered"; James W. Tuttleton, "S. in Russia: The
Rhetoric of Praise and Blame"; Charles C. Wal-
cutt, "Later Trends in Form: S., Hemingway,
Dos Passos"; Edmund Wilson, "From Classics
and Commercials"; James Woodress, "J. S.:
Hostage to Fortune"; Celeste Turner Wright,
"Ancient Analogues of an Incident in J. S."

383.   Fontenrose, Joseph Eddy. John Steinbeck: An

Introduction and Interpretation. New York: Barnes
and Noble, Inc., 1963. American Authors and Critics
Series, 8, ed. by John Mahoney.
Contents:
      Chronology
I.   Biographical Introduction
II.   The First Novels
III.   The Pastures of Heaven
IV.   Tortilla Flat
V.   Torgas Valley and Long Valley
VI.   The Grapes of Wrath
VII. Sea of Cortez
VIII. The Moralities
IX.   East of Eden and After
X.   Conclusion
      Bibliography

384.   French, Warren (ed.). A Companion to The Grapes
of Wrath. New York: Viking, 1963.
Contents: George Bluestone, "Novel into Film:
The G. of W."; Bernard Bowron, "The G. of W.:
A 'Wagons West' Romance"; The Editors of
Fortune, "I Wonder Where We Can Go Now";
Warren French, "Another Look at The G. of W.";
Warren French, "What Became of the Joads?";
Caroline A. Henderson, "Letters from the Dust
Bowl"; Joseph Henry Jackson, "The First Book
J. S. Has Written"; M. M. Leighton, "Geology
of Soil Drifting on the Great Plains"; B. R. Mc-
Elderry, Jr., "The G. of W.: In the Light of
Modern Critical Theory"; Carey McWilliams,
"The End of a Cycle"; Carey McWilliams, "Glory,
Glory, California"; R. Orlova, "Money against
Humanity: Notes on the work of J. S."; Theodore
Pollock, "On The Ending of The G. of W."; Mar-
tin Staples Shockley, "The Reception of The G. of W.
in Oklahoma"; J. S., "Their Blood Is Strong"
(reprint); Ivan Ray Tannehill, "Dusters and Black
Blizzards. "

385.   French, Warren G. John Steinbeck. New York:
Twayne Publishers, 1961 [U.S. Authors Series].
Contents:
      Chronology
1.   The Man Behind the Books
2.   Gatsby Sails the Carribbean
3.   Resurveying the Pastures of Heaven

4. Ways Out of the Wasteland
5. Morte d'Malory
6. Parsifal's Last Stand
7. End of a Dream
8. Adventures in the Long Valley
9. The Education of the Heart
10. Steinbeck Goes to War
11. The Intricate Music of Cannery Row
12. The Defective Pearl
13. The Lean Years
14. Mr. Steinbeck Goes to Town
    Notes and References
    Selected Bibliography

386. Hayashi, Tetsumaro. J. S.: A Concise Bibliography
      (1930-65). Introduction by Warren French. Metuchen,
      N. J.: Scarecrow Press, 1967.

387. Hayashi, Tetsumaro (ed.). S's Literary Dimension:
      A Guide to Comparative Studies. Metuchen, N. J.:
      Scarecrow Press, 1973.
         Contents: Joan Steele, "S. and Charles Dickens";
      John Ditsky, "S. and William Faulkner"; Peter
      Lisca, "S. and Ernest Hemingway"; Andreas K.
      Poulakidas, "S. and Nilos Kazantazakis"; Richard
      Peterson, "S. and D. H. Lawrence"; Richard
      Astro, "S. and Daniel Mainwaring"; John Gribben,
      "S. and John Milton"; Warren French, "S. and J. D.
      Salinger"; Sanford M. Marovitz, "S. and Adlai
      Stevenson"; George H. Spies, III, "S. and Robert
      Penn Warren"; Lawrence W. Jones, "S. and Emile
      Zola"; Peter Lisca, "A Survey of Steinbeck Criti-
      cism"; Tetsumaro Hayashi, "Steinbeck Scholarship:
      Recent Trends in the United States"; Tetsumaro
      Hayashi, "A Selected Bibliography."

388. Lisca, Peter (ed.). John Steinbeck, The Grapes of
      Wrath: Text and Criticism. New York: Viking
      Press, 1972.
         Contents: Editor's Preface; Chronology; the
      Itinerary of the Joads; Text; Criticism including
      Fortune, "I Wonder Where We Can Go Now" etc.;
      Frank J. Taylor, "California's Grapes of Wrath";
      Eric W. Carlson, "Symbolism in G. of W."; Wal-
      ter Fuller Taylor, "The G. of W. Reconsidered;
      Robert J. Griffin and William A. Freedman,
      "Machines and Animals: Pervasive Motifs in The

G. of W. "; Joseph Fontenrose, "The Grapes of
Wrath"; J. P. Hunter, "S's Wine of Affirmation
in G. of W. "; Carey McWilliams, "California Pas-
toral" etc.; Martin Shockley, "The Reception of
The G. of W. in Oklahoma"; Editor's Introduction:
The Pattern of Criticism; Frederic I. Carpenter,
"The Philosophical Joads"; Chester E. Eisinger
"Jeffersonian Agrarianism in G. of W. "; Peter
Lisca, "The Grapes of Wrath as Fiction"; Pascal
Covici, Jr., "Work and the Timeliness of The G.
of W. "; John R. Reed, "The G. of W. and the
Esthetics of Indigence"; Betty Perez, "House and
Home: Thematic Symbols in The G. of W. "; Two
Unpublished Documents including
   1. A Letter from S. to His Editor
   2. S's Suggestion for an Interview with Joseph
       Henry Jackson
Topics for Discussion and Papers
Bibliography

389.   Lisca, Peter. The Wide World of J. S. New
       Brunswick, N. J.: Rutgers University Press, 1958.
       Contents:
       Preface
        1. Introduction: The Failure of Criticism
        2. Cup of Gold
        3. To a God Unknown
        4. The Pastures of Heaven
        5. Tortilla Flat
        6. The Long Valley
        7. In Dubious Battle
        8. Of Mice and Men
        9. The Grapes of Wrath
      10. Sea of Cortez, War Writings, The Moon Is
           Down
      11. Cannery Row
      12. The Pearl
      13. The Wayward Bus
      14. Burning Bright
      15. East of Eden
      16. Sweet Thursday, The Short Reign of Pippin
           IV, Some Conclusion Notes
       Checklist of S's Published Work
       Index

390.   Marks, Lester J. Thematic Continuity in the Novels
       of John Steinbeck. The Hague, Netherlands: Mouton,

1969 (New York: Humanities Press,   1969).
Contents:
Introduction:
    I.   Three Thematic Patterns
          A Private Religion
          The Group Animal and Its Cells
          Non-Teleological Thinking and a Reverence
             for Life
    II. Cup of Gold
   III. To a God Unknown: The Yearning for Ritual
   IV. In Dubious Battle: Non Teleology and the
            Psychology of the Group
    V. A Few Words about "Something That Hap-
            pened"
   VI. The Grapes of Wrath
  VII. The War and a Few Years After
          The War Effort
          The Moon Is Down
          Transition: A Reaffirmation
 VIII. East of Eden: "Thou Mayest"
   IX. Conclusion: Three Novels and a Prize
Bibliography

391.   Moore, Harry Thornton.   The Novels of John Steinbeck: A First Critical Study.   Chicago: Normandie
House, 1939; Port Washington, New York; Kennikat,
1968.
      Contents:
      The Novels: A First Study
      A Biographical Sketch
      A Bibliographical Check-list
      A Note Concerning the Map

392.   O'Connor, Richard.   John Steinbeck (A Biography For
Young People).   New York: McGraw Hill Book Co.,
1970.
      Contents:
    1. The Native Son
    2. The Part-Time College Boy
    3. Breakthrough
    4. A First Taste of Success
    5. No Compromise
    6. "Migrant John"
    7. Watching A War Go By
    8. "Write Something Funny"
    9. Back to Eden
  10. A Prize from Stockholm

11.   The Journey Home
John Steinbeck's Books
Bibliography and Index

393.   Tedlock, Ernest W., Jr. and Wicker, C. V. (eds.).
Steinbeck and His Critics: A Record of Twenty-Five
Years. Albuquerque: University of New Mexico
Press, 1957 (Listed as SHC).
Contents: Joseph Warren Beach, "J. S.: Art and
Propaganda"; Joseph Warren Beach, "J. S.:
Journeyman Artist"; Frederick Bracher, "S. and
the Biological View of Man"; Edwin Berry Burgum,
"The Sensibility of J. S. "; Frederic I. Carpenter,
"J. S.: American Dreamer"; Frederic I. Carpen-
ter, "The Philosophical Joads"; Freeman Champ-
ney, "J. S., Californian"; Lewis Gannett, "J. S. 's
Way of Writing"; Lincoln R. Gibbs, "J. S.: Moral-
ist"; Stanley Edgar Hyman, "Some Notes on J. S. ";
John S. Kennedy, "J. S.: Life Affirmed and Dis-
solved"; Joseph Wood Krutch, "J. S. 's Dramatic
Tale of Three Generations"; Peter Lisca, "J. S.:
A Literary Biography"; Peter Lisca, "S. 's Fable
of The Pearl"; Peter Lisca, "The Wayward Bus--
A Modern Pilgrimage"; Claude-Edmonde Magny,
"S., On the Limits of the Impersonal Novel";
Blake Nevius, "S.: One Aspect"; Burton Rascoe,
"J. S. "; Woodburn O. Ross, "J. S.: Earth and
Stars"; Woodburn O. Ross, "J. S.: Naturalism's
Priest"; Antonia Seixas, "J. S. and The Non-
Teleological Bus"; Martin Staples Shockley, "Chris-
tian Symbolism in The G. of W. "; Martin Staples
Shockley, "The Reception of The G. of W. in
Oklahoma"; J. S., "Critics, Critics, Burning
Bright"; J. S., "A Letter on Criticism (February
5, 1955)"; J. S., "My Short Novels. "

394.   Watt, Frank William. John Steinbeck. London:
Oliver and Boyd, 1962.
[Writers and Critics Series, ed. A. Norman
Jeffares]. Also Evergreen Pilot EP 13. New
York: Grove Press, 1962.
Contents:
1.   Steinbeck and His Sea of Cortez
2.   The Long Valley
3.   The Angry Thirties
4.   The Later Steinbeck
5.   A Note on the Critics
     Bibliography

B. MONOGRAPHS, BOOKLETS, AND PAMPHLETS (395-418)

395.	Alexander, Charlotte. J. S. 's The Grapes of Wrath.
	New York: Monarch Press, 1965.
	[Monarch Notes and Study Guides Series 692-4].

396.	Bennett, Robert. The Wrath of J. S. , or St. John
	Goes to Church. Los Angeles: Albertson Press,
	1939.
	[Pamphlet]. Also in Monthly Record. [n. v.]
	(June, 1950), [n. p.]. [Reprinted by Folcroft
	Press, Gordon Publishers and Haskell House Pub-
	lishers in 1971].

396.	_____. Wrath of John Steinbeck. New York:
	Haskell House, 1939 [Reprint].

397.	Burrows, Michael. John Steinbeck and His Films.
	London: Primestyle, 1970.

398.	Carey, Gary. The Grapes of Wrath Notes. Lincoln,
	Nebraska: Bethany Press, 1965.

399.	_____. Of Mice and Men Notes. Lincoln,
	Nebraska: Cliffs, 1970.

400.	Cooperman, Stanley. Review and Notes and Study
	Guide to Steinbeck. New York: Monarch Press,
	1964.
	[Monarch Review Notes and Study Guide Series
	647].

401.	Fitzwater, Eva. The Pearl Notes. Lincoln,
	Nebraska: Cliffs, 1970.

402.	Gale, Robert L. Barron's Simplified Approach to
	S. 's The G. of W. New York: Barron, 1967.

403.	Gannett, Lewis. John Steinbeck, Personal and Bib-
	liographical Notes. New York: Viking Press, 1939.

403(a).	_____. J. S.: Personal and Bibliographic Notes.
	Lansdowne, Pa.: Lansdowne Press, 1939 (1971).

404.	Garcia, Reloy. S. and D. H. Lawrence: Fictive
	Voices and the Ethical Imperative (Steinbeck Mono-
	graph Series, No. 2, 1972). Muncie, Indiana:

Steinbeck Society of America, Ball State University, 1972.

405.   Goethals, Thomas R. The Grapes of Wrath: A
        Critical Commentary. New York: American R.D.M.
        Corporation, 1963.

406.   Gray, James. John Steinbeck (University of Minne-
        sota Pamphlets of American Writers, No. 94).
        Minneapolis: University of Minnesota Press, 1971.

407.   Hartrangt, Marshall V. Grapes of Gladness. Los
        Angeles: DeVorss & Co., 1939.
        [California's refreshing & inspiring answer to
        J. S.'s The Grapes of Wrath, with extracts from
        the reviews of The Grapes of Wrath by Burton
        Rascoe, John D. Barry, & Thomas W. McManns].

408.   Hayashi, Tetsumaro (ed.). John Steinbeck: A Guide
        to the Doctoral Dissertations (1946-1969) Steinbeck
        Monograph Series, No. 1, 1971, Muncie, Ind.: Ball
        State University, 1971.

409.   Hayashi, Tetsumaro and Siefker, Donald L. (com-
        pilers). The Special Steinbeck Collection of the
        Ball State University Library, A Bibliographical
        Handbook. Muncie, Indiana: John Steinbeck Society
        of America, BSU, 1972.

410.   Highland, Frederick C. The Red Pony and The
        Pearl. New York: American R.D.M. Corporation,
        1965.

411.   Jackson, Joseph Henry. Why Steinbeck Wrote 'The
        Grapes of Wrath,' New York: Limited Editions Club,
        1940.

412.   Liedloff, Helmut. Steinbeck in German Translational
        Practices. Southern Illinois University Monographs,
        Humanities Series, No. 1. Carbondale and Edwards-
        ville: Southern Illinois University, 1965.

413.   Lippman, Bertram. Of Mice and Men, A Critical
        Commentary. New York: American R.D.M. Cor-
        poration, 1964.

414.   Miron, George Thomas. The Truth About John

Steinbeck and the Migrants.   Los Angeles: Haynes
Corporation, 1939.

415.   Monarch Review Notes and Study Guide Series   see
        Alexander, Charlotte; Cooperman, Stanley; and
        Schwerner, Armand.

416.   Pratt, John Clark.   John Steinbeck: A Critical
        Essay. Grand Rapids, Michigan: William B.
        Eerdmans, 1970.

417.   Schwerner, Armand.   J. S.'s Of Mice and Men.
        New York: Monarch Press, 1965.

417(a).   _____.   John Steinbeck's The Red Pony and The
        Pearl. New York: Monarch Press, 1965.

418.   Study-Aid Series.   Notes on John Steinbeck's The
        Pearl.   London: Methuen, 1964 (1966) (28-page
        pamphlet).

C. DOCTORAL DISSERTATIONS (419-438)

419.   Alexander, Stanley Gerald.   "Primitivism and
        Pastoral Form in John Steinbeck's Early Fiction,"
        University of Texas, 1965.   DA, 26 (1966), 2201.

420.   Astro, Richard.   "Into the Cornucopia: Steinbeck's
        Vision of Nature and the Ideal Man," University of
        Washington, 1969.   DA in SN, 2 (1969), 41-42;
        DAI, 30 (1969), 251-A--2518-A.

421.   Bleeker, Gary.   "Setting and Animal Tropes in the
        Fiction of John Steinbeck," University of Nebraska,
        1969. SQ, 3 (1970), 38-39; DAI, 30 (1969), 2998-A.

422.   Casimir, Louis J., Jr.   "Human Emotion and the
        Early Novels of John Steinbeck," University of
        Texas, 1965.   DA, 27 (1966), 472-A.

423.   Ditsky, John Michael.   "Land-Nostalgia in the Novels
        of Faulkner, Cather, and Steinbeck," New York Uni-
        versity, 1967.   DA, 28 (July-September, 1967),
        1072-A; DA in SQ, 2 (1969), 68-69.

424.   Feied, Frederick.   "S's Depression Novels: The

Ecological Basis," Columbia University, 1968. DAI,
32 (July, 1971), 427-A--428-A.

425.   Freel, Eugene L.   "A Comparative Study Between
       Certain Concepts and Principles of Modern Psy-
       chology and the Main Writings of John Steinbeck,"
       New York University, 1946.   Also in Microfilm Ab-
       stracts, 7 (1947), 124.   New York University.

425(a). Gajewski, Anton.   "S's Short Stories Between the Two
       World Wars," Adam Mickiewicz University, Poznan,
       Poland, 1971.

426.   Johnson, Charles Daniel.   "A Pedagogical Study in
       Contrastive Cultural Analysis Illustrated by Stein-
       beck's Travels with Charley in Search of America,"
       University of Michigan, 1966.   DA, 27 (April-June,
       1967), 3775-A.

427.   Kagan, Sheldon S.   " 'Goin' Down the Road Feelin'
       Bad'--John Steinbeck's The Grapes of Wrath and
       Migrant Folklore," University of Pennsylvania, 1971.
       DAI, 32 (February, 1972), 4507-A.

428.   Levant, Howard Stanley.   "A Critical Study of the
       Longer Fiction of John Steinbeck," Cornell Univer-
       sity, 1962.   SQ, 3 (1970), 19-21; DA, 23 (1962),
       633.

429.   Lisca, Peter.   "The Art of John Steinbeck: An
       Analysis and Interpretation of Its Development,"
       University of Wisconsin, 1955.   DA, 16 (1956), 965.

430.   Marks, Lester Jay.   "A Study of Thematic Continuity
       in the Novels of John Steinbeck," Syracuse Universi-
       ty, 1961.   DA, 22 (1961), 4351.

431.   Ogulnik, Maurice A.   "The Moral World of Stein-
       beck," University of Montreal, Canada, 1953.

432.   Perez, Betty L.   "The Collaborative Role of John
       Steinbeck and Edward F. Ricketts in the Narrative
       Section of Sea of Cortez," University of Florida,
       1972.

433.   Satyanarayana, M. R.   "The Element of Compassion
       in the Works of John Steinbeck," Osmania Universi-
       ty, India, 1968.   SQ, 3 (1970), 77-78.

434.   Smith, Donald Boone. "The Decline in John Stein-
       beck's Critical Reputation since World War II: An
       Analysis and Evaluation of Recent Critical Practices
       with a Suggested Revision," University of New
       Mexico, 1967. DA, 27 (1967), 1449-A, 3149, 4074,
       6457, 9214.

435.   Taylor, Horace Platt, Jr. "The Biological Natural-
       ism of John Steinbeck," Louisiana State University,
       1961. DA, 22 (1962), 3674.

436.   Wallis, Prentiss Bascom, Jr. "John Steinbeck:
       the Symbolic Family," University of Kansas, 1966.
       DA, 27 (October-December, 1966), 1842-A.

437.   Wilson, James Robert. "Responses of College
       Freshmen to Three Novels" (J. D. Salinger, The
       Catcher in the Rye; John Steinbeck, The Grapes of
       Wrath; E. Hemingway, A Farewell to Arms), Uni-
       versity of California, 1963. DA, 24 (1963), 2465-
       2466.

438.   Young, Leo Vernon. "Values of the Young Charac-
       ters in the Fiction of Dos Passos, Hemingway, and
       Steinbeck," Stanford University, 1957. DA, 18
       (1958), 518-519.

         D. POEMS ABOUT STEINBECK (439-441)

439.   Ditsky, John. "John Steinbeck," SQ, 3 (1970), 79-
       80.

440.   Hayman, Lee Richard. "Field Trip," California
       State Poetry Quarterly, 1 (Fall, 1972), 17. "For
       John Steinbeck," Shore Review, 4 (1971), 12.

441.   Lisca, Peter. "In Memory of John Steinbeck," SN,
       2 (1969), 20-21.

         E. AUDIO-VISUAL MATERIAL (442-445)

442.   Columbia, ML-4756. "The Snake," "Johnny Bear"
       from The Long Valley. S. reads his own short

stories.
[Reference taken from Warren G. French's <u>John</u>
<u>Steinbeck</u>].

443.   Folkways Record #FH 5212. Woody Guthrie's <u>Dust</u>
        <u>Bowl Ballads</u> includes a resume of <u>The Grapes of</u>
        <u>Wrath</u> under the title "Tom Joad, Part I, and Part
        II."

444.   French, Warren. <u>The Grapes of Wrath</u> (Cassette,
        No. 102). DeLand, Florida: Everett /Edwards,
        1972.

445.   Thomas S. Klise Company. <u>Steinbeck's Losers, The De-</u>
        <u>pression Novels of John Steinbeck</u>. Filmstrip and record
        and reading script ($18.50; filmstrip with cassette and
        reading script, $19.50). Peoria, Ill.: Thomas S. Klise,
        Co., 1972.

F. FILM REVIEWS (446-667)

EAST OF EDEN (1952)--Warner Bros., (<u>1955</u>).

446.   <u>America</u>, 92 (March 19, 1955), 659. Review by
        Moria Walsh.

447.   <u>America Magazine,</u> 159 (April, 1955), 16.

448.   <u>Commonweal</u>, 61 (March 11, 1955), 604-605. Re-
        view by Philip T. Hartung, "Woe Is Me and Woe Is
        You."

449.   <u>Farm Journal</u>, 79 (April, 1955), 89.

450.   <u>Library Journal,</u> 80 (March 1, 1955), 555.

451.   <u>Look</u>, 19 (April 5, 1955), 100-101.

452.   <u>Manchester Guardian</u>. July 16, 1955. p. 5.

453.   <u>Manchester Guardian</u>. August 8, 1961. p. 3.

454.   <u>Monthly Film Bulletin</u>, 22 (July, 1955), 100.

455.   <u>Nation,</u> 180 (April 2, 1955), 294-295. Review by
        Robert Hatch.

456. National Parent Teacher, 49 (April, 1955), 39.
      Review by Mrs. Louis L. Bucklin.

457. New Republic, 132 (April 25, 1955), 22. Review by
      Delmore Schwartz.

458. New Statesman, 50 (July 16, 1955), 69-70. Review
      by William Whitebait. "The Big Drum."

459. New Statesman, 62 (August 11, 1961), 193. Review
      by Jonathan Miller. "Rural Dean."

460. New York Times, March 10, 1955, 32:3. "World
      Premiere, New York."

461. New York Times, March 10, 1955. 33:1.

462. New York Times, March 20, 1955. II, 1:7.

463. New York Times, March 20, 1955. II, 5:5.
      "Letters."

464. New Yorker, 31 (March 19, 1955), 129. Review by
      John McCarten. "S, Lay That Bible Down."

465. Newsweek, 45 (March 7, 1955), 90-91. "Kazan's S."

466. Punch, 229 (July 20, 1955), 83. Review by Richard
      Mallett.

467. Saturday Review, 38 (March 19, 1955), 25. Review
      by Lee Rogon. "Essay for Elia."

468. Scholastic, 66 (March 16, 1955), 46.

469. Sight and Sound, 25 (Summer, 1955), 32-34. Review
      by Derek Prouse.

470. Spectator, 195 (July 8, 1955), 49-50. Review by
      Penelope Houston.

471. Spectator, 207 (August 11, 1961), 206. Review by
      Isabel Quigley.

472. Speculum, 195 (July 8, 1955), 49.

473. Time, 65 (March 21, 1955), 98-100.

474. Times, July 11, 1955. p. 3. "East of Eden:
      Mr. E. Kazan's New Film."

475. Times. August 7, 1961. p. 12. "East of Eden
      Shown Again."

476. "Flight," an unreleased motion picture version. San
      Francisco, 1961. Independently produced.

THE FORGOTTEN VILLAGE (1941)

477. Commonweal, 35 (December 12, 1941), 198-99. Re-
      view by Philip T. Hartung. "Never a Dull Moment."

478. Monthly Film Bulletin, 11 (May 31, 1944), 56.

479. New Republic, 105 (December 8, 1941), 763. Review
      by Otis Ferguson. "Forgotten or Forgettable."

480. New Statesman, 27 (May 20, 1944), 336. Review by
      William Whitebait. "The Forgotten Village and Un-
      derworld at the Academy."

481. New York Times, January 26, 1941. IX, 5:6.
      "Filming Notes."

482. New York Times, March 23, 1941. IX, 4:1. "Excerpt
      from H. Kline's Diary Written During Filming
      Publication."

483. New York Times, May 4, 1941. IX, 4:1. "Release
      Delayed."

484. New York Times, August 22, 1941. 19:3. "Banned
      by New York State Censors Board."

485. New York Times, October 12, 1941. IX, 4:3. "Let-
      ters of Praise."

486. New York Times, November 15, 1941. 19:3. "New
      York State Regents Board Overrules Educational Dept.
      Motion Picture Censors Division Ban."

487. New York Times, November 19, 1941. 26:3.

488. New York Times, November 20, 1941. 26:4.

489. New York Times, November 23, 1941. IX, 5:2, 4.

"Review: Musical Score Discussed."

490. New Yorker, 17 (November 29, 1941), 91.

491. Newsweek, 18 (December 1, 1941), 70-71. "Censor Overruled."

492. Punch, 206 (May 24, 1944), 438. Review by Richard Mallett.

493. Spectator, 172 (May 19, 1944), 451. Review by Edgar Anstey. "The Forgotten Village at the Academy."

494. Theatre Arts, 25 (May, 1941), 336-343. Review by Herbert Kline. "An Account of Film Making in Mexico."

495. Theatre Arts, 25 (December, 1941), 883-884. Review by Hermine Rich Isaacs. "Fact Is Stronger Than Fiction."

496. Time, 38 (December 8, 1941), 96.

497. Times, 41 (May 11, 1944), 6. "Life in Mexico."

THE GRAPES OF WRATH (1939)--20th Century-Fox Film Corp. (1940).

498. Collier's, 105 (January 27, 1940), 23, 64, 67. Review by Frank Condon.

499. Commonweal, 31 (February 9, 1940), 348. Review by Philip T. Hartung. "Trampling But the Vintage."

500. Fortnightly, 145 (October, 1940), 409-16.

501. Life, 8 (January 22, 1940), 29-31. "Movie of the Week: The Grapes of Wrath Zanuck's Sharecroppers Are True to Life."

502. Life and Letters Today, 26 (September, 1940), 276.

503. Manchester Guardian, July 17, 1940. p. 4.

504. Monthly Film Bulletin, 7 (April 30, 1940), 56-57.

505. Nation, 150 (February 3, 1940), 137-38. Review by

Franz Hoellering.

506.   New Republic, 102 (February 12, 1940), 212-13. Re-
       view by Otis Ferguson. "Show for the People."

507.   New Statesman, 20 (July 27, 1940), 87. Review by
       William Whitebait. "A Fine Film: The G. of W. at
       the Odeon."

508.   New York Times, January 25, 1940. 17:2.

509.   New York Times, January 28, 1940. IX, 5:1.

510.   New York Times, February 4, 1940. IX, 5:2.
       "Comment on Mr. Quigley's ed. in Motion Picture."

511.   New York Times, February 25, 1940. 5:5. "Com-
       ment on Financial Returns."

512.   New York Times, December 23, 1940. 23:4.
       "Named Best 1940 Film by Motion Pictures National
       Review Board."

513.   New York Times, December 30, 1940. 20:2.
       "Named Best 1940 Film by New York Film Critics."

514.   Newsweek, 15 (February 12, 1940), 37-38. "The
       Saga of the Okies: The Grapes of Wrath Hits Screen
       as Powerful Social Drama."

515.   Punch, 198 (August 7, 1940), 142-43. Review by
       Penelope Knox.

516.   Saturday Review of Literature, 21 (February 10,
       1940), 16. Review by Thomas Burton. "Wine from
       These Grapes."

517.   Scholastic, 36 (February 5, 1940), 36.

518.   Sight and Sound, 9 (Spring, 1940), 14-15. Review
       by Herman Weinberg. "An Honest Film."

519.   Sight and Sound, 13 (February, 1948), 31-32. Re-
       view by William Patrick Wootten.

520.   Sociology & Social Research, 24 (May, 1940), 497.
       Review by E. S. B. "Social Photoplay."

521.   Spectator, 165 (July 26, 1940), [n.p.]. Review by
        Basil Wright. "The G. of W. at the Odeon."

522.   Speculum, 165 (July 26, 1940), 92.

523.   Time, 35 (February 12, 1940), 70-71. "The New
        Pictures."

524.   Times, July 19, 1940, p. 6.

LIFEBOAT   20th Century-Fox Film Corp. (1943).
        Steinbeck's script for Alfred Hitchcock's film, Lifeboat,
        which has never been published.

525.   Commonweal, 39 (January 28, 1944), 374-75. Re-
        view by Philip T. Hartung. "Water Water Every-
        where."

526.   Films and Filming, 16 (August, 1970), 57-61. Re-
        view by Raymond Durgnat. "The Strange Case of
        Alfred Hitchcock (pt. 7)--Missing Women."

527.   Hitchcock by Francois Truffaut. London: Panther
        Books, 1969; London: Secker & Warburg, 1968.
        p. 129.

528.   Life, 16 (January 31, 1944), 76-81. "Movie of the
        Week: Lifeboat: Hitchcock Throws Eight People &
        the Nazi who Torpedoed Them Together in an Open
        Boat."

529.   Manchester Guardian, June 6, 1944. p. 3.

530.   Monthly Film Bulletin, 11 (March 31, 1944), 31.

531.   Nation, 158 (January 22, 1944), 108. Review by
        James Agee.

532.   New Republic, 110 (January 24, 1944), 116. Review
        by Manny Farber. "Among the Missing: Hitchcock."

533.   New Republic, 110 (February 14, 1944), 211-12.
        Review by Manny Farber. "Theatrical Movies."

534.   New Statesman, 27 (March 25, 1944), 205-6. Review
        by William Whitebait. "Tunisian Victory and Lifeboat
        at the Odeon."

535.   New York Times, January 13, 1944.   17:1.

536.   New York Times, January 23, 1944.   II, 1.

537.   New York Times, January 23, 1944.   II, 3:2; January 30, 1944.   II, 3:1.

538.   New York Times, February 6, 1944.   II, 3:1.
       "Play Writing Discussed."

539.   New York Times, September 4, 1944.   12:6.   "Hissing of Picture Causes Melee, Buenos Aires Showing."

540.   New Yorker, 19 (January 15, 1944), 48+.

541.   New Yorker, 19 (February 5, 1944), 65.

542.   Newsweek, 23 (January 17, 1944), 66, 68.   "Lifeboat on Serson's Sea."

543.   Punch, 206 (March 29, 1944), 264.   Review by Richard Mallet.   "Implications."

544.   Sight and Sound, 18 (1953), 34-5.   Review by Peter Noble.

545.   Spectator, 172 (March 24, 1944), 267.   Review by Edgar Anstey.   "Lifeboat at the Odeon."

546.   Speculum, 72 (March 24, 1944), 267.

547.   Time, 43 (January 31, 1944), 94-6.

548.   Times, March 16, 1944, p. 6.

A MEDAL FOR BENNY--Paramount (1945).
   A film script (1946).

549.   Commonweal, 43 (May 18, 1945), 119.   Review by Philip T. Hartung.   "Choose Your Gal."

550.   Manchester Guardian, August 14, 1945.   p. 3.

551.   Monthly Film Bulletin, 12 (April 30, 1945), 50.

552.   New Statesman, 29 (May 26, 1945), 336.   Review by

William Whitebait. "A Medal for Benny at the Plaza."

553. Newsweek, 25 (April 30, 1945), 96. "S. 's Heroic Scum."

554. New Yorker, 21 (June 2, 1965), 64.

555. New York Times, May 24, 1945. 15:2.

556. New York Times, May 27, 1945. 1:8.

557. Punch, 208 (June 6, 1945), 480. Review by Richard Mallet.

558. Spectator, 174 (May 25, 1945), 474. Review by Edgar Anstey. "A Medal for Benny at the Plaza."

559. Theatre Arts, 29 (June, 1945), 368. Review by Parker Tyler.

560. Time, 45 (May 28, 1945), 54, 56.

561. Times, May 21, 1945. p. 8.

THE MOON IS DOWN (1942)--20th Century-Fox Film Corp. (1943).

562. Commonweal, 27 (April 9, 1943), 617. Review by Philip T. Hartung. "Ibsen! Thou Too Should Be Living."

563. Manchester Guardian, September 7, 1943. p. 3.

564. Monthly Film Bulletin, 10 (May 31, 1943), 54.

565. Nation, 156 (May 1, 1943), 642-43. Review by James Agee.

566. New Statesman, 26 (July 10, 1943), 59. Review by William Whitebait. "The Moon Is Down at the Rivoli."

567. New York Times, February 8, 1943. 17:2. "Mrs. Miniver; named by Motion Picture Arts & Sciences as 1942 Best Film."

568. New York Times, February 28, 1943. II, 3:4.

"Current British Life Scenes Rept. Inaccurate."

569. New York Times, March 5, 1943. 14:6. "Gets
     Motion Picture Arts & Sciences Academy 1942
     Award."

570. New York Times, March 15, 1943. 11:3. "The
     World Premiere, Toronto."

571. New York Times, March 27, 1943. 8:6.

572. New York Times, April 4, 1943. II, 3:1.

573. New York Times, May 8, 1943. 10:1. "Gets NYC
     Fed. of Women's Club Hon. Scroll."

574. New York Times, May 14, 1943. 17:1. "More the
     Merrier."

575. New York Times, May 16, 1943. II, 3:3. "More the
     Merrier."

576. Newsweek, 21 (April 5, 1943), 86, 88. "Bright
     'Moon'."

577. Punch, 205 (June 21, 1943), 59. Review by Richard
     Mallett. "The Invaders."

578. Speculum, 171 (July 16, 1943), 59.

579. Theatre Arts, 27 (May, 1943), 289-90. Review by
     Hermine Rich Isaacs.

580. Time, 39 (May 11, 1942), 47. "Biggest Cinema
     Story Price."

581. Time, 41 (April 5, 1943), 54, 56.

582. Times (London), "The Moon Is Down (Film)." July
     8, 1943. p. 6c.

583. Times, July 8, 1945. p. 6.

OF MICE AND MEN (1937)--Hal Roach Studio, Inc. (1940).

584. Collier's, 105 (January 6, 1940), 14-15. Review by
     Quentin Reynolds. "That's How Pictures Are Born."

585. Commonweal, 31 (January 19, 1940), 287. Review
      by Philip T. Hartung. "Tell Me About de Rabbits,
      George."

586. Life, 8 (January 8, 1940), 42-3. "Movie of the Week:
      Of Mice and Men: Famous Book and Play Is Filmed."

587. Manchester Guardian, April 11, 1940. p. 8.

588. Nation, 150 (January 20, 1940), 80-81.

589. New Republic, 102 (February 19, 1940), 247. Re-
      view by Otis Ferguson. "S: Other Vineyard."

590. New Statesman, 19 (April 13, 1940), 493-94. "Of
      Mice and Men at the Odeon."

591. New York Times, January 14, 1940. IX, 5:3.
      "Comment on Ad Brochure."

592. New York Times, February 17, 1940. 9:2.

593. New York Times, February 25, 1940. IX, 5:1.

594. New York Times, February 28, 1940. 7:4. "Banned
      in Australia."

595. New York Times, March 10, 1940. XI, 7:4. "A
      Copland on Musical Score."

596. New York Times, December 25, 1940. 15:1.
      "Christmas Eve Showing Barred, Fr. McClelland,
      Ala."

597. New Yorker, 16 (February 17, 1940), 77.

598. Newsweek, 15 (January 15, 1940), 32. "Of Mice and
      Men: Stark Tale of Bindle Stiffs Emerges as Moving
      Film."

599. Punch, 198 (April 24, 1940), 450. Review by
      Richard Mallett. "George, Lennie, and the Earl."

600. Spectator, 164 (April 19, 1940), 556. Review by
      Basil Wright. "Of Mice and Men at the Odeon."

601. Speculum, 164 (April 19, 1940), 556.

602. Time, 35 (January 15, 1940), 60, 62.

603. Times, April 15, 1940, p. 4.

THE PEARL (1947)--RKO Radio Pictures, Inc., (1948).
Spanish (original) and English versions of the same picture with the same cast and director. The Spanish version is about 10 minutes longer.

604. Commonweal, 47 (March 5, 1948), 522. Review by
Philip T. Hartung. "How the Other Half Lives."

605. Manchester Guardian, April 3, 1954. p. 3.

606. Monthly Film Bulletin, 21 (May, 1954), 72.

607. New Republic, 118 (March 1, 1948), 26. Review by
Robert Hatch.

608. New Statesman, 47 (April 10, 1954), 469. Review
by William Whitebait. "The Pearl and the Sea Around
Us at the Rialto."

609. New York Times, February 22, 1948. II, 1:8.

610. New York Times, February 18, 1948. 36:4.

611. New York Times Magazine, February 15, 1948. pp.
34-35. Review by Peggy LeBoutillier.

612. New Yorker, 24 (February 28, 1948), 56. Review
by John McCarten. "Steinbeck and a Pseudo-Docu-
mentary."

613. Newsweek, 31 (March 8, 1948), 83-84. "The Problem Pearl."

614. Spectator, 192 (April 2, 1954), 386. Review by
Virginia Graham. "The Pearl and the Sea Around Us
at the Rialto."

615. Time, 51 (March 1, 1948), 84, 86.

616. Times, April 5, 1954. p. 5.

THE RED PONY (1937)--Chas. K. Feldman Group Productions and Lewis Milestone Productions, (1949).

617. Commonweal, 49 (April 1, 1949), 611-12. Review
      by Philip T. Hartung. "Novel Into Film."

618. Good Housekeeping, 127 (December, 1948), 198.

619. Manchester Guardian, October 8, 1949. p. 5.

620. Monthly Film Bulletin, 16 (September 30, 1949), 158.

621. New Republic, 120 (March 21, 1949), 30-31. Review
      by Robert Hatch. "S. and Satan."

622. New Statesman, 38 (October 15, 1949), 424. Review
      by Gavin Lambert. "The Red Pony at the Plaza."

623. Newsweek, 33 (March 21, 1949), 89-90. "A Boy
      and His Pony."

624. New York Times, March 9, 1949. 33:2.

625. New York Times, March 13, 1949. II, 1:8.

626. New Yorker, 25 (March 19, 1949), 91. Review by
      John McCarten.

627. Rotarian, 74 (April, 1949), 37. Review by Jane
      Rockhart.

628. Spectator, 183 (October 14, 1949), 498. Review by
      Virginia Graham. "The Red Pony at the Plaza."

629. Time, 53 (March 28, 1949), 96, 98.

630. Times, October 10, 1949, p. 8. "A S. Story."

TORTILLA FLAT (1935)--Loew's Inc. (1942).

631. Commonweal, 36 (June 12, 1942), 182-83. Review
      by Philip T. Hartung. "The Meek and the Masterful."

632. Life, 12 (June 1, 1942), 39-41. "Hedy Lamarr
      Helps to Preserve the Glow of Steinbeck's Novel."

633. Manchester Guardian, October 10, 1942. p. 8.

634.   Monthly Film Bulletin, 9 (July 31, 1942), 91.

635.   New Republic, 106 (June 1, 1942), 766. Review by
       Manny Farber. "Not by the Book."

636.   New Statesman, 24 (October 17, 1942), 256. Review
       by William Whitebait. "Tortilla Flat at the Empire."

637.   Newsweek, 19 (June 1, 1942), 66. "Star-Studded
       Steinbeck."

638.   New York Times, May 22, 1942. 27:1.

639.   New Yorker, 18 (May 23, 1942), 63.

640.   Spectator, 169 (October 16, 1942), 359. Review by
       Edgar Anstey. "Tortilla Flat at the Empire."

641.   Speculum, 169 (October 16, 1942), 359.

642.   Time, 39 (May 18, 1942), 84-85.

643.   Times, October 12, 1942. "A S. Story."

VIVA ZAPATA!--20th Century-Fox Film Corp. (1950).
   Steinbeck's script for Marlon Brando's portrayal of a
   Mexican revolutionary hero, Emilio Zapata.

644.   France Illustration, No. 384 (February 14, 1953),
       236-37.

645.   Illustrated London News, 220 (April 19, 1952), 676.
       Review by Alan Dent. "Crudity & Finesse."

646.   Manchester Guardian, March 29, 1952. p. 3.

647.   Monthly Film Bulletin, 19 (April, 1952), 48.

648.   New Statesman, 43 (April 5, 1952), 402. Review by
       William Whitebait. "Viva Zapata! at the Marble Arch
       Odeon."

649.   Punch, 222 (April 9, 1952), 463. Review by
       Richard Mallet.

650.   Spectator, 188 (March 28, 1952), 397. Review by
       Virginia Graham. "Viva Zapata! at Odeon."

651.   Times, March 31, 1952. p. 2.

THE WAYWARD BUS (1947)--20th Century-Fox Film Corp.
   (1957).

652.   Catholic World, 185 (August, 1957), 385. Review by
        James F. Finley.

653.   Commonweal, 66 (June 21, 1957), 303-304. Review
        by Philip T. Hartung. "Boys Into Men--And Other
        Fables."

654.   Commonweal, 66 (July 19, 1957), 401-402. Paula
        Haigh. "Reply to the Review." See Hartung, Philip
        T. "Boys Into Men--And Other Fables," Common-
        weal, 66 (June 21, 1957), 303-304.

655.   Daily Express, March 13, 1957. p. 3. Review by
        David Lewin. "Joan Collins at Rebels Corner: On a
        Wayward Bus Ride with S."

656.   Illustrated London News, 231 (August 24, 1957), 314.
        Review by Alan Dent. "Weak New Films and a
        Strong Survivor."

657.   Manchester Guardian, July 20, 1957. p. 3.

658.   Monthly Film Bulletin, 24 (August, 1957), 106.

659.   National Parent Teacher, 52 (September, 1957), 34.
        Review by Mrs. Louis L. Bucklin.

660.   Newsweek, 49 (May 27, 1957), 119. " 'The Bus'--
        Over Hauled."

661.   New York Times, March 24, 1957. 5:8.

662.   New York Times, June 6, 1957. 35:2.

663.   New Yorker, 33 (June 15, 1957), 72. Review by
        John McCarten. "Halliday of the Yard."

664.   Punch, 233 (July 31, 1957), 141. Review by Richard
        Mallett.

665.   Spectator, 199 (July 26, 1957), 136. Review by
        Isabel Quigley. "The Wayward Bus (Rialto)."

666.   Time, 69 (June 17, 1957), 99-100.

667.   Times, July 22, 1957. p. 3.

        G. CRITICISM, BIOGRAPHY, BOOK REVIEWS
        (ARTICLES AND ESSAYS PUBLISHED IN
        PERIODICALS AND BOOKS) (668-2140)

668.   Aaron, Daniel. "The Radical Humanism of J. S.:
        The Grapes of Wrath Thirty Years Later," SR, 51
        (September 28, 1968), 26-7, 55-6.

669.   Abels, Cyrilly. Bookman, 75 (December, 1932),
        877-78 [PH] (R).

670.   Abramson, Ben. "J. S.," Reading and Collecting, 1
        (December, 1936), 4-5, 18.

671.   _____. Style. West Cornwall, Conn.: William
        S. Covington, 1970. 24pp.
        [A tribute to S.].

672.   Adams, James Donald. "J. S.--Main Street and the
        Dust Bowl," The Shape of Books to Come. New
        York: Viking Press, 1948. pp. 131-43.

673.   _____. New York Times Book Review, January
        14, 1945. 7, 2 [Cannery Row] (R).

674.   _____. New York Times Book Review, March 2,
        1947. 7, 2 [The Wayward Bus] (R).

675.   Adams, Scott. Library Journal, 73 (April 15, 1948),
        658.
        [A Russian Journal] (R).

676.   Adey, Alvin. Current History, 2 (April, 1942), 143-
        44.
        [The Moon Is Down, play] (R).

677.   Adrian, Daryl. "S.'s New Image of America and
        the Americans," SQ, 3 (1970), 83-92.
        [America and Americans].

678.   "After Number One," Times Literary Supplement,

(July 7, 1961), 413.
[The Winter of Our Discontent] (R).

679. Agee, James. Agee on Films. London: McDowell
      and Obolensky, 1958.
      [The Moon Is Down, p. 36; Lifeboat, pp. 71-2;
      The Pearl, p. 301; and "A Medal for Benny," pp.
      169-87].

680. Agate, James. "That Naughty Academy" and
      "Frenzy," Around Cinemas (2nd Series). London:
      Home and Van Thal, 1948. pp. 273-77.
      [The Forgotten Village].

681. Alexander, Stanley. "Cannery Row: S.'s Pastoral
      Poem," WAL, 2 (1968), 281-95.

682. _____. "The Conflict of Form in Tortilla Flat,"
      AL, 40 (1968), 58-66.

683. Allen, Walter. "The Grapes of Wrath," Tradition &
      Dream: The English & American Novel From the
      Twenties and Our Time. London: Phoenix House,
      1963. pp. 164-66; Also in The Modern Novel in
      Britain & The United States. New York: Dutton,
      1964.

684. _____. "In Dubious Battle," The Modern Novel in
      Britain & The United States. New York: Dutton,
      1964. pp. 161-66.

685. _____. Tradition & Dream: The English & Amer-
      ican Novel From the Twenties to Our Time. London:
      Phoenix House, 1963. (Reprinted as The Modern
      Novel in Britain & The United States. N.Y.: Dutton,
      1964), pp. 161-66 in both editions.

686. _____. The Urgent West. London: John Baker,
      1969.
      [Proposes a parallel between The Grapes of Wrath
      and Nathaniel West's The Day of the Locust].

687. "America and Americans (1966)," Choice, 4 (1967),
      279.

688. "America and Americans," TLS, December, 1966, p.
      1120.

689.   "America the Beautiful," Times Literary Supplement,
        (December 1, 1966), 1120.
        [America and Americans] (R).

690.   American Literature Abstracts, 3 (June, 1970), 157-
        58.
            1. Houghton, Donald E. "Westering in The Lead-
            er of the People," WAL, 4 (Summer, 1969),
            117-24.
            2. Van DerBeets, Richard. "A Pearl Is a Pearl
            Is a Pearl," CEA Critic, 32 (1970), 9.

691.   Anderson, Hilton. "Hawthorne's Roger Malvin's
        Burial," Explicator, 38 (1969), Item 12 ["Flight].

692.   _____. "S.'s 'Flight'," Explicator, 38 (1969),
        Item 12.

693.   Angoff, Allan (ed.). "J. S.," American Writing
        Today: Its Independence and Vigor. New York: New
        York University Press, 1957. Passim.

694.   Angoff, Charles. North American Review, 247
        (Summer, 1939), 387.
        [G. of W.] (R).

695.   Antico, John. "A Reading of S.'s 'Flight'," MFS,
        11 (Spring, 1965), 45-53.

696.   Apseloff, Stanford S. "Book Publishing in America
        by Charles A. Madison," SQ, 3 (1970), 17-19.
        [S. and Pascal Covici].

697.   Armitage, Merle. "J. S.," Accent on America.
        New York: E. Weyhe, 1944. pp. 271-72.

698.   Arrowsmith, J. E. S. London Mercury, 28 (July,
        1933), 268.
        [PH] (R).

699.   "Article on Russian Review of The Moon Is Down," New
        York Times, December 22, 1942. p. 23.

700.   Asselineau, Roger. "Warren French's J. S.,"
        Etudes Anglaises, 16 (1963), 216 (R).

701.   "Assisting J. S.," Newsweek, 47 (June, 1956), 56.

702. "Associated Farmers of Kern County, California, Approve Ban on The Grapes of Wrath," Wilson Library Bulletin, 14 (October, 1939), 102.

703. Astro, Richard. "J. S. by Richard O'Connor," SQ, 4 (Fall, 1971), 107-109 (R).

704. _____. "J. S.: Prospectus for a Literary Biography," SQ, 4 (Summer, 1971), 76-80.

705. _____. "Journal of a Novel by J. S.," SQ, 3 (1970), 107-110 (R).

706. _____. "S. and Mainwaring: Two Californians for the Earth," SQ, 3 (1970), 3-11.

707. _____. "S. and Ricketts: Escape or Commitment in The Sea of Cortez?" WAL, 6 (1971), 109-21.

708. _____. "S. Conference," SQ, 3 (1970), 23-24.

709. _____. "S. Country: An Editorial Preface," SQ, 4 (Summer, 1971), 67.

710. _____. "S.'s Bittersweet Thursday," SQ, 4 (Spring, 1971), 36-48.
[Sweet Thursday].

711. _____. "S.'s Post-War Trilogy: A Return to Nature and the Natural Man," TCL, 16 (1970), 109-22.

712. "At Home and Abroad," Times Literary Supplement, November 6, 1948, p. 621.
[The Pearl] (R).

713. Atkinson, Brooks. New York Times Book Review, December 12, 1937. 11:3.
[Of Mice and Men, play] (R).

714. _____. New York Times Book Review, October 29, 1950. 2:1.
[Burning Bright, play] (R).

715. _____. New York Times, November 24, 1937. p. 20.
[Of Mice and Men, play] (R).

716. _____. New York Times, October 19, 1950. p. 40.

[Burning Bright, play] (R).

717. _____. "Of Mice and Men," Broadway Scrapbook.
New York: Theatre Arts, 1947.

718. Atkinson, Oriana. New York Times Book Review,
May 9, 1948. 7:3.
[A Russian Journal] (R).

719. Atkinson, Ted. "J. S., America and Americans,"
SQ, 2 (1969), 66-68.

720. _____, "Warren French (ed.), A Companion to
The Grapes of Wrath," SN, 5 (1968), 7-8.

721. "Attempts to Suppress The Grapes of Wrath," Publishers' Weekly, 136 (September 2, 1939), 777.

722. "The Author J. S.," The Booklover's Answer, 2
(November-December, 1962). Passim.

723. "Authors and Others," Publishers' Weekly, 128 (July
27, 1935), 223.

724. "Awards; Nobel Prize in Literature," Wilson Library
Bulletin, 37 (December, 1962), 321.

725. B., A. Canadian Forum, 37 (July, 1957), 89.
[SRP] (R).

726. Baker, Carlos. "Forty Years of Pulitzer Prizes."
Princeton University Library Chronicle, 18 (Winter,
1957), 55-70.

727. _____. "The Grapes of Wrath," "Steinbeck of
California," Delphian Quarterly, 23 (April, 1940),
43-4.

728. _____. "In Dubious Battle Revalued," New York
Times Book Review, July 25, 1943). pp. 4, 16 (R).

729. _____. New York Times Book Review, February
16, 1947. 7:1.
[The Wayward Bus] (R).

730. _____. New York Times Book Review. November

30, 1947. 7:4.
[The Pearl] (R).

731. _____. New York Times Book Review, June 13,
1954. 7:4.
[Sweet Thursday] (R).

732. _____. New York Times Book Review, June 25,
1961. 7, p. 3.
[The Winter of Our Discontent] (R).

733. _____. "Of Mice and Men, S. of California,"
Delphian Quarterly, 23 (April, 1940), 42.

734. _____. "The Pulitzer Prizes, 1917-1957; Fiction
Awards," Columbia Literary Columns, 6 (May,
1957), 30-4.

735. _____. "S. at the Top of His Form," New York
Times Book Review, November 30, 1947. pp. 4, 52.

736. _____. "S. of California," Delphian Quarterly,
23 (April, 1940), 40-5.

737. _____. "Tortilla Flat, S. of California," Delphian
Quarterly, 23 (April, 1940), 41-2.

738. Baker, Howard. "The Grapes of Wrath, In Praise
of the Novel," Southern Review, 5 (1940), 787-90.
(The Fiction of Huxley, S., et al.).

739. _____. "In Praise of the Novel," Southern Review, 5 (1939-1940), 778-800.

740. Baker, Nelson M. Novelist's America: Fiction as
History, 1910-1940. Syracuse, N.Y.: Syracuse University Press, 1971. Passim.

741. Barbour, Brian M. "Paul McCarthy, 'House and
Shelter as Symbol in The Grapes of Wrath'," SN, 1,
v (1968), 11-13. (A review of an article published
in South Dakota Review).

742. _____. "Tetsumaro Hayashi, John Steinbeck: A
Concise Bibliography (1930-65)," SQ, 2 (1969), 63-
66.(R).

743. Barney, Virginia. New York Times Book Review,

October 1, 1933. p. 18.
[To a God Unknown] (R).

744.   Barron, Louis. Library Journal, 79 (June 1, 1954),
       1052.
       [Sweet Thursday] (R).

745.   Barry, Iris. New York Herald Tribune Books,
       April 18, 1948. p. 3.
       [A Russian Journal] (R).

746.   Beach, Joseph Warren. "Chrysanthemums,"
       American Fiction: 1920-1940. New York: Mac-
       millan, 1941. pp. 311-14. Also in SHC, pp. 80-
       91, 260-65.

747.   _____. "Eight Novelists Between Wars,"
       Saturday Review of Literature, 23 (March 29, 1941),
       3.

748.   _____. "The Grapes of Wrath," American Fic-
       tion: 1920-1940. New York: Macmillan, 1942.
       pp. 327-47. Also in SHC, pp. 260-65.

748(a). _____. "J. S.: Art and Propaganda," SIIC,
       pp. 250-65.

749.   _____. "J. S.: Journeyman Artist," American
       Fiction: 1920-1940. N.Y.: Macmillan, 1941. pp.
       309-47. Also in SHC, pp. 80-91.

750.   _____. "Tortilla Flat," American Fiction: 1920-
       1940. pp. 317-22.

751.   "Belgian Information Center Issued Bill of Complaints
       on The Moon Is Down," New York Times, April 28,
       1942. p. 19.

752.   Belmont, Clive. "Gripes of Wrath," Hollywood
       Tribune, 1 (August 7, 1939), 1-2.

753.   Benet, William Rose. S. R. of Literature, 12
       (June 1, 1935), 12.
       [Tortilla Flat] (R).

754.   _____. S. R. of Literature, 13 (February 1,
       1936), 10.
       [In Dubious Battle] (R).

Criticism, Biography, Book Reviews 87

755. Bennett, Jack Arthur W. (ed.). Essays on Malory.
Oxford: Clarendon Press, 1963. p. vii.

756. Berkelman, R. G. "George Sterling on 'The Black
Vulture'," AL, 10 (May, 1938), 223-24.

757. "Bernie Byrenes Files Breach of Contract Suit
Against J. S., L. Milestone, and Meredith,"
New York Times, February 24, 1948. p. 22.

758. Berry, J. Wilkes. "Enduring Life in The Grapes of
Wrath," CEA Critic, 33 (1971), 18-19.

759. Bidwell, Martin. "J. S.: an Impression," Prairie
Schooner, 12 (Spring, 1938), 10-15.

760. Bigsby, C. W. E. "Two Types of Violence,"
University Review (Kansas City), 32 (1965), 129-36.
[S. and Hemingway].

761. "Biographical Notes," Scholastic, 43 (December 6,
1943), 18; 44 (April 24, 1944), 22.

762. "Biographical Sketch," Publishers' Weekly, 128 (July
27, 1935), 223.

763. "Biographical Sketch," SR, 30 (February 15, 1947),
14.

764. "Biographical Sketch," Wilson Bulletin for Librarians,
11 (March, 1937), 456.

765. Birney, Earl. "The Grapes of Wrath," Canadian
Forum, 19 (June, 1939), 94.

766. "The Birth of S.," Wilson Library Bulletin, 13
(April, 1939), 540.

767. Blair, Walter, et al. (eds.). "J. S.," The Lit. of
the United States. 3 vols. Chicago: Scott, Fores-
man, 1953. pp. 783-84. Passim.

768. Blake, Nelson Morehouse. "The Lost Paradise,"
Novelists' America: Fiction as History, 1910-1940.
pp. 133-62.
[The Grapes of Wrath].

769.   Blanck, Jacob (ed.). "American First Editions,"
       Publishers' Weekly, 131 (April 17, 1937), 1701
       (J. S. Checklist by Lawrence C. Powell).

770.   Blankenship, Russell. "J. S. and The Sociological
       Novel," American Literature as an Expression of the
       National Mind. New York: Holt, Rinehart & Winston,
       1958. pp. 745-49.

771.   Block, Maxine (ed.). "J. S.," Current Biography.
       N.Y.: H. W. Wilson, 1940. pp. 757-59.

772.   Bloomfield, Paul. Manchester Guardian. December
       5, 1942. p. 4.
       [East of Eden] (R).

773.   Blotner, Joseph L. "J. S.: The Party Organizer,"
       The Political Novel. Garden City, N.Y.: Doubleday,
       1955. p. 14.

774.   _____. The Modern American Political Novel
       1900-1960. Austin and London: University of Texas
       Press, 1966. Passim.

775.   Bluefarb, Sam. "The Joads: Flight into the Social
       Soul," The Escape Motif in the American Novel:
       Mark Twain to Richard Wright. Columbus: Ohio State
       University Press, 1972. pp. 95-112.
       [The G. of W.].

776.   Bluestone, George. "The Grapes of Wrath," Novels
       into Film. Baltimore: Johns Hopkins Press, 1957.
       pp. 147-69. Also in Davis (ed.), pp. 102-21;
       French (ed.), pp. 165-89.

777.   Bode, Elroy. "The World on Its Own Terms: A
       Brief for S., Miller, and Simemon," Southwest Re-
       view, 5 (1968), 406-16.

778.   Bois, William. New York Times, April 15, 1957.
       p. 27.
       [SRP] (R).

779.   Booklist, 29 (December 1, 1932), 116.
       [PH] (R).

780.   Booklist, 35 (April 15, 1939), 271.
       [G. of W.] (R).

781.   Booklist, 35 (October 1, 1938), 48.
        [LV] (R).

782.   Booklist, 37 (July 1, 1941), 513.
        [The Forgotten Village] (R).

783.   Booklist, 38 (January 1, 1942), 153.
        [Sea of Cortez] (R).

784.   Booklist, 38 (March 15, 1942), 252.
        [The Moon Is Down, Novel] (R).

785.   Booklist, 39 (December 15, 1942), 132.
        [Bombs Away] (R).

786.   Booklist, 41 (January 1, 1945), 140.
        [Cannery Row] (R).

787.   Booklist, 43 (February 15, 1947), 186.
        [The Wayward Bus] (R).

788.   Booklist, 44 (December 15, 1947), 152.
        [The Pearl] (R).

789.   Booklist, 44 (May 15, 1948), 311.
        [A Russian Journal] (R).

790.   Booklist, 47 (September 1, 1950), 3.
        [Burning Bright, Play] (R).

791.   Booklist, 47 (November 1, 1950), 98.
        [Burning Bright, Play] (R).

792.   Booklist, 48 (October 15, 1951), 68.
        [Sea of Cortez] (R).

793.   Booklist, 48 (July 15, 1952), 369.
        [East of Eden] (R).

794.   Booklist, 49 (September 19, 1952), 33.
        [East of Eden] (R).

795.   Booklist, 50 (April 15, 1954), 309; 50 (June 15,
        1954), 401.
        [Sweet Thursday] (R).

796.   Booklist, 53 (March 1, 1957), 345.
        [SRP] (R).

797.   Booklist, 53 (April 15, 1957), 428.
       [SRP] (R).

798.   Booklist, 55 (September 1, 1958), 8; (November 1,
       1958), 122.
       [Once There Was a War] (R).

799.   Booklist, 57 (June 1, 1961), 606, 636.
       [The Winter of Our Discontent] (R).

800.   Booklist, 58 (July 1, 1962), 748; 58 (July 15, 1962),
       784.
       [Travels with Charley] (R).

801.   Bookmark, 3 (May, 1942), 17.
       [The Moon Is Down, Novel] (R).

802.   Bookmark, 12 (October, 1952), 10.
       [East of Eden] (R).

803.   Bookmark, 16 (May, 1957), 191.
       [SRP] (R).

804.   Bookmark, 20 (July, 1961), 234.
       [The Winter of Our Discontent] (R).

805.   "Books into Films," Publishers' Weekly, 147 (Janu-
       ary 13, 1945), 150.

806.   Boren, Lyle H.   "The Grapes of Wrath," Congres-
       sional Record, 76th Congress, 3rd Session, Pt. 13,
       86 (1940), 139-40.

807.   Boren, Lyle H.   "The Grapes of Wrath," Donohue
       (ed.), pp. 27-9.

808.   Boston Transcript.   January 29, 1936.   p. 2.
       [In Dubious Battle] (R).

809.   Bowden, Edwin T.   "The Commonplace and the Gro-
       tesque," The Dungeon of the Heart.   New York:
       Macmillan, 1961.   pp. 138-49.   Also in Donohue (ed.),
       pp. 195-203.

810.   _____.   "The Grapes of Wrath," The Dungeon of
       the Heart: Human Isolation and the American Novel.
       New York: Macmillan, 1961.   pp. 138-49.

811.   Bowen, James K.   "The Wide World of John Stein-
       beck by Peter Lisca," SQ, 3 (1970), 72-75 (R).

812.   Bowron, Bernard.   "The Grapes of Wrath: A
       'Wagons West' Romance," Colorado Quarterly, 3
       (Summer, 1954), 84-91.

813.   Boyle, Robert H.   Commonweal, 60 (July 9, 1954),
       351.
       [Sweet Thursday] (R).

814.   Boynton, Percy H.   "Cup of Gold," America in Con-
       temporary Fiction.   pp. 242-43.

815.   _____.   "The Grapes of Wrath," America in Con-
       temporary Fiction.   University of Chicago Press,
       1940.   pp. 251-57.

816.   _____.   "J. S.," America in Contemporary Fic-
       tion.   University of Chicago Press, 1940.   pp. 241-
       57.

817.   _____.   "Of Mice and Men," America in Con-
       temporary Fiction.   pp. 248-50.

818.   _____.   "The Pastures of Heaven," America in
       Contemporary Fiction.   pp. 244-46.

819.   _____.   "To a God Unknown," America in Con-
       temporary Fiction.   pp. 244-46.

820.   Bracher, Frederick.   "California's Literary Regional-
       ism," American Quarterly, 7 (Fall, 1955), 275-85.

821.   _____.   "S. and the Biological View of Man,"
       The Pacific Spectator, 2 (Winter, 1948), 14-29.
       Also in SHC, pp. 183-96.

822.   Braley, Berton.   "Acknowledgment (to J. S.),"
       Morgan Sails the Caribbean.   New York: Macmillan,
       1934.   pp. vii-viii.
       [The author explains his indebtedness to Steinbeck's
       Cup of Gold].

823.   Bradley, Sculley, et al. (eds.).   "J. S.," The Amer-
       ican Tradition in Literature.   New York: W. W.
       Norton, 1962.   2, 1399-1401.

824.   Bregy, Katherine. "Of J. S.," America, 71 (August 19, 1944), 496-97.

825.   Brewster, Dorothy and Burrell, John A. "J. S.: Artist with a Message," Modern World of Fiction. New Jersey: Littlefield & Adams & Co., 1953.

826.   Bridgman, Richard. The Colloquial Style in America. New York: Oxford University Press, 1966. p. 4.

827.   Brighouse, Harold. Manchester Guardian, June 9, 1933. p. 7.
        [PH] (R).

828.   _____. Manchester Guardian, March 27, 1935. p. 7.
        [To a God Unknown] (R).

829.   _____. Manchester Guardian, September 14, 1937. p. 5.
        [Of Mice and Men] (R).

830.   _____. Manchester Guardian, June 26, 1942. p. 3.
        [The Moon Is Down] (R).

831.   _____. Manchester Guardian, November 28, 1947. p. 3.
        [The Wayward Bus] (R).

832.   Brooke, Jocelyn. New Statesman, 42 (August 18, 1951), 184-85.
        [Burning Bright] (R).

833.   Brown, Clarence. "Callus Behind the Fiction," New Republic, 161 (December 20, 1969), 26+.

834.   _____. "Journal of a Novel," New Republic, 161 (December 20, 1969), 26.

835.   _____. Library Journal, 95 (March 1, 1970), 899.
        [J. of a Novel].

836.   Brown, Daniel R. "A Monolith of Logic Against Waves of Nonsense," Renascence, 16 (Fall, 1963), 48-51.

837.   Brown, Dening. "The Grapes of Wrath," Soviet

Attitudes Toward American Writing. Princeton University Press, 1962. pp. 74-80, 139-40, 162-64, 177-78, & Passim.

838. _____ . "J. S.," Soviet Attitudes Toward American Writing. Princeton, N.J.: Princeton University Press, 1962. Passim.

838(a). _____ . "Soviet Criticism of American Proletarian Literature of the 1930's," American Contributions to the Fourth International Congress of Slavicists, Moscow, September, 1958. The Hague: Mouton, 1958. p. 2.
[G. of W.].

839. Brown, D. Russell. "The Natural Man in J.S.'s Non-Teleological Tales," Ball State University Forum, 7 (Spring, 1966), 47-59.

840. Brown, John Mason. Book-of-the Month Club News, 35 (Midsummer, 1962), 1.
[Travels with Charley] (R).

841. _____ . "Mr. S.'s Of Mice and Men," Two on the Aisle: Ten Years of the American Theatre in Performance. New York: W. W. Norton, 1938. pp. 183-87.

842. _____ . "Upright Bus," Saturday Review of Literature, 30 (April, 1947), 24-7.
[The Wayward Bus] (R).

843. Browning, Chris. "Grape Symbolism in The Grapes of Wrath," Discourse, 11 (1968), 129-40.

844. Bruce, R. McElderry, Jr. Thomas Wolfe. New York: Twayne, 1964. p. 172.

845. Bruender, George M. "The Shape of S.," SR [n.v.] (March 8, 1969), 24.
[Letters to the Editor].

846. Brunn, Robert R. Christian Science Monitor, September 25, 1952. p. 11.
[East of Eden] (R).

847. Bruno, Francesco, "J. S.," Ausonia, 12 (1963), 41-3.

848.   Brustein, Robert. "America's New Culture Hero:
       Feelings Without Words," Commentary, 25 (February,
       1958), 123-29.

849.   Brynes, Asher. "A Man Who Lived with Failure,"
       New Republic, 145 (August 21, 1961), 24.
       [The Winter of Our Discontent] (R). See also
       The Grapes of Wrath.

850.   Bunzel, John H. "Welcoming Address."
       [Welcome to S. Country: A Conference and Film
       Festival], SQ, 4 (Summer, 1971), 69-73.

851.   Burbank, Rex. "In Dubious Battle and The Grapes
       of Wrath," Thornton Wilder. New York: Twayne,
       1961. pp. 79-80.

852.   Burgum, Edwin Berry. "Fickle Sensibility of J. S.,"
       The Novel and the World's Dilemma. New York:
       Oxford University Press, 1947. pp. 272-91. Also
       in SHC, pp. 104-18.

853.   _____. "The Grapes of Wrath," The Novel and
       The World's Dilemma. New York: Oxford Universi-
       ty Press, 1947. pp. 283-88. Also in SHC, pp. 112-
       16.

853(a). _____. "The Sensibilities of J. S.," Science and
       Society, 10 (Spring, 1946), 132-47. Also in SHC,
       pp. 104-18.

854.   _____. "The Moon Is Down," SHC, pp. 116-18.

855.   _____. "Of Mice and Men," SHC, pp. 109-12.

856.   Burke, Kenneth. The Philosophy of Library Form.
       Baton Rouge: Louisiana State University Press, 1941.
       Passim.

857.   Burnham, David. Commonweal, 36 (April 24, 1942),
       14.
       [The Moon Is Down, Play] (R).

858.   "Business Journal," Time, 51 (January 26, 1948), 58f.

859.   Butcher, Fanny. Chicago Sunday Tribune Magazine of
       Books, June, 1961. p. 1.
       [The Winter of Our Discontent] (R).

860. _____. Chicago Sunday Tribune Magazine of Books, July 29, 1962. p. 1.
[Travels with Charley] (R).

861. Butler, E. M. Catholic World, 155 (May, 1942), 253-54.
[The Moon Is Down, Novel] (R).

862. "Buys 2 NYC. E. 78th St. Houses," New York Times, November 7, 1945. p. 30.

863. Calder-Marshall, A. "Novels of J. S.," Fortnightly, 152 (September, 1939), 295-304.

864. California Citizens Association Report. "Was The Grapes of Wrath Answered?" in French (ed.), pp. 138-39.

865. Calta, Louis. New York Times, December 5, 1958. p. 38.
[Of Mice and Men, Musical Version] (R).

866. Calverton, V. F. "J. S.: Fulfillment Without Promise," Modern Monthly, 10, (June, 1938), 11-12, 16.

867. _____. "S., Hemingway, and Faulkner," Modern Quarterly, 11 (Fall, 1939), 36-44.

868. Canadian Forum, 27 (May, 1947), 45.
[The Wayward Bus] (R).

869. Canby, Henry Seidel. "The Right Question," S.R. of Literature, 21 (March 23, 1940), 8.

870. Canby, Henry S. Saturday Review of Literature, 15 (February 27, 1937), 7.
[Of Mice and Men, Novel] (R).

871. Cannon, Gerald. "The Pauline Apostleship of Tom Joad," College English, 24 (December, 1962), 222-24. Also in Donohue (ed.), pp. 118-22.

872. Capa, Robert. "A Legitimate Complaint," an inter-chapter between chapters 6 and 7 of A Russian Journal. New York: Bantam, 1970. pp. 145-48.

873.   "Career," New York Times, February 11, 1940, 9:4.

874.   Carlson, Eric W. "Symbolism in The G. of W.,"
       College English, 19 (January, 1958), 172-75. Also
       in Donohue (ed.), pp. 96-102. Also in Lisca (ed.).
       pp. 748-56.

875.   Carpenter, Frederic I. "Cup of Gold," SHC, pp.
       69-71.

876.   _____. "J. S.: American Dreamer," Southwest
       Review, 26 (July, 1941), 454-67. Also in SHC, pp.
       68-79.

877.   _____. "J. S.: The Philosophical Joads,"
       American Literature & the Dream. New York:
       Philosophical Library, 1955. pp. 167-75. Also in
       College English, 2 (January, 1941), 315-25. Also in
       SHC, pp. 241-49.

878.   _____. "Of Mice and Men," SHC, pp. 76-77.

879.   _____. "The Pastures of Heaven," SHC, pp. 71-73.

880.   _____. "The Philosophic Joads," College English,
       2 (December, 1941), 315-25. Also in Donohue (ed.),
       pp. 80-9; Lisca (ed.), pp. 708-19; SHC, pp. 241-49.

881.   _____. "The Red Pony," SHC, pp. 77-8.

882.   _____. "To a God Unknown," SHC, pp. 73-4.

883.   _____. "Tortilla Flat," SHC, pp. 74-5.

884.   Caskey, J. Homer. Saturday Review of Literature,
       20 (May 20, 1939), 9 (a Letter).
       [G. of W.].

885.   Catholic World, 155 (May, 1942), 253.
       [The Moon Is Down, Novel] (R).

886.   Cattani, R. J. "Journal of a Novel," Christian
       Science Monitor, January 2, 1970. p. 11.

887.   Caughey, John Walton. "Current Discussion of
       California's Migrant Labor Problem," Pacific His-
       torical Review, 8 (September, 1939), 347-54.
       [The Grapes of Wrath].

888. Chamberlain, John. Current History, 42 (July, 1935),
      7.
          [Tortilla Flat] (R).

889. _____. Current History, 43 (March, 1936), iv.
          [In Dubious Battle] (R).

890. _____. New York Times, March 6, 1942. p. 19.
          [The Moon Is Down, Novel] (R).

891. Chametzky, Jules. "The Ambivalent Endings of The
      G. of W.," MFS, 11 (Spring, 1965), 35-44. Also in
      Donohue (ed.), pp. 232-44.

892. Champney, Freeman. "Critics in Search of an
      Author," Antioch Review, 18 (Fall, 1958), 371-75.

893. _____. "J. S., Californian," Antioch Review, 7
      (September, 1947), 345-62. Also in SHC, pp. 135-51;
      Davis (ed.), pp. 18-35.

894. Chancellor, Richard. Spectator, 183 (July 29, 1949),
      152.
          [A Russian Journal] (R).

895. Chapin, Chester F. "Pepé Torres: A S. 'Natural',"
      College English 23 (May, 1962), 676.
          ["The Flight"].

896. Charques, R. D. Spectator, 189 (November 28, 1952),
      744.
          [East of Eden] (R).

897. Chase, Richard. "Radicalism in the American Novel,"
      Commentary, 23 (January, 1947), 65-71.

898. Chattani, R. J. Choice, 7 (October, 1970), 1944.
          [Journal of a Novel].

899. Chicago Daily Tribune, November 19, 1932. p. 14.
          [PH] (R).

900. _____. June 1, 1935. p. 14.
          [Tortilla Flat] (R).

901. Chicago Sun Book Week, January 7, 1945. p. 6.
          [Cannery Row] (R).

902.   Chicago Sun Book Week, September 16, 1945. p. 2.
        [The Red Pony] (R).

903.   Chicago Sun Book Week, November 23, 1947. p. 7.
        [The Pearl] (R).

904.   Chicago Sunday Tribune, October 26, 1958.   p. 10.
        [Once There Was a War] (R).

905.   Christian Century, 50 (September 20, 1933), 1179.
        [To a God Unknown]. (R).

906.   Christian Century, 79 (May 30, 1961), 693.
        [The Winter of Our Discontent] (R).

907.   Christian Science Monitor, May 6, 1939.   p. 13.
        [G. of W.] (R).

908.   _____. March 6, 1942.   p. 18.
        [The Moon Is Down, Novel] (R).

909.   _____. September 25, 1952.   p. 11.
        [East of Eden] (R).

910.   _____. October 17, 1958,   p. 9.
        [Once There Was a War] (R).

911.   _____. S June 29, 1961.   p. 7.
        [The Winter of Our Discontent] (R).

912.   _____. August 2, 1962.   p. 7.
        [Travels with Charley] (R).

913.   "Christian Symbolism in The Grapes of Wrath: A
        Discussion," College English, 19 (January, 1958),
        369.

914.   "John Steinbeck: A Concise Bibliography, by T.
        Hayashi," Choice, 4 (December, 1967), 1103 (R).

915.   Churchill, Winston S.   The Second World War: Vol-
        ume 4, The Hinge of Fate.   London: Cassell, 1951.
        Appendix C.
        [May 27, 1942; the Premier's recommendation
        about The Moon Is Down].

916.   Clark, Eleanor.   Nation, 164 (March 29, 1947), 370-
        73.

[The Wayward Bus] (R).

917. Clarke, Mary Washington. "Bridging the Generation
Gap: The Ending of S.'s The Grapes of Wrath,"
Forum (Houston), 8 (Summer, 1970), 16-17.

918. _____. "A Review of Joseph Fontenrose's J. S.,"
Western Folklore, 24 (1965), 126-27 (R).

919. Clough, Wilson O. "The Leader of the People,"
The Necessary Earth: Nature and Solitude in American Literature. Austin: University of Texas Press,
1964. pp. 148-49.

920. Coan, Otis W. and Richard G. Lillard. America
in Fiction. Palo Alto, California: Stanford University, 1949. pp. 64, 73, 132, 171.

921. Cody, W. F. "J. S. Will Get You If You Don't Watch
Out," Saturday Review of Literature, 28 (July 7,
1945), 18-19.
[A parody of S.'s writing style, especially of
[Cannery Row].

922. Colby, Harriet. New York Herald Tribune Books,
June 2, 1935. p. 4.
[Tortilla Flat] (R).

923. Coleman, John. Spectator, 201 (September 26, 1958),
412.
[The Log from the Sea of Cortez] (R).

924. Collier, Peter. "The Winter of J. S.," Ramparts,
6 (July, 1967), 59-61.

925. "Columnists: The Eye of the Veteran," Time, 88
(December 30, 1966), 41.
[S. in S. Vietnam].

926. Commager, Henry Steele. The American Mind.
New Haven: Yale University Press, 1950. pp. 271-
73.

927. Commonweal, 27 (December 10, 1937), 191.
[Of Mice and Men, Novel] (R).

928. _____. "Red Meat and Red Herrings," 30

(October 13, 1939), 562-63. Also in Donohue (ed.),
71-75.

929. _____ . 41 (January 26, 1945), 378.
[Cannery Row] (R).

930. Condon, Eddie. "Tortilla in B Flat," Flair [n.v.]
(January, 1951), pp. 114-15.
[This article includes a montage by William Ward
Beecher and a photograph of Steinbeck by Robert
Capa].

931. Condon, Frank. "Grapes of Raps; Hollywood Makes
a Picture, Strictly Under Blankets," Collier's, 105
(January 27, 1940), 23ff.

932. "Conference Set on S.'s Works," San Jose Mercury-
News, November 22, 1970. p. 30.

933. Conterno, Larry, Catholic World, 194 (November,
1961), 125-26.
[The Winter of Our Discontent] (R).

934. Cooperman, Stanley. "Cannery Row," Review Notes
and Study Guide to Steinbeck. New York: Monarch
Press, 1964. pp. 62-75.

935. _____ . "East of Eden," Review Notes and Study
Guides. pp. 76-95.

936. _____ . "Of Mice and Men," Review Notes and
Study Guide to Steinbeck. pp. 25-40.

937. _____ . "The Pearl," Review Notes and Study
Guide to Steinbeck. pp. 16-24.

938. _____ . "The Winter of Our Discontent," Review
Notes and Study Guide to Steinbeck. pp. 96-110.

939. Corin, Fernand. "S. and Hemingway: A Study in
Literary Economy," Revue Des Langues Vivantes,
24 (January-February and March-April, 1958), 60-
75, 153-63.
[The Pearl] (R).

940. Cosham, Ralph H. "S.: Imaginative Realist,"
San Jose Mercury-News, November 4, 1962. p. 15.

941.   Cournas, John and Sybil Norton. Famous Modern
       American Novelists. New York: Dodd, Mead, 1952.
       pp. 153-57.

942.   Court, Franklin. "Thematic Design in the Novels of
       John Steinbeck by Lester J. Marks," SQ, 4 (Fall,
       1971), 110-12 (R).

943.   Cousins, Norman. Saturday Review of Literature,
       25 (March 14, 1942), 6.
       [The Moon Is Down, Novel] (R).

944.   _____. Saturday Review of Literature, 28 (March
       17, 1945), 14.
       [Cannery Row] (R).

945.   _____. Saturday Review of Literature, 30 (March
       8, 1947), 22-3.
       [The Wayward Bus] (R).

946.   _____. Saturday Review, 33 (October 28, 1950),
       26-7.
       [Burning Bright, Novel] (R).

947.   Covici, Pascal, Jr. "From Commitment to Choice:
       Double Vision and the Problem of Vitality for J. S.,"
       The Fifties: Fiction, Poetry, Drama, ed. Warren
       French. Deland, Florida: Everett Edwards, 1970.
       pp. 63-71.

948.   _____. "In Memoriam: J. S.," SN, 2 (1969), 18.

949.   _____ (ed.). "Introduction," The Portable Stein-
       beck. New York: Viking Press, 1946. pp. vii-xxx.

950.   _____. "J. S. and the Language of Awareness,"
       The Thirties: Fiction, Poetry, Drama, ed. by
       Warren French. Deland, Florida: Everett Edwards,
       1967. pp. 47-54.

951.   _____. "Work and the Timeliness of The G. of
       W.," Lisca (ed.), pp. 814-24.

952.   Cowley, Malcolm. "American Tragedy," New Re-
       public, 98 (May 3, 1939), 382.

953.   _____. "A Farewell to the 1930s," Their Back

on Us.....A Contemporary Chronicle of the 1930s,
ed. Henry Dan Pipper. Carbondale: Southern Illinois University Press, 1967. pp. 347-54. Also in
Donohue (ed.), pp. 20-6.

954.   . New Republic, 98 (May 3, 1939), 382-3.
    [G. of W.] (R).

955.   . "Sherwood Anderson's Epiphanies,"
London Magazine, 7 (July, 1960), 61-66.

956.   . "S," The Literary Situation. New York:
Viking, 1955. Passim.

957.   Cox, Martha Heasley. "S. Country: A Conference
        and Film Festival," SQ, 4 (Summer, 1971), 68.

958.   Crandell, R. F. New York Herald Tribune Books,
        June 1, 1941. p. 6.
        [The Forgotten Village] (R).

959.   "A Crock of Chrysanthemums," San Francisco
        Chronicle, December 24, 1968.
        [A series of epigrams, a Herb Caen "exclusive"].

960.   Crockett, H. Kelly. "Bible and The Grapes of
        Wrath," College English, 24 (December, 1962), 193-
        99. Reply with Rejoinder by T. F. Dunn, College
        English, 24 (April, 1963), 566-67. Also in Donohue
        (ed.), pp. 105-14.

961.   Crockett, H. Kelly. "The Other Cheek," College
        English, 24 (April, 1963), 567.

962.   Cummins, P. D. "The Grapes of Wrath: John
        Steinbeck," 100 Great Books: Masterpieces of All
        Time. London: Odhams Books, 1966, pp. 596-601
        (R).

963.   Cunliffe, Marcus. "Fiction Since World War I,"
        The Literature of the United States. London:
        Penguin, 1954. Passim.

964.   Cuppy, Will. New York Herald Tribune Books.
        August 18, 1939. p. 12.
        [Cup of Gold] (R).

965.   "Cutting Down the Laurels; Nobel Prize for Literature,"

New Republic, 147 (November 10, 1962), 8.

966. Daiches, David. "S.," A Study of Literature for Readers and Critics. Ithaca: Cornell University, 1948. pp. 63-4, 132.

967. Daily Telegraph, No. 292, 1970, pp. 40-1, 43, 46. [J. of a Novel].

968. Davis, Elmer. Saturday Review of Literature, 18 (September 24, 1938), 11. [LV] (R).

969. _____. "The S. Country," Saturday Review of Literature, 18 (September 24, 1938), 11.

970. Dawson, Margaret C. New York Herald Tribune Books. October 23, 1932. p. 2. [PH] (R)

971. _____. New York Herald Tribune Books. September 24, 1933. p. 17. [To a God Unknown] (R).

972. "Death of a Racket," Spectator, 194 (April 8, 1955), 430-31.

973. Delisle, Arnold F. "Style and Idea in S.'s 'The Turtle'," Style, 4 (Spring, 1970), 135-54. [Chapter 3 of G. of W.].

974. DeMott, Benjamin. Hudson Review, 14 (Winter, 1961-62), 622. [The Winter of Our Discontent] (R).

975. DeMott, Robert. "Joseph Fontenrose, John Steinbeck," SN, 1, v (1968), 1-6 (R).

976. _____. "Warren French (ed.), The Thirties: Fiction, Poetry, Drama," KAL, 11 (1968), 91-4 (R).

977. Dent, Alan. Punch, 206 (June 23, 1943), 532. [The Moon Is Down] (P.R.).

978. De Roos, Robert. "Cannery Row--Now Popular Nostalgia," San Francisco Sunday Examiner and Chronicle,

This World,   July 26, 1970.   p. 28.

979.   De Schweinitz, George.   "S. and Christianity,"
       College English, 19 (May, 1958), 369.   Also in
       Donohue (ed.), pp. 103-4.
       [The Grapes of Wrath].

980.   "Determined Author: J. E. S.," New York Times,
       Western Edition.   October 26, 1962. p. 7.

981.   Detweiler, Robert.   "Christ and the Christ Figure
       in American Fiction," Christian Scholar, 47 (Sum-
       mer, 1964), 111-24.
       [The Grapes of Wrath].

982.   DeVolld, Walter L.   "Steinbeck in German Transla-
       tion by Helmut Liedoff," SQ, 3 (1970), 75-6 (R).

983.   _____ .   "Zum Problem des Kritischen Realismus
       bei John Steinbeck by Hildegard Schuman," SQ, 3
       (1970), 14-17 (R).

984.   De Voto, Bernard.   "American Novels: 1939,"
       Atlantic, 165 (January, 1940), 66-74.

985.   _____ .   "Dubious Battle in California," Nation,
       143 (September 12, 1936), 302-4.

986.   _____ .   New York Herald Tribune Books, Febru-
       ary 16, 1947. p. 1.
       [The Wayward Bus] (R).

987.   _____ .   The World of Fiction.   Boston: Houghton
       Mifflin Co., 1950.   Passim.

988.   No entry.

989.   Dickinson, Asa Don.   "S.," The Best Books of the
       Decade 1936-1945: Another Clue to the Literary
       Lobybrinter.   New York: H. W. Wilson Co., 1948,
       pp. 208-10.

990.   Didion, J.   National Review, 12 (January 16, 1962),
       33.
       [The Winter of Our Discontent] (R).

991.   Dietrich, R. F. and Sundell, Roger H.   Instructor's

Manual for The Art of Fiction. New York: Holt, Rinehart and Winston, 1967. ["The Chrysanthemums," pp. 33-40].

992. Ditsky, John. "Faulkner Land and S. Country," Astro and Hayashi (eds.), pp. 11-23.

993. _____. "From Oxford to Salinas: Comparing Faulkner and S.," SQ, 2 (1969), 51-55.

994. _____. "Music From a Dark Cave: Organic Form in S.'s Fiction," Journal of Narrative Technique, 1 (January, 1971), 59-67.

995. "Divorced," New York Times, March 19, 1943. p. 21 (Carol Henning).

996. Dodds, John W. "The Mediocre American," Huntington Library Quarterly, 22 (May, 1959), 163-7.

997. Dolbier, Maurice. "A Porch on Fire Island, a Hill in Mysore," New York Herald Tribune Book Review, February 1, 1959. p. 2.

998. Donohue, Agnes McNeill. "The Endless Journey to No End; Journey and Eden Symbolism in Hawthorne and S.," Donohue (ed.), pp. 257-66.

999. "Double Beating Views on American Soldiers, Reply to the Editor of L'Unita," Time, 60 (July, 1952), 48.

1000. "Double Vodka," Times Literary Supplement, April 23, 1949. p. 259.
[A Russian Journal] (R).

1001. Dougherty, Charles T. "The Christ-Figure in G. of W.," College English, 24 (December, 1962), 224-6. Also in Donohue (ed.), pp. 115-17.

1002. Doughty, Howard H., Jr. New York Herald Tribune Books, December 7, 1941. p. 3.
[Sea of Cortez] (R).

1002(a). Downs, Robert B. (ed.). The First Freedom. Chicago: A. C. A., 1960. pp. 284-85.

1003. Dreiser, Theodore. The Letters of Theodore

Dreiser, ed. Robert H. Elias. University of Pa. Pr.,
1959. 4, 800, 845, 868-9, 958.

1004.   "Dubious Battle in California," Nation, 143 (September 12, 1936), 302-4.

1005.   DuBois, W. "Success Story," New York Times Book
Review, September 6, 1953. p. 8.

1006.   Duchene, Anne. Manchester Guardian. October 26,
1954. p. 4.
[Sweet Thursday] (R).

1007.   Duffus, R. New York Times Book Review, December
28, 1941, 6:3.
[Sea of Cortez] (R).

1008.   _____. New York Times Book Review, March 8,
1942. 6:27.
[The Moon Is Down, Novel] (R).

1009.   Duffy, Charles. Commonweal, 35 (March 27, 1942),
569-70.
[The Moon Is Down, Novel] (R).

1010.   Duhamel, P. Albert. "Love in the Modern Novel,"
Catholic World, 191 (April, 1960), 31-5.

1011.   Dunaway, Philip, and Melvin Evans (ed.). "J. S.,"
Treasury of the World's Great Diaries. Garden City,
N.Y.: Doubleday, 1957. pp. 316-23.

1012.   Dunn, Thomas F. "Bible and The Grapes of Wrath,"
College English, 24 (April, 1963), 566-7. See H. K.
Crockett's article on the same subject.
[The Grapes of Wrath].

1013.   _____. "The G. of W.," College English, 24
(April, 1963), 566-7. Also in Donohue (ed.), pp.
123-5.

1014.   Durant, Will and Ariel (eds.). Interpretations of
Life: A Survey of Contemporary Literature. N.Y.:
Simon & Schuster, 1970 [n. p.].

1015.   Dusenbury, Winifred L. "S.: Of Mice and Men," The
Themes of Loneliness in Modern American Drama.

University of Florida Press, 1960. pp. 45-50.

1016. Dvorak, Jermila. Books Abroad, 36 (Winter, 1962),
80.
[The Winter of Our Discontent] (R).

1017. Dvorak, Wilfred Paul. "Notes Towards the Education
of the Heart," Iowa English Year Book, 10 (1965),
46-9.

1018. Eastman, Max. "J. S.--Genevieve Tabois," American
Mercury, 54 (June, 1942), 754-6.

1019. "East of Eden, a Best-seller," Facts on File, 12
(October 31-November 6, 1952), 355.

1020. "East of Eden, a Movie, Was Produced by Warner
Bros.," Facts on File, 15 (April 7-13, 1955), 127.

1021. The Editors of Fortune. "I Wonder Where We Can Go
Now," Fortune, [n.v.], (April, 1939), [n.p.] Also
in French (ed.), pp. 31-42; Lisca (ed.), pp. 623-42.

1022. Eisinger, Charles E. "Jeffersonian Agrarianism in
G. of W.," University of Kansas City Review, 14
(Winter, 1947), 149-54. Also in Donohue (ed.), pp.
143-50; Lisca (ed.), pp. 720-8.

1023. _____. "The Moon Is Down," Fiction
of the Forties. University of Chicago Press, 1963.
pp. 50-1, 100-101.

1024. _____. "S.," Fiction of the Forties. Chicago &
London: The University of Chicago Press, 1964.
pp. 4, 10, 48, 50-1, 100-101, 331, 333, 369.

1025. "Elected American Arts & Letters Academy Member,"
New York Times, November 24, 1948. p. 44.

1026. "Elected to the American Academy of Arts & Letters,"
Time, 52 (December 6, 1948), 42.

1027. Ellison, Jayne. "Dog Thieves Mourn S.," Dayton
Daily News. December 22, 1968. [n.p.].

1028. Ellithorpe, Harold. "A View of S.," Author and

Journalist, 47 (December, 1962), 15-16.

1029.   Ethridge, James M. (ed.). "S.," Contemporary
         Authors: A Bio-Bibliographical Guide to Current
         Authors & Their Works, Detroit: Gale Research Co.,
         1963. 2, 184.

1030.   Ewen, A. J. "100 Best American Novels--15,"
         Books and Bookman, [n. v.] November, 1962, p. 75.
         [Tortilla Flat].(R).

1031.   _____. "100 Best American Novels--16," Books
         and Bookman, [n. v.] December, 1962, p. 41.
         [The Grapes of Wrath] (R).

1032.   _____. "100 Best American Novels--16," Books
         and Bookman, [n. v.] December, 1962. p. 41.
         [Of Mice and Men] (R).

1033.   "Exploring Home," Times Literary Supplement,
         November 2, 1962. p. 843.
         [Travels with Charley] (R).

1034.   Fadiman, Clifton. "East of Eden," Book-of-the-Month
         Club News, September, 1952. p. 6 (R).

1035.   _____. New Yorker, 15 (April 15, 1939), 81.
         [G. of W.] (R).

1036.   _____. New Yorker, 17 (December 6, 1941), 133.
         [Sea of Cortez] (R).

1037.   _____. New Yorker, 18 (March 7, 1942), 52.
         [The Moon Is Down, Novel] (R).

1038.   _____. "S. Again," New Yorker, 18 (April 4,
         1942), 55.

1039.   Fairley, Barker. Canadian Forum, 21 (August, 1941),
         153.
         [The Forgotten Village] (R).

1040.   _____. "J. S. and the Coming Literature,"
         Sewanee Review, 50 (April, 1942), 145-61.

1041.   Farrell, James T. "The End of a Literary Decade,"

American Mercury, 48 (December, 1939), 408-14.

1042. Farrelly, John. New Republic, 117 (December 23, 1947), 28.
[The Pearl] (R).

1043. Fausset, Hugh l'A. Manchester Guardian. November 9, 1945. p. 3.
[Cannery Row] (R).

1044. Fazia, A. Della. "Nobel Prize, 1962 and the Bridge on the Drina Revisited," Books Abroad, 37 (Winter, 1963), 24-6.

1045. Feeney, William J. Extension, 55 (September, 1961), 15.
[The Winter of Our Discontent] (R).

1046. Fenton, Charles A. "The Writers Who Came Out of the War," SR, 40 (August 3, 1957), 5-7, 24.

1047. "The Fiction Award," Saturday Review of Literature, 22 (May 11, 1940), 5.

1048. Fiedler, Leslie A. Love and Death in the American Novel. New York: Stein and Day, 1966. p. 458.

1049. _____. "S.," Waiting for the End. New York: Stein and Day Publishers, 1964. Passim.

1050. "Film Studios Bid for New Novel, Wayward Bus," New York Times, November 3, 1946. 2:4.

1051. Finkelstein, Sidney. Existentialism and Alienation in American Literature. New York: International Publishers, 1967. Passim.

1052. Fischer, Louis. Saturday Review of Literature, 31 (May 15, 1948), 13.
[A Russian Journal] (R).

1053. Fitzgerald, F. Scott. The Letters of F. Scott Fitzgerald, ed. Andrew Turnbull. London: Bodley Head, 1964. pp. 73, 280, 288, 581.

1054. Floyd, Carlisle. "Of Mice and Men, an Opera," Opera News, 34 (September 6, 1969), 20-1.

1055.   "La Follett Committee Investigation Based on The
         Grapes of Wrath," Time, 34 (August 21, 1939), 10.

1056.   Fontenrose, Joseph. "The Grapes of Wrath," Lisca
         (ed.), pp. 748-800.
            [Originally from his book: John Steinbeck, 1963.
            pp. 67-83].

1057.   _____. "Memorial Statement on J. S.," SN, 2
         (1969), 19-20.

1058.   _____. "Sea of Cortez," J. S.: An Introduction
         and Interpretation. New York: Rinehart and Winston,
         1963. pp. 84-97. Also in Davis (ed.), pp. 122-34.

1059.   Fortune. "I Wonder Where We Can Go Now, etc.,"
         Fortune, [n. v.] (April, 1939), [n.p.]. Also in Lisca
         (ed.), pp. 623-42.

1060.   Forum, 90 (November, 1933), viii.
            [To a God Unknown] (R).

1061.   Forum, 102 (July, 1939), 4.
            [G. of W.] (R).

1062.   Foster, William. "S's Dog Show," Sunday Times,
         October 7, 1962, p. 33.
            [Travels with Charley] (R).

1063.   Fraser, Jack. "J. S.: As Colorful as the Men He
         Wrote About," San Jose Mercury-News Sunday Maga-
         zine, March 2, 1969. pp. 8-12.

1064.   _____. " 'Tortilla Flat' and Its Paisanos Gone,"
         San Jose Mercury-News, September 4, 1960. p. 6.

1065.   Frazier, George. "J. S.! J. S.! How Still We See
         Thee Lie, and Lie, and Lie," Esquire, 72 (1969),
         150-1, 269, 271, 274-5.

1066.   Freiman, Ray (ed.). "Some Random and Randy
         Thoughts in Books," The Author Looks at Format.
         New York: Trade Borre Clinic, 1950-51.

1067.   French, Warren. "L'Affaire Lettuceberg, Early
         Working Title of The Grapes of Wrath," John Steinbeck.
         p. 24.

1068. _____ . American Literary Scholarship, An
Annual/1967, ed. James Woodress. Duke University
Press, 1969. Passim.

1069. _____ . American Literary Scholarship, An Annual/
1968, ed. James Woodress. Duke University Press,
1970. pp. 193-4.

1069(a). _____ . Ibid., 1969. pp. 216-17.

1070. _____ . "Another Look at The G. of W.," Colorado
Quarterly, 3 (Winter, 1955), 337-43. French (ed.),
pp. 217-24.

1071. _____ . "The Education of the Heart," John Steinbeck. New York: Twayne, 1961. pp. 107-12. Also
in Donohue (ed.), pp. 204-8.

1072. _____ . "End of a Dream," J. S. New York:
Twayne, 1961. pp. 72-9. Also in Davis (ed.), pp.
63-9.

1073. _____ . "The First Theatrical Productions of
Steinbeck's Of Mice and Men," American Literature,
36 (January, 1965), 525-7.

1074. _____ . "In Memoriam: Lawrence William
Jones," SQ, 4 (Spring, 1971), 35.

1075. _____ . "J. S.," American Winners of the Nobel
Literary Prize, ed. Warren French and Walter E.
Kidds. Norman: University of Oklahoma Press,
1968. pp. 193-223.

1076. _____ . "J. S.," Fifteen Modern American Au-
thors: A Survey of Research and Criticism, ed.
Jackson R. Bryer. Durham, North Carolina: Duke
University Press, 1969. 369-87.

1077. _____ . "J. S. (1902-1968)," The Politics of
Twentieth-Century Novelists, ed. George A. Panichas.
New York: Hawthorn Books, 1971.
[Foreword by John W. Aldridge, pp. 296-306,
Passim].

1078. _____ . "Message: J. S. (February 27, 1902-
December 20, 1968)," SN, 2 (1969), 3-9.

1079. _____ . The Social Novel at the End of an Era.
See Trimmer, Joseph F., SQ, 2 (1969), 37-41.

1080. _____ . "S.," Encyclopedia Americana.   25,
612.   New York: Americana Corp., 1964.

1081. _____ . "S.," (The Grapes of Wrath, Cannery
Row, The Pastures of Heaven), J. D. Salinger.
New York: Twayne Publishers, Inc., 1963.   pp.
43-84, 106.

1082. _____ . "S.'s Winter Tale," MFS, 11 (Spring,
1965),   66-74.

1083. _____ . "The Time the Wolves Ate the Vice-
Principal," (Possibly an inter-chapter omitted
from Cannery Row, 1947), John Steinbeck.   pp. 129-
31.

1084. _____ . "Tortilla Flat," John Steinbeck.   pp. 22-
3, 53-61, Passim.   Preface to Modern Library
Edition, p. 54; Play, p. 24.   Film, p. 23.

1085. _____ . "What Became of the Joads?"   French
(ed.), pp. 93-101.
        [From his J. S. (1961), p. 107].

1086. Frey, John R.   "Postwar German Reactions to
American Literature," Journal of English and German Philology, 54 (April, 1955), 173-94.

1087. Friede, Donald.   The Mechanical Angel.   New
York: Knopf, 1948.   pp. 126-32.   Passim.

1088. Friedman, Norman.   " 'Flight': What Makes a
Short Story Short?"   MFS, 4 (Summer, 1958), 113-
14.

1089. Frietzsche, Arthur H.   "S. as a Western Author,"
Proceedings of the Utah Academy of Sciences, Arts,
and Letters, 42 (1965), 11-13.

1090. Frohock, W. M.   "East of Eden," The Novel of
Violence in America.   pp. 141-3.

1091. Frohock, W. M.   "The Grapes of Wrath," The
Novel of Violence in America.   pp. 129-33.

1092.   . "In Dubious Battle," The Novel of
Violence in America.   pp. 134-7.

1093.   . "J. S.--The Utility of Wrath," The
Novel of Violence in America.   Dallas, Texas:
Southern Methodist University Press, 1950.   pp.
129-33.

1094.   . "J. S.'s Men of Wrath," Southwest Review, 31 (Spring, 1946), 144-52.

1095.   Fukuma, Ken-ichi.   " 'Man' in S.'s Works,"
Kyushu American Literature, 7 (1964), 21-30.

1096.   Fuller, Edmund.   "East of Eden," Man in Modern
Fiction.   New York: Random House, 1958.   pp. 25-
9.

1097.   . "J. S.," Man in Modern Fiction: Some
Minority Opinions on Contemporary American
Writing.   New York: Random House, 1958.
Passim.

1098.   Fuller, Edward.   "Afterward," in his and Blanche Jen-
nings Thompson (eds.), Four Novels For Appreciation.   New York: Harcourt, Brace, 1960.   pp.
656-60.
[The Pearl].

1099.   Fytton, Francis.   "The Car as a Character,"
London Magazine, 6 (May, 1966), 36-50.

1100.   Galbraith, John K.   "J. S.:   Footnote for a
Memory," Atlantic, 224 (1969), 65-7.

1101.   . "S.," Economics, Peace and Laughter.
Boston: Houghton Mifflin, 1971.   pp. 317-29
[Chapter 8].

1102.   Gallagher, Jim.   "A Corridor of Greatness (S.
Country and S.'s Books)," Peninsula Living.
February 13, 1971.   pp. 6-9, 27-8.

1103.   Ganapathy, R.   "S.'s Of Mice and Men: A Study
of Lyricism Through Primitivism," Literary Criterion, 5 (Winter, 1962), 101-4.

1104. Gannett, Lewis. "Introduction," in PS (1958).
       pp. vii-xviii.

1105.   . "J. S.," in Preface to Cup of Gold.
       New York: Collier, 1936. pp. v-viii.

1106.   . New York Herald Tribune Books, July
       29, 1962. p. 3.
       [Travels with Charley] (R).

1107.   . "J. S.: Novelist at Work," Atlantic,
       176 (December, 1944), 55-60.

1108. Garcia, Reloy. Proletarian Writers of the Thirties,
       ed. David Madden. SQ, 4 (Winter, 1971), 19-21
       (R).

1109. Gardiner, Harold C. America, 55 (July 22, 1961),
       554.
       [The Winter of Our Discontent] (R).

1110.   . "Novelist to Philosopher?" In All Con-
       science: Reflections on Books and Culture.
       Garden City, New York: Hanover House, 1959.
       pp. 136-8.
       [East of Eden].

1111.   . "The Wayward Bus," In All Conscience.
       New York: Hanover House, 1959. pp. 131-6.

1112. Garrison, W. W. Christian Century, 59 (April 29,
       1942), 561-2.
       [The Moon Is Down, Novel] (R).

1113. Gassner, John. Current History, 2 (May, 1942),
       228.
       [The Moon Is Down, Novel] (R).

1114.   . Current History, 2 (May, 1942), 228-32.
       [The Moon Is Down, Play] (R).

1115. Geismar, Maxwell. American Moderns. London:
       W. H. Allen, 1958. pp. 151-3.
       [The Pearl] (R).

1116.   . American Moderns. London: W. H.
       Allen, 1958. pp. 153-5.
       [Burning Bright] (R).

1117.   . American Moderns. London: W. H.
Allen, 1958. pp. 155-6.
[The Short Reign of Pippin IV] (R).

1118.   . American Moderns. London: W. H.
Allen, 1958. pp. 164-7.
[East of Eden] (R).

1119.   . "Cup of Gold," Writers in Crisis. pp.
246-8.

1120.   . "Decline of the Classic Moderns,"
Nation, 180 (May 7, 1955), 402-4.

1121.   . "Further Decline of the Moderns:
J. S.," American Moderns; From Rebellion to
Conformity. New York: Hill and Wang, 1958.
pp. 151-6, 164-7. Passim.

1122.   . "In Dubious Battle," Writers in Crisis:
The American Novels Between Two Wars. Boston:
Houghton Mifflin. 1942. pp. 260-3.

1123.   . "J. S.," American Moderns: From
Rebellion to Conformity. New York: Hill and
Wang, 1958. pp. 151-6, 164-7.

1124.   . "J. S.: Of Wrath of Joy," Writers
in Crisis: The American Novel, 1925-1940.
Boston: Houghton Mifflin, 1942. pp. 237-70.

1125.   . Ibid., in Donohue (ed.), pp. 134-42.

1126.   . "Of Mice and Men," Writers in Crisis.
pp. 256-60.

1127.   . "PH," Writers in Crisis. pp. 242-6.

1128.   . "The Pearl," American Moderns.
pp. 151-3.

1129.   . Saturday Review of Literature, 30
(October 21, 1950), 14.
[Burning Bright, Play] (R).

1130.   . Saturday Review of Literature, 30
(November 22, 1947), 14.
[The Pearl] (R).

1131.   . "The Short Reign of Pippin IV, "
American Moderns. pp. 155-6.

1132.   . "To a God Unknown, " Writers in Crisis.
248-52.

1133.   . "Tortilla Flat, " Writers in Crisis.
pp. 252-6.

1134.   Gentry, Curt. "A Perceptive S. Study, " John
Steinbeck: Introduction and Interpretation, by Joseph
Fontenrose. San Francisco Chronicle, This World,
April 19, 1964, p. 40 (R).

1135.   George, Daniel. Spectator, 198 (May 31, 1957),
726-7.
[The Short Reign of Pippin IV] (R).

1136.   Gerber, Rudolph J. America, 107 (August 4, 1962),
569.
[Travels with Charley] (R).

1137.   "German Documents Reveal That Hitler Cited the
Novel, The Grapes of Wrath as Example of Living
Conditions in U.S., " New York Times, April 8,
1947. p. 13.

1138.   Gerould, Gordon Hall. "S., " The Patterns of
English and American Fiction. Boston: D. C. Heath,
1942. pp. 490-1.

1139.   Gerstenberger, Donna. "S. 's American Waste
Land, " MFS, 11 (Spring, 1965), 59-65.

1140.   "Gets King Haakon's Liberty Cross, " New York
Times. November 16, 1946. p. 17.

1141.   "Gets Norwegian Award for The Moon Is Down, "
New York Times, January 21, 1947. p. 21.

1142.   Gibbs, Lincoln R. "J. S., Moralist, " Antioch Review, 2 (June, 1942), 172-84. Also in SHC, pp.
92-103.

1143.   . "Tortilla Flat, " SHC, pp. 95-7.

1144.   Gibson, Wilfred. Manchester Guardian, September

8, 1939. p. 3.
[The Grapes of Wrath] (R).

1145.   Gide, André. "In Dubious Battle," Journals of André
        Gide, IV, 1939-49, tr. Justin M. O'Brien. New
        York: Knopf, 1951. p. 48. Also in Davis (ed.),
        pp. 47-8.

1146.   _____. The Journals of André Gide. tr. by
        Justin O'Brien. New York: Knopf, 1941.
        [September 27, 1940 and July 29, 1941].

1147.   Gierasch, Walter. "S.'s The Red Pony II: 'The
        Great Mountains'," Explicator, 4 (1946), Item 39.

1148.   Gilder, Rosamond. Theatre Arts, 26 (May, 1942),
        287.
        [The Moon Is Down, Play] (R).

1149.   Gill, Brendan. New Yorker, 30 (July, 1954), 63-4.
        [Sweet Thursday] (R).

1150.   Gilroy, Harry. New York Times Book Review,
        September 16, 1951. 7:6.
        [Sea of Cortez] (R).

1151.   "God and Man in Stockholm," America, 108 (Janu-
        ary 5, 1963), 4.

1152.   Goldhurst, William. "Of Mice and Men: J. S.'s
        Parable of The Curse of Cain," WAL, 6 (Summer,
        1971), 123-35.

1153.   Goldman, Eric F. New York Times Book Review,
        July 29, 1962. 7:5.
        [Travels with Charley] (R).

1154.   Goldsmith, Arnold L. "Thematic Rhythm in The
        Red Pony," College English, 26 (February, 1965),
        391-4. Also in Davis (ed.), pp. 70-4.

1155.   Golemba, Henry L. "S.'s Attempt to Escape the
        Literary Fallacy," MFS, 15 (1969), 231-9.

1156.   Goodman, Theodore R. New York Times Book Re-
        view, October 29, 1950. 2:3.
        [Burning Bright, Play] (R).

1157.   Goodrich, Norma L. "Bachelors in Fiction, Through
        J. S. and Jean Giono," Kentucky Romance Quarter-
        ly, 14 (1967), 367-78.

1158.   Gordon, Ernest. "The Winter of Our Discontent,"
        Princeton Seminary Bulletin, 15 (1962), 44-7.

1159.   Gorer, Geoffrey. New Statesman, 37 (June 25,
        1949), 683.
        [A Russian Journal] (R).

1160.   "Government Bans 182 Books Including Some By H. A.
        Smith, J. S., H. Spring, and A. Murphy," New
        York Times, January 21, 1956. 8.

1161.   Graef, Richard. Catholic World, 156 (February,
        1943), 635.
        [Bombs Away] (R).

1162.   "The Grapes Has First Birthday," Publishers Week-
        ly, 137 (April 13, 1940), 1493-4.
        [On The Grapes of Wrath].

1163.   "The Grapes of War: S. Prose from England,"
        Newsweek, 22 (July 5, 1943), 94-6.

1164.   "The Grapes of Wrath," American Writing Today.
        pp. 398-9.

1165.   "The Grapes of Wrath: Association of Farmers of
        Kern County Seeks California Ban," New York
        Times, August 23, 1939. 17.

1166.   "The Grapes of Wrath Banned By Buffalo Library,"
        Publishers' Weekly, 136 (August 12, 1930), 453.

1167.   "The Grapes of Wrath Banned in Kansas City,"
        New York Times, August 19, 1939. 8.

1168.   "The Grapes of Wrath: Career," New York Times,
        May 7, 1940. 20:24.

1169.   "The Grapes of Wrath: Cited in Article on Cali-
        fornia Migratory Labor," New York Times, August
        27, 1939. 7:10.

1170.   "The Grapes of Wrath Cited in P. V. McNutt

Article," New York Times, March 17, 1942.   7, 12.

1171.   "The Grapes of Wrath," Collier's, 104 (September 2, 1939), 54.

1172.   "The Grapes of Wrath Consigned to Flames By Library Board of East St. Louis, Illinois," Publishers' Weekly, 136 (November 25, 1939), 1944.

1173.   "The Grapes of Wrath: East St. Louis Library Orders Copies of The Grapes of Wrath Burned," New York Times, November 15, 1939. 21.

1174.   "The Grapes of Wrath Gets New Sales Stimulus," Publishers' Weekly, 136 (December 30, 1939), 2320.

1175.   "The Grapes of Wrath: He Gives Pulitzer Prize Checks to R. Lovejoy for Literary Career," New York Times, June 16, 1940.

1176.   "The Grapes of Wrath: He Wins American Booksellers Association Award," New York Times, February 14, 1940.

1177.   "The Grapes of Wrath: He Wins Pulitzer Prize," New York Times, May 7, 1940.

1178.   "The Grapes of Wrath: He Wins Social Work Today (Pub.) Award," New York Times, April 2, 1940.

1179.   "The Grapes of Wrath: Mrs. F. D. Roosevelt Holds He Did Not Exaggerate," New York Times, April 3, 1940.

1180.   "The Grapes of Wrath: Mrs. Roosevelt Comments on the Book," New York Times, December 8, 1939. 16.

1181.   "The Grapes of Wrath: Praised by Pearl Buck," New York Times, November 30, 1939.

1182.   "The Grapes of Wrath: Screen Rights Sold," New York Times, April 21, 1939.

1183.   "The Grapes of Wrath To Be Published," New York

Times, January 11, 1943. p. 2.

1184.   "The Grapes of Wrath: To Collaborate with H.
         Kleine on Film Production," New York Times,
         April 7, 1940. 9:5.

1185.   Gray, James. "Cannery Row," On Second Thought.
         Minneapolis: University of Minnesota Press, 1946.
         pp. 133-40.

1186.   _____. "A Local Habitation in J. S.," On
         Second Thought. Minneapolis: University of
         Minnesota Press, 1946. pp. 133-40.

1187.   _____. "S.," On Second Thought. Minneapolis:
         University of Minnesota, 1946. pp. 133-40.

1188.   Greet, T. Y., et al (eds.). "The Snake," The
         World of Fiction: Stories in Context. Boston:
         Houghton Mifflin, 1964. pp. 370-5.

1189.   Griffin, Robert J. and Freedman, William A.
         "Machines and Animals: Pervasive Motifs in G. of
         W.," JEGP, 62 (April, 1963), 569-80. Also in
         Donohue (ed.), pp. 219-31; Lisca (ed.), pp. 769-
         83.

1190.   Grommon, Alfred H. "Who Is The 'Leader of the
         People'?: Helping Students Examine Fiction,"
         English Journal, 48 (November, 1959), 449-56.

1191.   Gunther, John. New York Herald Tribune Books,
         March 8, 1942. p. 1.
             [The Moon Is Down, Novel]. (R)

1192.   Gurko, Leo. "The Joads in California," The Angry
         Decade. New York: Dodd, Mead, 1947. pp. 201-
         21. Also in Donohue (ed.), pp. 63-7.

1193.   _____. Nation, 175 (September 20, 1952), 235-6.
             [East of Eden] (R).

1194.   _____. "S.," Heroes, Highbrows and the Popular
         Mind. New York: Bobbs-Merrill, 1953. Passim.

1195.   _____. "S.'s Later Fiction," Nation, 175 (Sep-
         tember 20, 1952), 235-6.

1196.   _____ and Miriam. "The S. Temperament,"
Rocky Mountain Review, 9 (Fall, 1944), 17-22.

1196(a). Hagopian, John V. and Martin Dolch. "The Leader
of the People," Insight I: Analysis of American
Literature. Frankfurt Am. Main: Herschgroben-
Verlog, 1962   pp. 230-5.

1197.   Haines, Helen E. "S.," What's In a Novel. New
York: Ronald Press Co., 1935. Passim.

1198.   Hamby, James A. "S.'s The Pearl: Tradition and
Innovation," Western Review, 7 (1970), 65-6.

1199.   Hampson, John. Spectator, 175 (November 2, 1945),
418-20.
[Cannery Row] (R).

1200.   Harcourt, Peter. Time and Tide, 59 (June 22,
1961), 1031.
[The Winter of Our Discontent] (R).

1201.   Harcourt-Smith, Simon. New Statesman, 36 (November 6, 1948), 400-402.
[The Pearl] (R).

1202.   Hart, Eugene D. Library Journal, 66 (October 15,
1941), 903.
[Sea of Cortez] (R).

1203.   Hart, James D. (ed.). "S.," The Oxford Companion to American Literature. New York: Oxford
University Press, 1956. pp. 722-3.

1204.   _____ . "S.," What's In a Novel. New York:
Ronald Press Co., 1935. Passim.

1205.   Hartt, Julian N. "The Grapes of Wrath," The Lost
Image of Man. Baton Rouge: Louisiana State University Press, 1964. pp. 74-6.

1206.   _____ . "In Dubious Battle," The Lost Image of
Man. Baton Rouge: Louisiana State University
Press, 1964. pp. 74-6.

1207.   _____ . Yale Review, 52 (Winter, 1962), 305-306.

[The Winter of Our Discontent] (R).

1208.   Hartung, Philip T.   Commonweal, 34 (July 25, 1941), 329-30.
[The Forgotten Village] (R).

1209.   Harvard Law Review.   "Depression Migrants and the States," HLR, 53 (April, 1940), 1041-2.   Also in Donohue (ed.), pp. 30-1.

1210.   "Has Eye Surgery," New York Times, June 25, 1962.   p. 11.

1211.   Hashiguchi, Yasuo.   "Japanese Translations of S.'s Works (1939-69)," SQ, 3 (1970), 93-106.

1212.   Hastings, William T.   "J. S.," Syllabus of American Literature.   Chicago: University of Chicago Press, 1941.   pp. 103, 105-106.

1213.   Hatch, R. L.   "The Pearl, A Screen Play," New Republic, 118 (March 1, 1948), 26.

1214.   Hauck, Richard B.   "The Comic Christ and the Modern Reader," College English, 31 (1970), 498-506.
[Jim Casy in The Grapes of Wrath; Faulkner and others].

1215.   "Have We Gone Soft?   America--1960, A Symposium," Thurston N. Davis; Arthur M. Schlesinger, Sr.; Harry Golden; Reinhold Niebuhr.   New Republic, 142 (February 15, 1960), 11-15.

1216.   Havighurst, Walter.   "Flight," Instructor's Manual for Masters of the Modern Short Story.   New York: Harcourt, Brace, 1945.   pp. viii-ix.

1217.   Hayashi, Tetsumaro.   "The Agony and Ecstasy of Being an American: A Review of S.'s America and Americans," Indian P. E. N., [n.v.] (September, 1968), [n.p.] (R).

1218.   _____.   "A Brief Survey of J. S. Bibliographies," KAL, 9 (1966), 54-61.

1219.   _____.   "The Function of the Joad Clan in The

Grapes of Wrath," Modern Review. 20 (March, 1968), 158-9, 161-2.

1220.   . "Harry T. Moore, The Novels of John Steinbeck," SN, 1, ii (1968), 4 (R).

1221.   . "J. S.'s America and Americans," Lumina, 2 (1968), 34-6 (R).

1222.   . "J. S.'s America and Americans," The New York Nichibei. February 2, 1967. p. 8 (R).

1223.   . "John Steinbeck, America and Americans." SN, 1 (August, 1968), 4 (R).

1224.   . "J. S.'s America and Americans," Visvabharati Quarterly, 31 (1965-66), 404-406 (R).

1225.   . "J. S.'s The Grapes of Wrath: The Joad Clan and Women," Lumina, 4 (1961), 1-4.

1226.   . "Kenji Inoue and Y. Miyamoto (eds.), John Steinbeck's America and Americans (a Japanese edition in English)," SN, I, ii (1968), 4 (R).

1227.   . "The Principle of Continuity in The Grapes of Wrath," KAL, 10 (1967), 75-80.

1228.   . "Recent S. Studies in the United States," SQ, 4 (Summer, 1971), 73-6.

1229.   . "Robert Bennett, The Wrath of John Steinbeck (a pamphlet)," SN, I, 11 (1968), 2 (R).

1230.   . "S. Conference," SQ, 3 (1970), 23-4.

1231.   . "S.'s Women and the Principle of Continuity," Visvabharati Quarterly, 31 (1965-66), 201-206.

1232.   . "Thomas Goethals, John Steinbeck's The Grapes of Wrath: A Critical Commentary," SN, I, ii (1968), 3 (R).

1233. Hayman, Lee Richard. "Report from Salinas," SQ, 3 (1970), 43-4.

1234.   Hedgpeth, Joel. "Philosophy on Cannery Row,"
         Astro and Hayashi (eds.), pp. 89-129.

1235.   _____. "Sea of Cortez Revisited or Cannery
         Row Revisited," Pacific Discovery, 6 (1953), 28-30,
         (R).

1236.   Hedley, George. "S.," Background and Foregrounds.
         Mills College, Oakland: Eucalyptus Press, 1939.
         Passim.

1237.   Heiney, Donald W. "American Naturalism and the
         New Italian Writers," Twentieth Century Literature,
         3 (October, 1957), 135-41.

1237(a).   _____. "S.," Essentials of Contemporary Lit-
         erature. Great Neck, New York: Barron's Edu-
         cational Series, 1954. pp. 143-6.

1238.   _____. "The Red Pony," Recent American
         Literature. Great Neck, New York: Barron, 1958.
         pp. 234-5.

1239.   Hemenway, Robert. "American Literature in the
         Twentieth Century by Heinrich Straumann," SQ, 4
         (Spring, 1971), 55-6 (R).

1240.   Henderson, Caroline A. "Letters from the Dust
         Bowl," French (ed.), pp. 15-27.

1241.   Hersey, John. "J. S.," Proceedings. New York:
         American Academy of Arts and Letters and the
         National Institute of Arts and Letters, 1969 (Publi-
         cation No. 262, Part 3, Commemorative Tributes
         of the Academy). pp. 85-90.

1242.   Herzberg, Max J. and the Staff of The Thomas Y.
         Crowell Co. (eds.). "J. S.," The Reader's En-
         cyclopedia of American Literature. New York:
         Crowell, 1962. pp. 1079-80.

1243.   Hester, Sister Mary. "Mr. S.? Frankly, No,"
         Today, 17 (May, 1963), 23-6.

1244.   Hickey, Neil. "How Does the World See Us?"
         TV Guide, December 5-11, 1970, p. 8.
         [USIS Film, "An Impression of J. S.--Writer"].

1245.   Hicks, Granville. S. R., 44 (June 24, 1961), 11.
         [The Winter of Our Discontent] (R).

1246.   _____ . (ed.). "S.," Proletarian Literature in
         the United States. New York: International Pub-
         lishers, 1935. Passim.

1247.   _____ . "The Thirties: A Reappraisal," S. R.
         46 (May 4, 1963), 27-8.

1248.   Higashiyama, Masayoshi. "On Works of J. S.,
         A Great Modern Novelist," Kansai Gakuin Times,
         7 (1957), 15-28.

1249.   Hildebrand, William H. "The Social Rebel in
         American Literature, ed. Robert A. Woodward and
         James J. Clark," SQ, 4 (Fall, 1971), 112-13 (R).

1250.   Hinkel, Edgar J. and McCann, William E.
         Criticism of California Literature. Oakland, Cali-
         fornia: Alameda County Library, 1940. Official
         Project No. 665-08-3-85 of Work Project. Ad-
         ministration.
         [Mimeographed].

1251.   Hirose, Hidekazu. "The Growth of Jim Casy in
         The Grapes of Wrath," Studies in American Litera-
         ture (Chu-Shikoku American Literature Society), 6
         (1970), 43-51.

1251(a). _____ . "The 25th Chapter of The Grapes of
         Wrath and the Epilogue of Their Blood is Strong :
         Spring, 1938," The Chu-Shikoku American Litera-
         ture Society Bulletin, 11 (1970), 5-9.

1252.   Hobson, L. Z. "Trade Winds," S. R., 35 (August
         30, 1952), 4.

1253.   Hodgart, Matthew. New Statesman, 61 (June 30,
         1961), 1052-54.
         [The Winter of Our Discontent] (R).

1254.   Hoffman, Frederick J. The Modern Novel in Amer-
         ica, 1900-1950. Chicago: Henry Regney, 1951.
         pp. 160-8.

1255.   _____ . "Violence and Rhetoric in the 1930's,"

The Modern Novel in America. Chicago: Regnery,
1951. 160-8.

1256.   Hogan, William. San Francisco Sunday Chronicle
("This World Magazine"), July 29, 1962. p. 24.
[Travels with Charley] (R).

1257.   No entry.

1258.   Holiday, 32 (August, 1962), 12.
[Travels with Charley] (R).

1259.   Holman, Hugh. New Republic, 130 (June 7, 1954),
18-20.
[Sweet Thursday] (R).

1260.   Houghton, Donald E. " 'Westering' in 'The Leader of the People'," WAL, 4 (1969), 117-24.

1261.   Houlihan, T. Library Journal, 83 (September 15,
1958), 2436.
[Once There Was a War] (R).

1262.   Howard, Leon. "Power and the Past: J. S.,"
Literature and the American Tradition. Garden
City, New York: Doubleday, 1960. pp. 300-303.

1263.   Hughes, Riley. Catholic World, 176 (November,
1952), 150-1.
[East of Eden] (R).

1264.   _____. Catholic World, 179 (April, 1954), 393-4.
[Sweet Thursday] (R).

1265.   _____. Catholic World, 185 (July, 1957), 312.
[SRP] (R).

1266.   Huie, William Bradford. Saturday Review of
Literature, 25 (December 5, 1942), 22.
[Bombs Away] (R).

1267.   Hunter, Anne. Commonweal, 47 (January 23, 1948),
377.
[The Pearl] (R).

1268.   Hunter, J. P. "S.'s Wine of Affirmation in The
Grapes of Wrath," Essays in Modern American

Literature, ed. Richard E. Langford. Deland, Florida: Edwards, 1967. Also in Lisca (ed.), pp. 801-13.

1269. Hunter, J. Paul. "S.'s Wine of Affirmation in _The Grapes of Wrath_," Stetson Studies in the Humanities, 1 (1961), 76-89.

1270. "Hurt in Apartment Mishap," New York Times, May 16, 1947. p. 21.

1271. Hutchens, John K. New York Herald Tribune, June 23, 1961. p. 21. [The Winter of Our Discontent] (R).

1272. _____. "On an Author," New York Herald Tribune Book Review, September 21, 1952. p. 2.

1273. Hyman, Stanley E. "J. S. and The Nobel Prize," New Leader, 45 (December 10, 1962), 10-11.

1274. _____. "J. S. and the Nobel Prize," Standards: A Chronicle of Books for Our Time. New York: Horizon Press, 1966. pp. 113-17. [The Winter of Our Discontent].

1275. _____. "J. S., Of Invertebrates and Men," The Promised End: Essays and Reviews, 1942-62. Cleveland World Publishing, 1963. pp. 17-22.

1276. _____. New Republic, 106 (February 16, 1942), 242. [Sea of Cortez] (R).

1277. _____. "Some Notes on J. S.," Antioch Review, 2 (June, 1942), 185-200. Also in SHC, pp. 152-66.

1277(a). _____. "Some Trends in the Novel," College English, 20 (October, 1958), 1-9.

1278. "If I Were King," Time, 69 (April 15, 1957), 126. [SRP] (R).

1279. Inoue, Atsuko. "A Study of J. S.: The Group in His Fiction," Essays and Studies in British and

American Literature, (Tokyo Women's Christian
College), 11 (Winter, 1964), 49-99.

1280.   "Insufficient People," Times Literary Supplement.
November 29, 1947. p. 613.
[The Wayward Bus] (R).

1281.   "Interview with a Best-Selling Author, J. S.,"
Cosmopolitan, 122 (April, 1947), 18, 123f.

1282.   "Invasion," Times Literary Supplement, June 20,
1942. p. 305.
[The Moon Is Down] (R).

1283.   Isaacs, Edith J. R.   "Of Mice and Men," Theatre
Arts Anthology.   New York: Theatre Arts Books,
1950.   pp. 644-6.

1284.   _____.   Theatre Arts, 22 (January, 1938), 13-
16.
[Of Mice and Men, Play] (R).

1285.   _____.   "When Good Men Get Together,"
Theatre Arts Monthly, 22 (January, 1938), 13-16.

1286.   Isherwood, Christopher.   "The Grapes of Wrath,"
Exhumations.   London: Methuen, 1966.   pp. 25-7.
Harmondsworth: Penguin Books, 1969.   pp. 38-41
(R).

1287.   _____.   "The Tragedy of Eldorado," Kenyon
Review, 1 (Autumn, 1939), 450-3.   Also in
Donohue (ed.), pp. 76-9.

1288.   "It Started in a Garden," [East of Eden], Time,
September 22, 1952.   p. 110 (R).

1289.   "Izvestia pub. J. S. Letter apologizing to Soviet
writers who were his hosts during 1963 visit for mix
up over copies of his 1962 Nobel Prize speech and
mimeographed thank-you list he sent to them and
accidentally to others he had never met," New
York Times, August 30, 1964.   p. 24.

1290.   Jack, Peter Monro.   New York Times Book Review.   April 16, 1939.   7:2.
[G. of W.] (R).

1291. Jackson, Frank H. "Economics in Literature,"
       Duquesne Review, 3 (Spring, 1958), 80-5.
       [The Grapes of Wrath].

1292. Jackson, Joseph Henry. "The Finest Book J. S.
       Has Written," French (ed.), pp. 111-17.
       [From New York Herald Tribune Books, April
       16, 1939, p. 3] [G. of W.].

1293. _____. "Introduction" Of Mice and Men.
       New York: Random House, Modern Library, 1937.

1294. _____. "Introduction" The Grapes of Wrath.
       New York: Limited Edition Club and Heritage
       Press, 1940.

1295. _____. "Introduction" The Short Novels of
       John Steinbeck. New York: Viking Press, 1963.
       pp. vii-xv.

1296. _____. "Introduction" The Short Novels of
       John Steinbeck. pp. xii-xiii.
       [Cannery Row].

1297. _____. "Introduction," The Short Novels of
       John Steinbeck. pp. xiii-xiv.
       [The Pearl].

1298. _____. "J. S., a Portrait," Saturday Review
       of Literature, 16 (September 25, 1937), 11-12, 18.

1299. _____. "S.," Introduction to Of Mice and Men.
       New York: Random House, 1937.

1300. _____. "S.," Introduction to The G. of W.
       New York: Limited Edition Club and Heritage
       Press, 1940.

1301. _____. "S.," Preface to The Short Novels of
       John Steinbeck. New York: Viking Press, 1953.
       pp. vii-xv.

1302. _____. "The Moon Is Down," Introduction to
       The Short Novels of John Steinbeck. pp. xi-xii.

1303. _____. New York Herald Tribune Books, April
       16, 1939. p. 3.
       [G. of W.] (R).

1304.   . "The Red Pony," Introduction to The
        Short Novels of John Steinbeck.   p. xi.

1305.   . San Francisco Chronicle   "This World,"
        February 16, 1947. p. 17.
        [The Wayward Bus] (R).

1306.   . San Francisco Chronicle "This World,"
        April 18, 1948. p. 14.
        [A Russian Journal] (R).

1307.   . San Francisco Chronicle "This World,"
        October 27, 1950. p. 16.
        [Burning Bright, Novel] (R).

1308.   . San Francisco Chronicle "This World,"
        September 21, 1952. p. 20.
        [East of Eden] (R).

1309.   . "Tortilla Flat," Introduction to The
        Short Novels of John Steinbeck.   pp. viii-ix.

1310.   Jackson, Robert B.   Library Journal, 86 (June 15,
        1961), 2339.
        [The Winter of Our Discontent] (R).

1311.   Jaffe, Adrian H. and Virgil Scott.   "The Leader
        of the People," Studies in The Short Story.   New
        York: Dryden, 1947. pp. 172-81.

1312.   Janeway, Elizabeth.   New York Times Book Review.
        April 14, 1957. 7:6.
        [SRP] (R).

1313.   "J. S. and Others Named Honorary Consultants in
        American Literature," New York Times, May 29,
        1963. p. 40.

1314.   "J. S. Charges USSR Fears Truth Above All Else,"
        New York Times, June 27, 1952. p. 2.

1315.   "J. S. Gets Press Medal of Freedom," New York
        Times, September 15, 1964. p. 15.

1316.   "J. S. Hires Convention Leg Man," Editor and
        Publisher, 89 (June 16, 1956), 10.

1317.   "J. S. in USSR Under Cultural Program: S.

Moscow, " New York Times, October 22, 1963.
p. 34.

1318. "J. S. Made National Institute of Arts and Letters
Member, " New York Times, January 19, 1939.
p. 15.

1319. "J. S. , " National Review, 64 (January 28, 1969),
64.

1320. "J. S.: 1902-1968, " Newsweek, 72 (December 30,
1968), 55.

1321. "J. S.: 1902-1968, " Time, 92 (December 27, 1968),
61-2.

1322. "J. S. , One of the Kennedy Library Trustees, "
New York Times, January 14, 1964. p. 17.

1323. "J. S. , Social Novelist, " America, 120 (January
11, 1969), 32.

1324. "J. S. , Special Guest, " New York Times, September 3, 1947. p. 4; September 9, 1957. p. 3.

1325. "J. S. To Continue in Journalism, " Editor and
Publisher, 90 (April 27, 1957), 124.

1326. "J. S. To Get U. S. Medal of Freedom, " New
York Times, July 4, 1964. p. 1.

1327. "J. S. To Mexico City Literary Adaptations,
Actors Theatre, " New York Times, August 19,
1948. p. 42.

1328. "J. S. , " Wilson Library Bulletin, 11 (March,
1937), 456.

1329. "J. S. Wins Back Rights to His Novel, Cannery
Row, from Producer B. Bryants, " New York
Times, October 27, 1949. p. 38.

1330. Johnson, Curtis L. "S.: A Suggestion for Research, " MFS, 11 (Spring, 1965), 75-8.

1331. Johnson, Lady Bird. A White House Diary.
London: Weidenfeld and Nicholson, 1970. pp. 72,

155-7, 300-3, 421, 423, 719-20.

1332.   Johnson, Pamela Hansford. New Statesman, 54 (July
         13, 1957), 61-2.
         [The Short Reign of Pippin IV] (R).

1333.   "Joins New York Herald Tribune Syndicate," Time,
         41 (May 3, 1943), 49.

1334.   Jones, Claude Edward. "Proletarian Writing and
         J. S.," Sewanee Review, 48 (October-December,
         1940), 445-56.

1335.   Jones, E. B. C. New Statesman, 5 (June 10,
         1933), 764-5.
         [The Pastures of Heaven] (R).

1336.   Jones, Lawrence William. "Journal of a Novel,"
         Saturday Review, 52 (December 20, 1969), 25.

1337.   _____. "A Little Play in Your Head: Parable
         Form in J. S.'s Post-War Fiction," Genre, 3
         (1970), 55-63.

1338.   _____. New Republic, 161 (December 20, 1969),
         26.
         [J. of a Novel].

1339.   _____. "A Novel on S.'s Earliest Stories,"
         SQ, 2 (1969), 59-60.

1340.   _____. "Personal History," Saturday Review,
         52 (December 20, 1969), 25-6.

1341.   _____. "Random Thoughts from Paris: S.'s
         Un Américain à New York et à Paris," SQ, 3
         (1970), 27-30.

1342.   _____. "The Real Authorship of S.'s 'Verse',"
         SQ, 3 (1970), 11-12.

1343.   _____. "S. and Zola: Theory and Practice of
         the Experimental Novel," SQ, 4 (Fall, 1971), 95-
         101.

1344.   _____. "An Uncited Post-War S. Story: 'The
         Short Short Story of Mankind'," SQ, 2 (1970), 30-1.

1345.   . "Whole Life and the Holy Life: J. S.
        and the Riddle of Belief, " Religion in Life, 39
        1970), 559-66.

1346.   Jones, William M.   "S. 's 'Flight', " Explicator, 18
        (November, 1959), Item 11.

1347.   Justus, James H.   "The Transient World of Tor-
        tilla Flat, " Western Review, 7 (1970), 55-60.

1348.   Kalb, Bernard.   "The Author, " Saturday Review,
        35 (September 20, 1952), 11.

1349.   . "Biographical Note, " Saturday Review,
        35 (September 20, 1952), 11.

1350.   . "Trade Winds, " Saturday Review, 36
        (February 27, 1954), 8.

1351.   Kang, Pongshik.   "A Primitive Rhythm of Life in
        J. S., " Korea University Journal, 15 (1969), 11-31.

1352.   Karsh, Yousuf.   "S., " Portraits of Greatness.
        New York: Nelson, 1959.

1353.   Karsten, Ernest E., Jr.   "Thematic Structure in
        The Pearl, " English Journal, 54 (January, 1965),
        1-7.

1354.   Kauth, Priscilla Jane.   "Hemingway, S., Warren,
        Faulkner: The Sense of the Past, " Unpublished
        Master's Thesis, Stetson University, 1962.

1355.   Kawamura, Yoneichi.   "S. 's Humor and Pathos in
        Tortilla Flat and Cannery Row, " Hokkaido Univer-
        sity Essays in Foreign Languages and Literature,
        1 (December, 1953), 24-30.

1356.   Kazin, Alfred.   "J. S., " On Native Grounds: An
        Interpretation of Modern American Prose Litera-
        ture. New York: Reynal & Hitchcock, 1942.
        pp. 393-9.

1357.   . "The Revival of Naturalism, " On Native
        Grounds, pp. 393-9.

1358.   Kazumi, Kazushi. "Notes on The Grapes of Wrath,"
         English and American Literature Study, Aoyama
         Gakuin University, 8 (February, 1962), 1-17.

1359.   Keller, Dean H. "The Foreword by J. S. to
         Speeches of Adlai Stevenson," SQ, 3 (1970), 39-40.

1360.   _____. "S. at Club '21': An Unrecorded Es-
         say," SQ, 2 (1969), 69-70.

1361.   Kelley, H. Gilbert. Library Journal, 72 (February
         15, 1947), 321.
         [The Wayward Bus] (R).

1362.   Kellogg, Florence L. Survey Graphic, 25 (March,
         1936), 179.
         [In Dubious Battle] (R).

1363.   Kempton, Kenneth. "Chrysanthemums," Short
         Stories for Study. Cambridge: Harvard Universi-
         ty Press, 1953. pp. 120-4.

1364.   Kennedy, John S. "Burning Bright," SHC, pp. 131-
         3.
         [Novel].

1365.   _____. "The Grapes of Wrath," Fifty Years of
         the American Novel, ed. Harold C. Gardiner.
         New York: Scribner's, 1951. Passim.

1366.   _____. "J. S.: Life Affirmed and Dissolved,"
         Fifty Years of the American Novel, ed. Harold C.
         Gardiner. New York: Scribner's, 1951. pp. 217-
         36. Also in SHC, pp. 119-34.

1367.   Keown, Eric. "Of Mice and Men (Apollo)," Punch,
         196 (June 7, 1939), 640, (P.R.)

1368.   _____. Punch, 20 (July 5, 1961), 31.
         [The Winter of Our Discontent] (R).

1369.   _____. Punch, 20 (July 29, 1961), 31.
         [The Winter of Our Discontent] (R).

1370.   Kerr, Walter. The Commonweal, 53 (November
         10, 1950), 120.
         [Burning Bright. Novel] (R).

1371. _____. The Commonweal, 53 (November 10, 1950), 120.
[Burning Bright, Play] (R).

1372. "King for a Day," Times Literary Supplement, June 7, 1957. p. 345.
[The Short Reign of Pippin IV] (R).

1373. King, Robin. Spectator, 179 (December 19, 1947), 782-4.
[The Wayward Bus] (R).

1374. Kingery, Robert E. Library Journal. November 1, 1947. p. 1540.
[The Pearl] (R).

1375. Kingsbury, Stewart A. "S.'s Use of Dialect and Archaic Language," SN, 2 (1969), 28-33.

1376. Kinney, Arthur F. "The Arthurian Cycle in Tortilla Flat," MFS, 11 (Spring, 1965), 11-20.

1377. Klammer, Enno. "The Grapes of Wrath--A Modern Exodus Account," Cresset, 25 (February, 1962), 8-11.

1378. Kline, Herbert. "On J. S.," SQ, 4 (Summer, 1971), 80-8.

1379. Knapp, John. "Warren French, John Steinbeck," SN, I, v (1968), 9-10.

1380. Knickerbocker, Paine. "'Dark Watchers' Haunted the Shooting of 'Flight'," San Francisco Sunday Chronicle Datebook, January 17, 1960. p. 3.

1381. Knitz, S. J. "The Grapes of Wrath," Wilson Library Bulletin, 14 (October, 1939), 102, 165.

1382. Koike, Nobuo. "A Study of J. S. With Special Reference to the Works in the 30's," British and American Literature, Kansei Gakuin University, 3 (April, 1954), 57-90.

1383. Krim, Seymour. "When We Went to J. S.'s Funeral Service, This Is What Happened," London Magazine (New Series), 10 (1970), 130-3.

1384.   Kronenberger, Louis. "The Grapes of Wrath,"
         College Prose. pp. 424-7.

1385.   _____. "Hungry Caravan," College Prose, ed.
         Theodore Gates and Austin Wright. Boston: D. C.
         Heath, 1942. pp. 424-7.

1386.   _____. Nation, 148 (April 15, 1939), 440-1.
         [G. of W.] (R).

1387.   Kruppa, Hans-Günter. "J. S.: 'The Debt Shall Be
         Paid'," Die Neueren Sprachen, 18 (1969), 165-9.

1388.   Krutch, Joseph Wood. "East of Eden," SHC, pp.
         302-305. Also in "J. S.'s Dramatic Tale of Three
         Generations," New York Times Book Review,
         September 21, 1955.

1389.   _____. "J. S.'s Dramatic Tale of Three Genera-
         tions," New York Herald Tribune Book Review,
         September 21, 1952. p. 1. Also in SHC, pp. 302-
         305.

1390.   _____. Nation, 145 (December 11, 1942), 663.
         [The Moon Is Down, Novel] (R).

1391.   _____. Nation, 145 (December 11, 1937), 663-4.
         [Of Mice and Men, Play] (R).

1392.   _____. New York Herald Tribune Books. Septem-
         ber 21, 1952. p. 1.
         [East of Eden] (R).

1393.   _____. New York Herald Tribune Weekly Book
         Review. December 31, 1955. p. 1.
         [Cannery Row] (R).

1394.   _____. "S.," The American Drama Since 1918:
         An Informal History. New York: Random House,
         1939. pp. 128-30, 139.
         [Of Mice and Men; The Grapes of Wrath]; New
         York: George Braziller, 1957. pp. 73-133.

1395.   Kuhl, Art. "Mostly of The Grapes of Wrath,"
         Catholic World, 150 (November, 1939), 160-5.

1396.   Kunitz, Stanley J. (ed.). "J. S.," Twentieth Century

Authors: A Biographical Dictionary of Modern Literature. 1st Supplement. New York: H. W.
Wilson, 1955. pp. 954-5. 1338-9; 1942 ed.

1397. Kunitz, Stanley J. "Wine Out of These Grapes,"
Wilson Library Bulletin, 14 (October, 1939), 165.

1398. Lalley, J. M. New Yorker, 23 (February 22,
1947), 87-90.
[The Wayward Bus] (R).

1399. Langewiesche, Wolfgang. New York Herald Tribune
Books, December 6, 1942. p. 3.
[Bombs Away] (R).

1400. Lardner, John. New Yorker, 26 (October 28, 1950),
52-3.
[Burning Bright, Novel] (R).

1401. "Larger Than Life," Times Literary Supplement,
December 5, 1952. p. 789.
[East of Eden] (R).

1402. Lawson, John Howard. "The Grapes of Wrath,"
Film: The Creative Process. New York: Hill
and Wang, 1964. pp. 215-18, 358.

1403. _____. "Our Film and Theirs: The G. of W.
and Bonnie and Clyde," American Dialect, 5
(1968-69), 30-3.

1404. Leighton, M. M. "Geology of Soil Drifting on the
Great Plains," French (ed.), pp. 8-15.

1405. LeMaster, J. R. "Mythological Constructs in S.'s
To a God Unknown," Forum (University of Houston),
9 (Summer, 1971), 6-11.

1406. Leonard, Frank G. "Cozzens Without Sex; S.
Without Sin (Reader's Digest Condensed Books),"
Antioch Review, 18 (Summer, 1958), 209-19.
[East of Eden].

1407. No entry.

1408. "Letter on the Ban of The Grapes of Wrath," New

York Times, November 17, 1939. p. 20.

1409.   "Letter on The Moon Is Down," New York Times,
         April 5, 1942. 6:2.

1410.   Levant, Howard S. "Essays in Modern American
         Literature, ed. Richard E. Langford, Guy Owen and
         William E. Taylor," SQ, 3 (1970), 100-12 (R).

1411.   _____. "J. S.'s The Red Pony: A Study in Nar-
         rative Technique," Journal of Narrative Technique,
         1 (May, 1971), 77-85.

1411(a). _____. "Tortilla Flat: The Shape of J. S.'s
         Career," PMLA, 85 (1970), 1087-95.

1412.   _____. "The Unity of In Dubious Battle: Vio-
         lence and Dehumanization," MFS, 11 (Spring, 1965),
         21-33. Also in Davis (ed)., pp. 49-62.

1413.   Levenson, Samuel. "The Compassion of J. S.,"
         Canadian Forum, 20 (September, 1940), 185-6.

1414.   Levidova, I. "The Post-War Books of J. S.,"
         Soviet Review, 4 (Summer, 1963), 3-13.

1415.   Lewis, R. W. B. "East of Eden" in "J. S.: The
         Fitful Daemon," The Young Rebel in American
         Literature, ed. Carl Bode. London: Heinemann,
         1959. pp. 131-4.

1416.   _____. "J. S.: The Fitful Daemon," The
         Young Rebel in American Literature, ed. Carl
         Bode. London: Heinemann, 1959. pp. 121-41.
         Also in Davis (ed), pp. 163-75.

1417.   _____. "J. S.: The Fitful Daemon," The Young
         Rebel in American Literature, ed. Carl Bode.
         New York: Frederick A. Praeger, 1960. pp. 121-
         41. Also in Modern American Fiction: Essays in
         Criticism, ed. A. Walton Litz. New York:
         Oxford University Press, 1963. pp. 265-77.

1418.   _____. "The S. Perspective," The Picaresque
         Saint: Representative Figures in Contemporary
         Fiction. Philadelphia: Lippincott, 1958. pp. 179-
         93.

1419. Library Journal, 67 (February 15, 1942), 182.
[The Moon Is Down, Novel] (R).

1420. _____. 67 (September 1, 1942), 739.
[The Moon Is Down, Play] (R).

1421. _____, 68 (January 1, 1943), 37.
[Bombs Away] (R).

1422. Life, 12 (April 6, 1942), 32-4.
[The Moon Is Down, Novel] (R).

1423. Lisca, Peter. "The Dynamics of Community in
The Grapes of Wrath, " From Irving to Steinbeck:
Studies in American Literature, ed. Motley F.
Deakin and Peter Lisca. Gainesville: University
of Florida Press, 1972.

1424. _____ (ed.). "Editor's Introduction: The Pattern
of Criticism, " J. S.: The Grapes of Wrath, Text
and Criticism (1972), pp. 695-707.

1425. _____. "Escape and Commitment: Two Poles
of the S. Hero, " Astro and Hayashi (eds.), pp. 3-
22.

1426. _____. "The G. of W. as Fiction, " PMLA, 72
(1957), 296-309. Also in Donohue (ed.), pp. 166-
81. Enlarged in his The Wide World of J. S., pp.
144-177.

1427. _____. "The Grapes of Wrath as Fiction, "
The Modern American Novel; Essays in Criticism,
ed. Max Roger Westbrook. New York: Random
House, 1966. pp. 173-93. Also in Lisca (ed.),
pp. 729-47.

1428. _____. "J. E. S., " Collier's Encyclopedia,
1964. XXI, 518.

1429. _____. "J. E. S., " Encyclopaedia Britannica,
1964. XXI, 377.

1430. _____. John Steinbeck, Journal of a Novel.
MFS, 16 (Winter, 1970-71), 571-2 (R).

1431. _____. "J. S.: A Literary Biography, " SHC,
pp. 3-22.

1432.   . "A Letter on Criticism," Colorado
Quarterly, 4 (Autumn, 1955), 218-19.

1433.   . "Motif and Pattern in Of Mice and Men,"
MFS, 2 (Winter, 1956), 228-34.

1434.   . "S. and Hemingway," SN, 2 (1969), 9-
17. Reprinted in SPAN, 10 (1969), 34-6.

1435. No entry.

1436.   . "S.'s Fable of The Pearl," SHC. pp.
291-301.

1437.   . "S.'s Image of Man and His Decline as
a Writer," MFS, 11 (Spring), 1965), 3-10.

1438.   . "The Wayward Bus...A Modern Pilgrimage," SHC, pp. 281-90. First appeared in his
Ph.D. dissertation, "The Art of John Steinbeck,"
1955.

1439. Literary Digest, 121 (February 1, 1936), 28.
       [In Dubious Battle] (R).

1440.   , 124 (December 18, 1937), 34.
       [Of Mice and Men, Novel] (R).

1441.   , 124 (December 18, 1937), 34.
       [Of Mice and Men, Play] (R).

1442. "The Literary Life: Impersonated," Time, 40
(August 17, 1942), 62.

1443. "Literature Award," New York Times, Western
Edition. October 26, 1962. p. 6.

1444. Lockridge, Richard. New York Herald Tribune
Books. October 22, 1950. p. 4.
       [Burning Bright, Novel] (R).

1445. London Mercury, 32 (June, 1935), 1936.
       [To a God Unknown] (R).

1446.   , 36 (October, 1937), 595.
       [Of Mice and Men] (R).

1447. _____, 39 (April, 1939), 564.
       [The Long Valley] (R).

1448. Long, Louise. "The Grapes of Wrath," Southwest
       Review, 24 (July, 1939), 495-8.

1449. Longaker, Mark. Catholic World, 160 (March,
       1945), 570-1.
       [Cannery Row] (R).

1450. Longstreet, Stephen. "The Grapes of Wrath,"
       College Prose. pp. 428-30.

1451. Lowry, Malcolm. Selected Letters of Malcolm
       Lowry, ed. Harvey Breit and Margerie Bonner
       Lowry. London: Jonathan Cape, 1965. p. 145.

1452. Luccock, Halford E. "Of Mortgages and Migrants,"
       American Mirror: Social, Ethical and Religious
       Aspects of American Literature, 1930-1940. pp.
       179-85.

1453. _____. "S.," American Mirror: Social Ethical
       and Religious Aspects of American Literature,
       1930-40. New York: The Macmillan Co., 1940.
       pp. 179-85. Passim.

1454. Lutwack, Leonard. Heroic Fiction. Carbondale:
       Southern Illinois University Press, 1971. pp. 47-
       63.

1455. McCarthy, Desmond. "The American View of
       Nature: Play Of Mice and Men, Gate Theatre,"
       New Statesman, 17 (April 22, 1939), 605-606.
       (P.R.).

1456. McCarthy, Joe. "Costello's: The Wayward
       Saloon," Holiday, 26 (1959), 108-15.

1457. McCarthy, Mary. Nation, 142 (March 11, 1936),
       326-7.
       [In Dubious Battle] (R).

1458. McCarthy, Paul. "Backgrounds of American
       Literary Thought by Rod W. Horton and Herbert W.
       Edwards," SQ 3 (1970), 31-3 (R).

1459.   ."House and Shelter as Symbol in The
Grapes of Wrath," South Dakota Review, 5 (Winter,
1967-68), 48-67.

1460.   . "House and Shelter as Symbol in The
Grapes of Wrath," South Dakota Review. Review
by B. Barbour, SN, I, v (1968), 11-13 (R).

1461. McCormick, Benedict. "J. S.: An Evaluation,"
Way--Catholic Viewpoints, 19 (1939), 53-8, 113-15.

1462. MacDougall, James K. "Pseudonyms of Christ in
the Modern Novel by Edwin M. Moseley," SQ, 4
(Spring, 1971), 57-9 (R).

1463. McElderry, B. R., Jr. "The G. of W.: In the
Light of Modern Critical Theory," College English,
5 (March, 1944), 308-13. Also in Donohue (Ed.),
pp. 126-33; French (ed.), pp. 199-208.

1464.   . Thomas Wolfe. New York: Twayne,
1964. p. 172.

1465. McHugh, V. "J. S. Branches Out," American
Mercury, 47 (May, 1939), 113-15.

1466. McKenney, J. W. "J. S. Says a Great Teacher
Is One of the Great Artists," California Teachers'
Association Journal, 51 (November, 1955), 6f.

1467. McMahan, Elizabeth E. " 'The Chrysanthemums':
Study of a Woman's Sexuality," MFS, 14 (Winter,
1968-69), 453-8; Reply, G. Noonan, 15 (Winter,
1969-70), 542.

1468. McWilliams, W. Carey. "California Pastoral,"
Antioch Review, 2 (March, 1942), 103-21. Also in
Donohue (ed.), pp. 32-51; Lisca (ed.), pp. 657-79.

1469.   . "The End of a Cycle," French (ed.),
pp. 42-9.

1470.   . "Glory, Glory, California," French (ed.),
pp. 140-3.
       [From New Republic, 103 (July 22, 1940), 125.
       See also New Republic, 103 (September 2, 1940),
       305].

1471. _____. "Man, a Place, and a Time," American
West, 7 (1970), 4-8+.

1472. _____. "What's Being Done About The Goods?,"
New Republic, 100 (September 20, 1939), 178-80.
[The Grapes of Wrath].

1473. _____ and N. R. "J. S., Writer," Commonweal,
90 (May 9, 1969), 229-30.

1474. Madden, Charles F. (ed.). Talks with Authors.
Carbondale: Southern Illinois University Press,
1968. "Warren Beck on John Steinbeck," pp. 56-
72.

1475. Madeo, Frederick. " 'Flight'--An Allegorical
Journey," English Record, 14 (April, 1964), 55-8.

1476. _____. "Justice for S.," S. R., 53 (January
10, 1970), 35.
[Letter in praise of the late Lawrence W. Jones'
review of Journal of a Novel].

1477. Madison, Charles A. "Covici: S.'s Editor, Collaborator, and Conscience," Book Publishing in
America. New York: McGraw-Hill, 1966.

1478. _____. "Covici: S.'s Editor, Collaborator,
and Conscience," S. R., 49 (June 25, 1966), 15-16.

1479. _____. "The Friendship of Covici and S.,"
Chicago Jewish Forum, 24 (Summer, 1966), 293-6.

1480. Magill, Frank N. (ed.). "J. S.," Cyclopedia of
World Authors. New York: Salem Press, 1958.
pp. 1017-19.

1481. Magny, Claude-Edmonde. "J. S.'s East of Eden,"
Perspective USA, 5 (Fall, 1953), 146-52.

1482. _____. Perspective, November 5, 1953. Translated by Louise Varrese.
[East of Eden] (R).

1483. _____. "S., or the Limits of the Impersonal
Novel," tr. Francoise Gourier. SHC, pp. 216-30.
[First appeared in his L'Age du Roman
Americain].

1484.   Mair, John. New Statesman, 17 (February 18,
         1939), 250.
         [LV] (R).

1485.   "Making of a New Yorker," New York Times Maga-
         zine, February 1, 1953. 6, Pt. 3, p. 26; Febru-
         ary 22, 1953. 6, p. 4. Autobiography. Also in
         Empire City: A Treasure of New York, ed. A.
         Klein. New York: Rinehart, 1955. pp. 469-75.

1486.   Mallett, Richard. "The S. Party," Twentieth
         Century Parody, ed. Burling Lowrey. Introduced
         by N. Benchley. New York: Harcourt, Brace,
         1960. p. 81.

1487.   Maloney, Wiley. "The Sardine Trade Is Dying, and
         So Is 'Cannery Row,' " San Jose Evenings News.
         March 18, 1957. p. 34.

1488.   Manchester Guardian, April 13, 1939. p. 11.
         [Of Mice and Men] (P.R.)

1489.   _____. September 8, 1939. p. 3.
         [G. of W.] (R).

1490.   _____. June 26, 1942. p. 3.
         [The Moon Is Down, Novel] (R).

1491.   _____. June 10, 1943. p. 3.
         [The Moon Is Down] (P.R.)

1492.   _____. November 9, 1945. p. 3.
         [Cannery Row] (R).

1493.   _____. November 29, 1947. p. 3.
         [The Wayward Bus] (R).

1494.   _____. December 5, 1952. p. 4.
         [East of Eden] (R).

1495.   _____. October 26, 1954. p. 4.
         [Sweet Thursday] (R).

1496.   _____. June 4, 1957. p. 4.
         [SRP] (R).

1497.   _____. June 30, 1961. p. 7.

[The Winter of Our Discontent] (R).

1498. _____. September 21, 1962. p. 6.
[Travels with Charley] (R).

1499. Mandlebaum, Bernard. "J. S.'s 'The Snake':
The Structure of a Dream," English Record, 16
(1966), 24-6.

1500. Mangione, Jerre. New Republic, 83 (July 13,
1935), 285.
[Tortilla Flat] (R).

1501. "Man Plays God, Warns S.," San Jose Mercury,
December 11, 1962. p. 14.

1502. Mantle, Robert Burns. "Of Mice and Men," Contemporary American Playwrights. New York:
Dodd, Mead, 1938. pp. 3-6.

1503. Marchwardt, Albert H. "Regional and Social
Variations," Introductory Readings on Language,
ed. Wallace L. Anderson and Norman C. Stageberg.
New York: Holt, Rinehart and Winston, 1962.
pp. 327-8.
[S. and His Use of Dialects].

1504. Marcus, Mordecai. "The Lost Dream of Sex and
Childbirth in 'The Chrysanthemums,'" MFS, 11
(Spring, 1965), 54-8.

1505. Marks, Lester J. "East of Eden: 'Thou Mayest',"
SQ, 4 (Winter, 1971), 3-18.

1506. _____. "J. E. S.: 1902-1968," SN, 2 (1969),
21-2.

1507. Marovitz, Sanford E. "A Casebook on The Grapes
of Wrath, ed. Agnes McNeill Donohue," SN, 2 (1969),
33-7 (R).

1508. _____. "J. S. and Adlai Stevenson," SQ, 3
(1970), 51-62.

1509. "Married," Time, 41 (April 5, 1943), 76. (Gwyn
Conger).

1510. Marriott, Charles. Manchester Guardian, (January

29, 1937, p. 7.
[Cup of Gold] (R).

1511.   Marsh, Fred T. New York Times, June 2, 1935.
         p. 6.
         [Tortilla Flat] (R).

1512.   _____. New York Times, February 2, 1936,
         p. 7.
         [In Dubious Battle] (R).

1513.   Marshall, Margaret. Nation, 149 (November 25,
         1939), 576-9.
         [The G. of W.].

1514.   _____. Nation, 153 (July 12, 1941), 36.
         [The Forgotten Village] (R).

1515.   _____. Nation, 154 (March 7, 1942), 286.
         [The Moon Is Down, Novel] (R).

1516.   _____. Nation, 160 (January 20, 1945), 75-6.
         [Cannery Row] (R).

1517.   _____. Nation, 171 (October 28, 1950), 396.
         [Burning Bright] (P. R.).

1518.   Martin, Bruce K. " 'The Leader of the People'
         Reexamined, " Studies in Short Fiction, 7. (Summer,
         1971), 423-32.

1519.   Marx, Leo. "Two Kingdoms of Force," Massa-
         chusetts Review, 1 (October, 1959), 62-95.

1520.   Mathiessen, F. O. "Some Philosophers in the
         Sun, " New York Times, December 31, 1944. 1:18.

1521.   _____. New York Times Book Review, Decem-
         ber 31, 1944. VII, 1.
         [Cannery Row] (R).

1522.   Matsuda, Kazuko. "The Religious Background of
         S. 's Literature, " Hokkaido Educational University
         Quarterly, 20 (1970), 143-58; 21 (1971), 190-7 (in
         Japanese).

1523.   Matsutori, Mataki. "J. S.: All That Lives Is

Holy," <u>Kyushu Institute of Technology Report</u>, 8
(March, 1960), 1-6.
[<u>G. of W.</u>]

1524. Matthews, David K.   "Allegory and Determinism in
S.'s <u>Of Mice and Men,</u>" An Introduction to Fiction
by Robert Stanton.   New York: Holt, Rinehart and
Winston, 1965.   pp. 83-8.

1525. Mayberry, George.   <u>New Republic,</u> 112 (January 15,
1945), 89-90.
[<u>Cannery Row</u>] (R).

1526. Mayo, Thomas F.   "The Great Pendulum," <u>South-
west Review,</u> 36 (Summer, 1951), 190-201.

1527. "Medals of Freedom: J. S. President Johnson
gave Medals of Freedom, the highest civilian honor
a President can vest on to 25 men and 5 women on
September 14, 1964," <u>Facts on File</u>, 24 (October
10, 1964), 335.

1528. Mendelson, M.   "S.," Soviet Interpretation of Contemporary American Literature.   Washington, D.C.:
Public Affairs Press, 1948.   Passim.

1529. Metzger, Charles R.   "The Film Version of S.'s
The Pearl," <u>SQ</u>, 4 (Summer, 1971), 88-92.

1530. _____.   "S.'s Mexican Americans," Astro and
Hayashi (eds.), pp. 141-55.

1531. _____.   "S.'s Version of the Pastoral," <u>MFS,</u> 6
(Summer, 1960), 115-24.
[<u>Sweet Thursday</u>].

1532. Meyer, Roy W.   <u>The Middle Western Farm Novel in
the 20th Century.</u>   Lincoln: University of Nebraska
Press, 1965.   pp. 183, 196-7.

1533. Miller, William V.   "Steinbeck and His Critics, ed.
E. W. Tedlock, Jr. and C. V. Wicker," <u>SQ</u>, 3
(1970), 36-8 (R).

1534. Millett, Fred B.   "J. S.," <u>Contemporary American
Authors: A Critical Survey and 219 Bio-Bibliogra-
phies.</u>   New York: Harcourt, Brace, 1944. pp. 50,
596-7.

1535.   Miron. George Thomas. The Truth About John
Steinbeck and The Migrants. Los Angeles: Haynes
Corp., 1939.

1536.   "Mrs. Roosevelt Comments on The Grapes of
Wrath," Time, 35 (April 15, 1940), 17.

1537.   Mitgang, Herbert. New York Times Book Review,
November 16, 1958. 7:12.
[Once There Was a War] (R).

1538.   Mizener, Arthur. "Does a Moral Vision of the
Thirties Deserve a Nobel Prize?," New York Times
Book Review, December 9, 1962. pp. 4, 43-5.
Also in Donohue (ed.), pp. 267-72.
[East of Eden].

1539.   No entry.

1540.   _____. "Evaluating an Author's Vision of the
Thirties," New York Times, Western Edition.
December 10, 1962. p. 9.

1541.   _____. "The Grapes of Wrath," New York
Times Book Review. December 9, 1962. pp. 44-5.

1542.   _____. "In Dubious Battle " New York Times
Book Review. December 9, 1962. pp. 4, 43.

1543.   _____. New Republic, 127 (October 6, 1952), 21.
[East of Eden] (R).

1544.   _____. "The Novel in America: 1920-1940,"
Perspectives USA, 15 (Spring, 1956), 134-47.

1545.   _____. "The Pastures of Heaven," New York
Times Book Review. December 9, 1962. p. 4.

1546.   _____. "The Red Pony," New York Times Book
Review. December 9, 1962. p. 4.

1547.   _____. The Sense of Life in the Modern Novel.
Boston: Houghton Mifflin, 1964. pp. 6, 20, 128.

1548.   Mofett, Anita. New York Times. November 20,
1932. pp. 5, 16, 20.
[PH] (R).

1549. Moloney, M. F. "Half-faith in Modern Fiction," Catholic World, 171 (August, 1950), 349-50.

1550. Monroe, Elizabeth N. "The Grapes of Wrath," The Novel and Society. Chapel Hill: University of North Carolina Press, 1941. pp. 17-18 and Passim.

1551. Moon, Eric. Library Journal, 87 (June 15, 1962), 2378.
      [Travels with Charley] (R).

1552. _____. "America and Americans," Library Journal, 91 (December 1, 1966), 5962 (R).

1553. "The Moon Is Down at the Whitehall," New Statesman, 25 (June 19, 1943), 400 (P.R.)

1554. "The Moon Is Down Opens in Stockholm," Time, 41 (April 19, 1943), 42.

1555. "Moon Is Halfway Down," New Republic, 106 (May 18, 1942), 657.
      [The Moon Is Down, Novel] (R).

1556. Moore, Harry Thornton. "J. S. the Soft-Hearted Satirist," New Republic, 136 (May 27, 1959), 23-4.

1557. _____. "J. S.: A Memorial Statement," SN, 2 (1969), 23.

1558. _____. New Republic, 86 (February 19, 1936), 54.
      [In Dubious Battle] (R).

1559. _____. New Republic, 136 (May 27, 1957), 23-4.
      [SRP] (R).

1560. Moore, Ward. "Cannery Row Revisited, S. and the Sardine," Nation, 179 (October 16, 1954), 325-7.
      [Sweet Thursday and Cannery Row] (R).

1561. Moore, William L. "In Memoriam," SN, 2 (1969), 24.

1562.   "More Wrath; 'Phony Pathos' in Writings Flayed
        (Letter), " Time, 35 (March 25, 1940), 14.

1563.   Morioka, Sakae. "The Eigo Seinen (The Rising
        Generation), Special Number in Memory of the Late
        J. S., April, 1969, " SQ, 4 (Fall, 1971), 116-
        19. (A).

1564.   _____. Ichiro Ishi (ed.), Steinbekku (in Japan-
        ese). Tokyo: Kenkyusha, 1967. SN, I, 11 (August,
        1968), 3-4 (R).

1565.   _____. "J. S. 's Art, " English and American
        Language and Literature Studies, Kyushu University,
        3 (1953), 51-8.

1566.   _____. "Tetsumaro Hayashi's John Steinbeck:
        A Concise Bibliography (1930-65), " KAL, 10 (1967),
        104-105 (R).

1567.   Moritz, Charles (ed.). "J. S., " Current Biography.
        New York: Wilson, 1940. pp. 757-9.

1568.   Morris, Alice S. New York Times Book Review,
        October 22, 1950. 7:4.
        [Burning Bright, Novel] (R).

1569.   Morris, Harry. "The Pearl: Realism and Alle-
        gory, " English Journal, 52 (October, 1963), 487-
        95, 503. Also in Davis (ed.), pp. 149-62.

1570.   _____. "The Pearl: Realism and Allegory, "
        Scholarly Appraisals of Literary Works Taught in
        High Schools by Stephen Dunning and Henry W.
        Sams, ed. National Council of Teachers of English.
        Champaign, Illinois: NCTE, 1965. p. 83.
        [A selected bibliography for S. 's The Pearl].

1571.   Morris, Lloyd R. "The Grapes of Wrath, " Post-
        script to Yesterday. New York: Random House,
        1947. pp. 167-71.

1572.   _____. "Heritage of a Generation of Novelists:
        Anderson and Dreiser, Hemingway, Faulkner, Far-
        rell and S., " New York Herald Tribune Weekly
        Book Review, 25 (September 25, 1949), pp. 12-13,
        74.

1573.   _____. "Seven Pillars of Wisdom," Postscript
to Yesterday: America: Last Fifty Years. New
York: Random House, 1947. pp. 134-71.

1574.   Morsberger, Robert E. "In Defense of 'Westering',"
WAL, 5 (Summer, 1970), 143-6.
[On "The Leader of the People" in LV].

1575.   Moseley, Edwin M. "Christ as the Brother of
Man: S's G. of W.," Pseudonyms of Christ in the
Modern Novel. Pittsburgh: University of Pittsburgh Press, 1962. pp. 163-75. Also in Donohue
(ed.), pp. 209-18.

1576.   Mott, Frank L. "S.," Golden Multitudes. New
York: Macmillan, 1947. p. 259, Passim.

1577.   Moult, Thomas. Manchester Guardian, February
14, 1939. p. 7.
[The Long Valley] (R).

1578.   Munro, Thomas. "The Failure Story: An Evaluation," Journal of Aesthetics & Art Criticism, 17
(March, 1959), 362-87.

1579.   _____. "The Failure Story: A Study of Contemporary Pessimism," Journal of Aesthetics &
Art Criticism, 17 (December, 1958), 143-68.

1580.   Munz, Charles Curtis. Nation, 153 (December 20,
1941), 647.
[Sea of Cortez] (R).

1581.   Nagle, J. M. "View of Literature Too Often Neglected: The Pearl," English Journal, 58 (1969),
399-407.

1582.   Naipaul, V. S. "Cannery Row Revisited," Daily
Telegraph Magazine, No. 285 (April 3, 1970), 24-
30. Reprinted in his The Overcrowded Barraloon
and Other Articles. London: Andre Deutsch, 1972.
pp. 155-68.

1583.   Nakachi, Akira. "The Grapes of Wrath: A Novel
of Mankind," Taira Technical Junior College Reports of Study, 1 (1961), 1-15.

1584.   Nathan, G. J.   "Burning Bright," Theatre Book of
         the Year, 1950-1951. Toronto: MacClelland, 1952.
         pp. 67-70.

1585.   Nation, 135 (December 7, 1932), 574.
         [PH] (R).

1586.   _____.   137 (October 18, 1933), 456.
         [To a God Unknown] (R).

1587.   _____.   179 (July 10, 1954), 37.
         [Sweet Thursday] (R).

1588.   Nebberger, Richard.   "Who Are the Associated
         Farmers?" Survey Graphic, 28 (September, 1939),
         517-21, 555-7.

1589.   Needham, Wilbur.   "Racketeer Reviewers and
         J. S.," Black and White, 1 (June, 1939), 28-31.

1590.   Nelson, Harlan S.   "S.'s Politics Then and Now,"
         Antioch Review, 27 (1967), 118-33.

1591.   Neville, Helen.   Nation, 140 (June 19, 1935), 720.
         [Tortilla Flat] (R).

1592.   Nevius, Blake.   "S.: One Aspect (His Attitude
         Toward Illusion)," Pacific Spectator, 3 (Summer,
         1949), 302-10. Also in SHC. pp. 197-205.

1593.   New Republic, 77 (December 20, 1933), 178.
         [To a God Unknown] (R).

1594.   _____, 108 (January 18, 1943), 94.
         [Bombs Away] (R).

1595.   "Newsfronts: Nobelist Novelist Who Got an Ignoble
         Reception," Life, 53 (November 9, 1962), 100.

1596.   Newsweek, 9 (February 27, 1937), 39.
         [Of Mice and Men, Novel] (R).

1597.   _____, 19 (April 20, 1942), 72.
         [The Moon Is Down, Novel] (R).

1598.   _____, 31 (March 8, 1948), 83-4.
         [The Pearl] (R).

1599.   _____, 36 (October 30, 1950), 78.
              [Burning Bright, Novel] (R).

1600.   _____, 36 (October 30, 1950), 78.
              [A musical by Richard Rodgers and Oscar Ham-
              merstein II, based on S.'s Burning Bright, Play].

1601.   _____, 57 (June 26, 1961), 96.
              [The Winter of Our Discontent] (R).

1602.   _____, 60 (July 30, 1962), 77.
              [Travels with Charley] (R).

1603.   "New York Censors Ban The Forgotten Village,"
              Time, 38 (September 1, 1941), 54.

1604.   New Yorker, 14 (September 24, 1938), 92.
              [LV] (R).

1605.   _____, 15 (April 15, 1939), 101.
              [G. of W.] (R).

1606.   _____, 17 (June 7, 1941), 77.
              [The Forgotten Village] (R).

1607.   _____, 17 (December 6, 1941), 133.
              [Sea of Cortez] (R).

1608.   _____, 18 (March 7, 1942), 59; 18 (April 4,
              1942), 63.
              [The Moon Is Down, Novel] (R).

1609.   _____, 18 (November 28, 1942), 96.
              [Bombs Away] (R).

1610.   _____, 20 (January 6, 1945), 62.
              [Cannery Row] (R).

1611.   _____, 23 (December 27, 1947), 59.
              [The Pearl] (R).

1612.   _____, 24 (May 1, 1948), 91.
              [A Russian Journal] (R).

1613.   _____, 27 (October 6, 1951), 125-26.
              [Sea of Cortez] (R).

1614.   , 30 (July 10, 1954), 63.
        [Sweet Thursday] (R).

1615.   , 33 (April 13, 1957), 164.
        [SRP] (R).

1616.   , 34 (November 8, 1958), 203.
        [Once There Was a War] (R).

1617.   , 37 (September 16, 1961), 177.
        [The Winter of Our Discontent] (R).

1618.   , 38 (September 8, 1962), 152.
        [Travels with Charley] (R).

1619.   , "Our Man in Helsinki," New Yorker, 39
        (November 9, 1962), 43-5. Also in Donohue (ed.),
        pp. 273-7.

1620.   New York Evening Post. September 28, 1929. p. 7.
        [Cup of Gold] (R).

1621.   , October 29, 1930. p. 7.
        [Cup of Gold] (R).

1622.   , October 29, 1930. p. 3.
        [PH] (R).

1623.   New York Herald Tribune Books, August 18, 1929.
        p. 12.
        [Cup of Gold] (R).

1624.   , October 23, 1932. p. 2.
        [PH] (R).

1625.   , September 24, 1933. p. 17.
        [To a God Unknown] (R).

1626.   , June 2, 1935. p. 4.
        [Tortilla Flat] (R).

1627.   , February 2, 1936. p. 6.
        [In Dubious Battle] (R).

1628.   , September 18, 1938. p. 7.
        [LV] (R).

1629. _____, April 16, 1939. p. 3.
       [G. of W.] (R).

1630. _____, June 1, 1941. p. 6.
       [The Forgotten Village] (R).

1631. _____, December 7, 1941. p. 3.
       [Sea of Cortez] (R).

1632. _____, March 8, 1942. p. 1.
       [The Moon Is Down, Novel] (R).

1633. _____, December 6, 1942. p. 3.
       [Bombs Away] (R).

1634. _____, November 4, 1945. p. 6.
       [The Red Pony] (R).

1635. "New York Herald Tribune Article on Visit to USSR
       Criticized by Izvestia," New York Times, March
       18, 1948. p. 14.

1636. New York Herald Tribune Book Review, February 8,
       1959. p. 10.
       [Once There Was a War] (R).

1637. New York Times, October 1, 1933. p. 18.
       [To a God Unknown] (R).

1638. _____, March 4, 1947. p. 23.
       [The Wayward Bus] (R).

1639. "New York Times and New York Herald Tribune
       Conflicting Reviews Cited in State Department
       Broadcast to USSR," New York Times, February
       18, 1947. p. 18; February 19, 1947. p. 24.

1640. New York Times Book Review, June 1, 1941. pp. 6,
       8, 18.
       [The Forgotten Village] (R).

1641. New York Times, November 15, 1963. p. 5.
       [The Moon Is Down, Play] (R).

1642. Nichols, Lewis. "Talk With J. S.," New York
       Times Book Review, September 28, 1952. p. 30.

1643.   ____. "The Writers in the Sand," New York
            Times Book Review, August 4, 1968. Section 7,
            pp. 8, 10.

1644.   Nicholson, Norman. Man and Literature. London:
         S. C. M. Press, 1944. p. 138.
         [The Grapes of Wrath and Of Mice and Men].

1645.   Nimitz, Jack. "Ecology in The Grapes of Wrath,"
         Hartford Studies in Literature, 2 (1970), 165-8.

1646.   "Nobel Prize Presented," Facts on File, 22 (De-
         cember 20-26, 1962), 466.

1647.   "Nobel Prize Winners...," New York Times,
         Western Edition. December 11, 1962. p. 3.

1648.   Noonan, Gerald. "A Note on 'The Chrysanthemums',"
         MFS, 15 (1969), 542.

1649.   North, Paul H., Jr. "Another Note on the Armed
         Services Edition (ASE)," American Book Collector,
         15 (November, 1964), 25.

1650.   Nossen, Evon. "The Beast-Man Theme in the
         Works of J. S.," Ball State University Forum, 7
         (1966), 52-64.

1651.   Nye, Russel B. "The Grapes of Wrath--an Analy-
         sis," Civilization, Past and Present, ed. T. Walter
         Thompson and Alastair M. Taylor. Chicago:
         Scott, Foresman, 1961. 2, 564-5.

1652.   Nyren, Dorothy (ed.). "S.," A Library of Literary
            Criticism: Modern American Literature. New
            York: Frederick Ungar Publishing Company, 1960.
            pp. 465-8.
         P. 466: Edmund C. Richards, NAR, (June, 1937),
            p. 409.
         Burton Rascoe, EJ (March, 1938), pp. 213-14.
         T. K. Whipple, NR (October 12, 1938), p. 294.
         P. 466: Edmund Wilson, NR (December 9, 1940),
            pp. 785-6.
         Maxwell Geismar, Writers in Crisis (Houghton),
            1942. p. 260.
         Woodburn O. Ross, CE (May, 1949), pp. 436-7.
         P. 467: Blake Nevius, PS (Summer, 1949), pp.
            307-308.

W. M. Frohock, The Novel of Violence in America.
(S.M. University Press, 1950, 1957), p. 147.
Joseph Henry Jackson, Introduction to The Short
Novels of John Steinbeck. (Viking, 1952), pp. vii-
viii.
Hugh Holman, NR (June 7, 1954), p. 20.
Claude-Edmunde Magny in SHC, pp. 225-7.

1653. "Obituary--J. S.," Current Biography, 30 (1969),
48.

1654. "Obituary," New York Times, December 21, 1968.
p. 1+.

1655. "Obituary," Publishers' Weekly, 194 (December 30,
1968), 48-9.

1656. O'Brien, E. D. Illustrated London News, 233
(October 11, 1958), 620.
[The Log from the Sea of Cortez] (R).

1657. _____. Illustrated London News, 235
(December 26, 1959), [n. p.].
[Once There Was a War] (R).

1658. _____. Illustrated London News, 239 (July 8,
1961), 70.
[The Winter of Our Discontent] (R).

1659. _____. Illustrated London News, 241 (October
6, 1962), 534.
[Travels with Charley] (R).

1660. O'Brien, Kate. Spectator, 163 (September 15, 1939),
386.
[The Grapes of Wrath] (R).

1661. _____. Spectator, 169 (July 10, 1942), 44.
[The Moon Is Down] (R).

1662. "Of Mice and Men at Gate Theatre," Times, April
13, 1939. p. 10. (P.R.).

1663. "Of Mice and Men: Criticism," Life and Letters
Today, 22 (July, 1939), 93-4.

1664.   "Of Mice and Men: Criticism," New Statesman and
        Nation, 17 (April 22, 1939), 605-608.

1665.   "Of Mice and Men: Criticism," Spectator, 162
        (April 21, 1939), 668.

1666.   "Of Mice and Men (Play): Feature and Article,"
        New York Times, April 24, 1938. 10:1.

1667.   "Of Mice and Men (Play): G. George Comments,"
        New York Times, April 24, 1938. 10:1.

1668.   "Of Mice and Men (Play): New York Drama Critics
        Circle Award Presented," New York Times, April
        25, 1938. p. 19.

1669.   "Of Mice and Men (Play) Receives Critics Award,"
        Time, 31 (April 25, 1938), 39.

1670.   "Of Mice and Men (Play): S. Interviewed," New
        York Times, December 5, 1937. p. 7.

1671.   "Of Mice and Men (Play) Wins New York Drama
        Critics Circle Award," New York Times, April 19,
        1938. p. 23.

1672.   "Of Mice and Men: S. in South Vietnam," The
        Times of India (December 14, 1966). Asian Student
        (December 24, 1966). p. 7.

1673.   O'Hara, F. H. "Melodrama with a Meaning," Today
        in American Drama. Chicago: University of
        Chicago Press, 1939. pp. 142-89.

1674.   "Old S.," Newsweek, 57 (June 26, 1961), 96.

1675.   Oliver, H. J. "J. S.," Australian Quarterly, 23
        (June, 1951), 79-83.

1676.   Olson, Clarence E. "Fame Revisited: Nobel Award
        Has Interrupted S.'s Pursuit of Privacy," St. Louis
        Post Dispatch (Sunday Pictures), December 2, 1962.
        pp. 56-9.

1677.   O'Malley, Frank. Commonweal, 46 (April 25, 1947),
        43-4.
            [The Wayward Bus] (R).

1678.   "On Ernie Pyle as War Correspondent," Time, 44
         (July 17, 1944), 65.

1679.   "On Monkey Hill," Times Literary Supplement,
         December 21, 1935.   p. 877.
         ⌐ [Tortilla Flat] (R).

1680.   "Organization of World Video," Time, 52 (July 19,
         1948), 65.

1681.   "Organizes World Video to Produce T.V. Shows:
         Comment," Time, 52 (July 19, 1948), 65.

1682.   "Original Typescript of Book, The Grapes of Wrath,
         Discussed," New York Times, February 1, 1942.
         6, 22.

1683.   "Original Typescript of Book, The Grapes of Wrath,
         Given to The Library of Congress," New York
         Times, December 25, 1941.   p. 31.

1684.   Orlova, R.   "Money Against Humanity: Notes on the
         Work of J. S.," tr. Armin Moskovic.   In French
         (ed.), pp. 152-9.

1685.   Orvis, Mary.   "The Grapes of Wrath," The Art of
         Writing Fiction.   New York: Prentice-Hall, 1948.
         196-200.

1686.   Osborn, Paul (ed.).   "Dialogue Script; East of
         Eden," Study of Current English (Tokyo), 10 (Sep-
         tember, 1955), 16-32.

1687.   Osborne, William R.   "The Texts of S.'s 'The
         Chrysanthemums'," MFS, 12 (Winter, 1966-67),
         479-84.

1688.   "Our Man in Helsinki," New Yorker, 39 (November
         9, 1963), 43-5.

1689.   Paton, Alan and Pope, Liston.   "The Novelist and
         Christ," S.R., 37 (December 4, 1954), 15-16, 56-9.

1690.   Paul, Louis.   New York Herald Tribune Books,
         February 28, 1937.
         [Of Mice and Men, Novel] (R).

1691.   Peattie, Donald Culross. Saturday Review of Litera-
         ture, 24 (December 27, 1941), 5.
             [Sea of Cortez] (R).

1692.   Peller, Lili E. "Daydreams and Children's Favor-
         ite Books," Psychoanalytic Study of the Child, 14
         (1946), 414-33.

1693.   "PEN Am. Center Invites 6 USSR Writers to Visit
         U.S.: Invitation Sent By J. S. and E. Albee,"
         New York Times, June 8, 1964. p. 26.

1694.   Perez, Betty L. "House and Home: Thematic
         Symbols in The G. of W.," Lisca (ed.), pp. 840-53.

1695.   Peterson, Richard. "American Winners of the Nobel
         Literary Prize, ed. Warren French and Walter
         Kidds," SQ, II (1969), 61-3 (R).

1696.   Peterson, Virginia. New York Herald Tribune,
         June 25, 1961. p. 29.
             [The Winter of Our Discontent] (R).

1697.   Phillips, William. "Male-ism and Moralism:
         Hemingway and S.," American Mercury, 75 (October,
         1952), 93-8.
             [East of Eden].

1698.   Pickrel, Paul. Harper's, 225 (August, 1962), 91.
             [Travels with Charley] (R).

1699.   "Pipe Dream, By R. Rodgers and O. Hammerstein
         II; J. S. on His Novel Sweet Thursday from Which
         Musical Was Adapted," New York Times, November
         27, 1955. 2, p. 1; December 11, 1955. 2, p. 1.

1700.   "Pipe Dream, A Musical Comedy By Oscar Ham-
         merstein II (Books and Lyrics) and Richard Rogers
         (Music) Based on J. S.'s Novel, Sweet Thursday
         Was Produced," Facts on File, 15 (December 1-7,
         1955), 403.

1701.   "Play at Apollo Theatre," Times (May 25, 1939), p. 14.
             [Of Mice and Men] (P.R.).

1702.   Plomer, William. Spectator, 155 (December 6, 1935),
         960.
             [Tortilla Flat] (R).

1703.   _____. Spectator, 156 (May 6, 1936), 850.
         [In Dubious Battle] (R).

1704.   "Plush Stuff," Newsweek, 42 (October 19, 1953), 114.

1705.   Poindexter, Anne. "A Lot Has Changed in S.
         Country and a Lot Hasn't," Los Angeles Times
         West Magazine, October 11, 1970. pp. 8-14.

1706.   Poling, Daniel A. Christian Herald, 83 (November,
         1961), 100.
         [The Winter of Our Discontent] (R).

1707.   Pollock, Theodore. "On the Ending of The G. of
         W.," MFS, 4 (Summer, 1958), 177-8. Also in
         Donohue (ed.), pp. 182-4; French (ed.), pp. 224-6.

1708.   Poole, Robert. "Resurgent S.," Books and Book-
         man, [n.v.] July, 1961, p. 191.
         [The Winter of Our Discontent] (R).

1709.   Poore, Charles. "Introduction," The Grapes of
         Wrath. New York: Harper's Modern Classics,
         1951. pp. vii-xv.

1710.   _____. New York Times, April 14, 1939. p. 27.
         [G. of W.] (R).

1711.   _____. New York Times, September 15, 1939. p. 27.
         [Cup of Gold] (R).

1712.   _____. New York Times, September 15, 1939. p. 27.
         [In Dubious Battle] (R).

1713.   _____. New York Times, December 5, 1941. p. 21.
         [Sea of Cortez] (R).

1714.   _____. New York Times, September 22, 1951. p. 15.
         [Sea of Cortez] (R).

1715.   _____. New York Times, June 10, 1954. p. 29.
         [Sweet Thursday] (R).

1716.   "Portrait," Newsweek, 31 (February 9, 1948), 76.

1717.   "Portrait of J. S.," New York Times, April 19,
         1938. p. 23.

1718.   "Portrait," Saturday Night, 69 (July 24, 1954), 13.

1719.   "Portrait," Saturday Night, 76 (August 5, 1961), 27.

1720.   Poulakidas, Andreas K.   "Christos Lambrinos,
'J. S.: His Death, A Loss for World Literature',"
(T).   SQ, 4 (Spring, 1971), 61-2 (translated eulogy).

1721.   _____.   "S., Kazantzakis, and Socialism," SQ
3 (1970), 62-72.

1722.   Powell, Lawrence Clark.   A B Bookman's Weekly.
November 2, 1970.   p. 1285.
[The Grapes of Wrath].

1723.   _____.   "Birth of S.," Wilson Bulletin for Librarians, 13 (April, 1939), 540.

1724.   _____.   "S.," Books in My Baggage.   Cleveland
and New York: World Publishing, 1960.   pp. 87,
175, 208, 238.

1725.   _____.   "J. S.," Black and White, 1 (1939),
16-17.

1726.   _____.   "S.," Southwestern Book Trails; A
Reader's Guide to the Heartland of New Mexico and
Arizona.   Albuquerque, New Mexico: Horn and
Wallace, 1963.   p. 31.

1727.   Prescott, Orville.   In My Opinion.   Indianapolis:
Bobbs-Merrill, 1952.   pp. 58-64.

1728.   _____.   New York Times, November 27, 1942.
[Bombs Away] (R).

1729.   _____.   New York Times, January 2, 1945.
[Cannery Row] (R).

1730.   _____.   New York Times, February 17, 1947.
[The Wayward Bus] (R).

1731.   _____.   New York Times, November 24, 1947.
[The Pearl] (R).

1732.   _____.   New York Times, April 16, 1948.   p. 21.
[A Russian Journal] (R).

1733.   _____.   New York Times, October 20, 1950,

p. 25.
[Burning Bright, Novel] (R).

1734. _____. New York Times, September 19, 1952.
p. 21.
[East of Eden] (R).

1735. _____. New York Times, June 23, 1961.   p. 27.
[The Winter of Our Discontent] (R).

1736. _____. New York Times, July 27, 1962. p. 23.
[Travels with Charley] (R).

1737. _____. "Outstanding Novels," Yale Review, 36
(Autumn, 1947), 765.

1738. _____. "Squandered Talents: Lewis, S.,
Hemingway, O'Hara," In My Opinion.   Indianapolis:
Bobbs-Merrill, 1952.   pp. 50-74.

1739. _____. Yale Review, 36 (Summer, 1947), 765-6.
[The Wayward Bus] (R).

1740. "President and Mrs. Johnson Go by Helicopter to
Camp David for Weekend; among Guests are Mr.
and Mrs. J. S.," New York Times, July 18, 1965.
I, 27.

1741. Priestley, J. B.   "S.," Literature and Western
Man.   New York: Harper and Brothers, 1960.
p. 433.
[The Grapes of Wrath].

1742. Pritchett, V. S. New Statesman, 16 (September
25, 1937), 448-9.
[Of Mice and Men] (R).

1743. _____. Spectator, 154 (April 5, 1935), 580.
[To a God Unknown] (R).

1744. "Producer-Director of The Forgotten Village,"
Time, 38 (December 8, 1941), 96.

1745. "Pulitzer Award," Scholastic, 36 (May 20, 1940),
28.

1746. "Pulitzer Fiction Awards," Saturday Review of

Literature, 22 (May 11, 1940), 5f.

1747.   "Pulitzer Prize Recipient," Time, 35 (May 13, 1940),
         77.

1748.   "Queer Fish," Times Literary Supplement, October
         10, 1958, p. 575.
         [The Log From the Sea of Cortez] (R).

1749.   Quennell, Peter. New Statesman, 11 (May 2, 1936),
         670.
         [In Dubious Battle] (R).

1750.   Quinn, Arthur Hobson, et al. "S.," The Literature
         of the American People. New York: Appleton-
         Century-Crofts, 1951. pp. 958-61.

1751.   Rascoe, Burton. "But---Not---Ferdinand," News-
         week, 13 (April 13, 1939), 46.

1752.   _____. "Excuse It, Please," Newsweek, 13
         (May 1, 1939), 38.

1753.   _____. "J. S.," English Journal, 27 (March,
         1938), 205-16. Also in SHC, pp. 57.67.

1754.   Raven, Simon. "False Prophets," Spectator, 206
         (June 30, 1961), 960.
         [The Winter of Our Discontent] (R).

1755.   Ray, David. "Many Keys to S.," Nation, 184 (April
         20, 1957), 346-7.
         [SRP] (R).

1756.   "R. Lardner, Jr. Banned By Film Company for
         Congressional Contempt Charges, Will Produce Film
         with J. S. and B. Meredith," New York Times,
         June 11, 1948, p. 27.

1757.   Raymund, Bernard. "Cannery Row," Writers of
         Today, ed. Denys Val Baker. London: Sidgwick and
         Jackson, 1946. pp. 136-7.

1758.   _____. "J. S.," Writers of Today. pp. 122-38.

1759.   _____. "Of Mice and Men," Writers of Today,
         p. 127.

1760.   _____. "The Grapes of Wrath," Writers of Today. pp. 127-36.

1761.   _____. "Tortilla Flat," Writers of Today,
pp. 125-7.

1762.   "Recording Writers," New York Times Magazine,
October 11, 1953. p. 44.

1763.   Redfern, James. "The Moon Is Down at the Whitehall," Spectator, 170 (June 18, 1943), 567 (P.R.).

1764.   Redman, Ben Ray. "The Case of J. S.," American
Mercury, 154 (May, 1947), 624-30.

1765.   _____. Saturday Review, 40 (April 13, 1957), 14.
[SRP] (R).

1766.   "Red Meat and Red Herrings; Excerpt from Reviews
of The Grapes of Wrath," Commonweal, 30 (October
13, 1939), 562-3.

1767.   "The Red Pony, a Screen Play," Good Housekeeping,
127 (December, 1948), 198.

1768.   Reed, John R. "The G. of W. and the Esthetics of
Indigence," Lisca (ed.), pp. 825-939.

1769.   Reich, Charles R. "Study Questions for The Red
Pony," Exercise Exchange, 9 (April, 1962), 3-4.

1770.   Rexroth, Kenneth. Afterword to Frank Norris,
McTeague. New York: New American Library,
1964 (Signet). Contains Reference to J. S. in Con-
nection with "The Boys in the Back Room" by
Edmund Wilson.

1771.   Reynolds, Quentin. "S.," The Curtain Rises. New
York: Random House, 1944. Passim.

1772.   Richards, Edmund C. "The Challenge of J. S.,"
North American Review, 243 (Summer, 1937), 406-
13.

1773.   Richardson, Maurice. New Statesman, 48 (November 6, 1954), 589-90.
[Sweet Thursday] (R).

1774.   Richter, Conrad. "America and Americans," Harper,
        233 (1966), 133 (R).

1775.   Ricketts, Toni Jackson (Antonia Seixas). "J. S. and
        the Non-Teleological Bus," What's Doing On the
        Monterey Peninsula, 1 (March, 1947). Also in SHC,
        pp. 275-80.

1776.   _____. See Seixas, Antonia.

1777.   Rideout, Walter S. "S.," The Radical Novel in the
        United States 1900-1954. Cambridge, Massachusetts:
        Harvard University Press, 1956. Passim.

1778.   Rivers, William. Saturday Review, 45 (September
        1, 1962), 31.
        [Travels with Charley] (R).

1779.   Roane, Margaret C. "Cannery Row," Wisconsin
        Studies in Contemporary Literature, 5 (Summer,
        1964), 127-8.

1780.   _____. "Flight," Wisconsin Studies in Contempor-
        ary Literature, 5 (Summer, 1964), 129-30.

1781.   _____. "J. S. As A Spokesman for the Mental-
        ly Retarded," Wisconsin Studies in Contemporary
        Literature, 5 (Summer, 1964), 127-32.

1782.   _____. "Of Mice and Men," Wisconsin Studies
        in Contemporary Literature, 5 (Summer, 1964), 130.

1783.   _____. "Tortilla Flat," Wisconsin Studies in
        Contemporary Literature, 5 (Summer, 1964), 129.

1784.   Robin, A. "Living Legends," Today's Health, 41
        (April, 1963), 5.

1785.   Robles, M. "Cain--An Unfortunate?," Modern
        Language (London), 50 (1960), 57-9.
        [Cain in Unamuno, Baudelaire, Beckett, and S.].

1786.   Roland, Bartel. "Proportioning in Fiction: The
        Pearl and Silas Marner," English Journal, 56
        (April, 1967), 542-6.

1787.   Rolo, Charles. Atlantic, 190 (October, 1952), 94

[East of Eden] (R).

1788.   Rosenblatt, Louise M.   "S.," Literature as Exploration. New York: D. Appleton-Century, 1938.
Passim.

1789.   Ross, Woodburn O.   "J. S.: Earth and Stars,"
The University of Missouri Studies in Honor of
A. H. R. Fairchild. Columbia: University of
Missouri Press, 1946. 21, 179-97. Also in SHC,
pp. 167-82.

1790.   _____. "J. S.: Naturalism's Priest," College
English, 10 (May, 1949), 432-8. Also in SHC, pp.
206-15.

1791.   _____ and A. Wallace Doyle. "The Leader of
the People," Short Stories in Context. New York:
American Book Company, 1953. pp. 16-19.

1792.   _____. "To a God Unknown," in "John Stein-
beck: Earth and Stars," SHC, pp. 172-3. Also in
University of Missouri Studies in Honor of A. H. R.
Fairchild, ed. Charles T. Prouty. Columbia,
Missouri: University of Missouri Press, 1946.

1793.   Roth, Claire J. Library Journal, 76 (October 1,
1951), 1565-6.
[Sea of Cortez] (R).

1794.   Rothman, Nathan L. "A Small Miracle," Saturday
Review of Literature, 27 (December 30, 1944), 5.
[Cannery Row].

1795.   Rubin, Louis D. and John Rees Moore (eds.).
"S.," The Idea of an American Novel. New York:
Thomas Y. Crowell, 1961. pp. 172-3.

1796.   Rugoff, Milton. New York Herald Tribune Books,
June 13, 1954. p. 1.
[Sweet Thursday] (R).

1797.   Rundell, Walter, Jr. "The Grapes of Wrath,"
"Steinbeck's Image of the West," The American
West, 1 (Spring, 1964), 4-8 and Passim.

1798.   _____. "S.'s Image of the West," American
West, 1 (Spring, 1964), 4-17, 79.

1799.   Sale, William, et al (eds). "Breakfast," Critical
        Discussions for Teachers Using Short Stories: Tra-
        dition and Direction. Norfolk, Connecticut: New
        Directions, 1949. pp. 50-2.

1800.   San Francisco Chronicle, December 14, 1947, p. 16.
        [The Pearl] (R).

1801.   _____. October 17, 1958. p. 33.
        [Once There Was a War] (R).

1802.   Sanford, Charles L. "Classics of American Reform
        Literature," American Quarterly, 10 (Fall, 1958),
        295-311.

1803.   Sartre, Jean-Paul. "American Novelists in French
        Eyes," Atlantic, 178 (August, 1946), 114-18.

1804.   Saturday Review of Literature, 9 (November 26,
        1932), 275-6.
        [PH] (R).

1805.   Saturday Review (London), 160 (November 23, 1935),
        501.
        [Tortilla Flat] (R).

1806.   Satyanarayana, M. R. " 'And Then the Child Be-
        comes a Man': Three Initiation Stories of J. S.,"
        Indian Journal of American Studies, 1 (November,
        1971), 87-93.

1807.   _____. "J. S.'s Lonely Valley," Banathali
        Patrika, 4 (July, 1968), 43-52.

1808.   _____. "S. and Shakespeare," American Studies
        Research Center News Letter (India), 10 (1966), 28.
        [The Winter of Our Discontent and Macbeth].

1809.   Saw, Sally. "Religious Symbols in S.'s Grapes,"
        Joad Newsletter, 1 (January, 1963), 1-2 (Mimeo-
        graph).

1810.   Sawey, Orlan. "Another Look at East of Eden."
        ASTC Faculty Publications (Formerly ASTC Bulletin),
        [n.v.], 1964. pp. 54-8.

1811.   "S. Bischoff Acquires Screen Rights to Book, Cup

of Gold," New York Times. December 16, 1945.
II, 5.

1812. No entry.

1813. "Scandinavian Trip," Time, 48 (November 11, 1946),
49.

1814. Scherman, David. "America and Americans," New
York Times Book Review. December 4, 1966. p.
46 (R).

1815. _____, and Redlich, Rosemarie. Literary Amer-
ica: A Chronicle of American Writers from 1607-
1952 with 173 Photographs of the American Scene
That Inspired Them. New York: Dodd, Mead and
Co., 1952. pp. 166-7.
["Route 66" from The Grapes of Wrath].

1816. Schorer, Mark. New York Times Book Review.
September 21, 1952. 7:1.
[East of Eden] (R).

1817. _____. "Technique as Discovery," Forms of
Modern Fiction, ed. W. Van O'Connor. Blooming-
ton: Indiana University Press, 1959. pp. 9-29.

1818. Schramm, Wilber L. "Careers at Cross Roads,"
Virginia Quarterly Review, 15 (October, 1939), 628-
32.

1819. _____. "The Chrysanthemums," Fifty Best
American Short Stories, 1915-1939, ed. Edward J.
O'Brien. Boston: Houghton Mifflin, 1939. pp.
925-7.

1820. Scott, J. D. New Statesman, 44 (December 6,
1952), 698-9.
[East of Eden] (R).

1821. Scott, Walter. "Personality Parade," Parade:
The Sunday Newspaper Magazine. December 2, 1961.
pp. 2, 10.

1822. Scoville, Samuel. "The Weltanschauung of S. and
Hemingway: An Analysis of Themes," English
Journal, 56 (1967), 60-3.
[The Pearl and The Old Man and the Sea].

1823.   Scully, Frank. "S.," Rogues' Gallery: Profiles of
         My Eminent Contemporaries. Hollywood: Murray
         and Gee, 1943. pp. 37-55.

1824.   _____. "S. Au Naturel," Hollywood Tribune.
         August 21, 1939. pp. 5, 14-15.

1825.   Seixas, Antonia. See Ricketts, Toni Jackson.

1826.   _____ (Toni Jackson Ricketts). "J. S. and the
         Non-Teleological Bus," SHC, pp. 275-80.
         [Originally in What's Doing on The Monterey
         Peninsula, 1 (March, 1947)].

1827.   Shannon, David A. (ed.). The Great Depression.
         Englewood Cliffs, N.J.: Prentice, 1960.

1828.   Shaw, Peter. "S.: The Shape of a Career,"
         Saturday Review, 52 (February 8, 1969), 10-14+.

1829.   Shedd, Margaret. "Of Mice and Men," Theatre
         Arts, 17 (October, 1937), 774-8.

1830.   Shimada, Saburo. "A Study of J. S.'s To a God
         Unknown," Beacon Study in English Language and
         Literature, 5 (1964), 23-5.

1831.   Shockley, Martin S. "Christian Symbolism in
         G. of W.," College English, 18 (November, 1956),
         87-90. Also in Donohue (ed.), pp. 90-5; SHC;
         pp. 266-74.

1832.   _____. "The Reception of G. of W. in Oklahoma,"
         American Literature, 15 (January, 1944), 351-61.
         Also in Donohue (ed.), pp. 52-62; French (ed.), pp.
         117-31; Lisca (ed.), pp. 680-91; SHC, pp. 231-40.

1833.   Short, Raymond and Sewall, Richard B. "The
         Leader of the People," A Manual For Teachers
         Using "Short Story For Study." New York: Holt,
         1960. pp. 16-17; 3rd ed., 1956. pp. 1-2.

1834.   "The Short Reign of Pippin IV," Library Journal, 82
         (March 15, 1957), 753 (R).

1835.   Shorter, Eric. "Bresslaw's Best in S. (Review of
         Revival of Of Mice and Men, New Theater, Bromley,

England," Daily Telegraph, August 26, 1970. p. 11,
Column 6 (R).

1836.   Shrodes, Caroline, et al. Instructor's Manual for
Reading for Understanding. New York: Macmillan,
1968.
["The Chrysanthemums," pp. 33-4].

1837.   Sillen, Samuel. "Censoring G. of W.," New Masses, 32 (September 12, 1939), 23-4; Also in Donohue
(ed.), pp. 3-7.

1838.   Simpson, Claude M. and Nelvin, Allan (eds.). "The
Chrysanthemums," The American Reader. Boston:
Heath, 1941. pp. 864-5.

1839.   Singer, Burns. Listener, 65 (June 29, 1961), 1145.
[The Winter of Our Discontent] (R).

1840.   Singleton, Ralph H. "The Red Pony," Instructor's
Manual for Two and Twenty: A Collection of Short
Stories. New York: St. Martin's Press, 1962.
pp. 13-14.

1841.   _____ (ed.). Two and Twenty: A Collection of
Short Stories. New York: St. Martin's Press,
1962. pp. 236-8 contain bibliographical information.

1842.   Sister Mary Hester. See Hester, Sister Mary.

1843.   "Sixth American Writer to Win The Nobel Prize for
Literature," Illustrated London News, 141 (November 3, 1962), 715.

1844.   Slade, Leonard A., Jr. "The Use of Biblical
Allusions in The Grapes of Wrath," CLAJ, 11 (1968),
241-7.

1845.   Slochower, Harry. "The Grapes of Wrath," No Voice
is Wholly Lost. pp. 299-306.

1846.   _____. "John Dos Passos and J. S., Contrast-
ing Notions of the Communal Personality," Byrd-
cliffe Afternoons, ed. C. E. Jones. Woodstock,
New York: Overlook Press, 1940. pp. 11, 21.

1847.   _____. "The Promise of America," No Voice Is

Wholly Lost. New York: Creative Age Press, 1945.
pp. 299-308. Also in his Literature and Philosophy
Between Two World Wars: The Problem in a War
Culture. New York: Citadel Press, 1964. pp. 299-
306.

1848. _____. "Towards a Communal Personality," No
Voice Is Wholly Lost. London: Dobson, 1946.
pp. 242-8.

1849. Smith, Bernard. New York Herald Tribune Books,
February 2, 1936. p. 6.
[In Dubious Battle] (R).

1850. Smith, Bobby. "The Beast-Man Theme in the Work
of J. S.," by Evon Nossen. Ball State University
Forum, 7 (Spring, 1966), 52-64. SQ, 3 (1970), 40-1
(R).

1851. _____. "The Natural Man in J. S.'s Non-Teleological Tales," by D. Russell Brown. Ball State
University Forum, 7 (Spring, 1966), 47-52. SQ, 3
(1970), 67-77 (R).

1852. Smith, Cecil. "Viewing TV: Henry Fonda in Police
Series," San Jose Mercury-News. November 29,
1960. p. 6, TV.

1853. Smith, Eleanor Touhey. Library Journal, 77 (August,
1952), 1303.
[East of Eden] (R).

1854. _____. Library Journal, 82 (March 15, 1957),
753.
[SRP] (R).

1855. Smith, Harrison. Saturday Review of Literature, 30
(February 15, 1947), 14.
[The Wayward Bus] (R).

1856. Smith, H. A. "Is J. S. Literary?," Teacher's College Journal, 13 (January, 1942), 61-3.

1857. Smith, James Stell. "Life Looks at Literature,"
American Scholar, 27 (Winter, 1952-58), 24-42.

1858. Smith, Stevie, Spectator, 181 (October 29, 1948),

570.
[The Pearl] (R).

1859. Smith, Thelma M. and Ward L. Miner. "J. S.,"
Transatlantic Migration: The Contemporary Ameri-
can Novel in France. Durham: Duke University
Press, 1955. pp. 24-5; 161-78.

1860. Snell, George. "Cannery Row," The Shapes of
American Fiction: 1798-1947. New York: Dutton,
1947. pp. 196-7.

1861. _____. "J. S.: Realistic Whimsy," The
Shapes of American Fiction: 1798-1947. pp. 159-66,
187-97.

1862. _____. "The Pastures of Heaven," The Shapes
of American Fiction: 1798-1947. pp. 190-1.

1863. _____. "To a God Unknown," The Shapes of
American Fiction: 1798-1947. pp. 189-90.

1864. _____. "Tortilla Flat," The Shapes of American
Fiction: 1798-1947. pp. 191-2.

1865. Snyder, Philip J. "The Radical Novel in the United
States (1900-1954) by Walter B. Rideout," SQ, 4
(Spring, 1971), 60-1 (R).

1866. Soskin, William. New York Herald Tribune Books,
September 18, 1938. p. 7.
[LV] (R).

1867. Spearman, S. J. Arthur. " 'The Grapes of Wrath'
Called Communistic; Product of a Fevered Brain;
Brands Novel Lecherous," Los Angeles Examiner,
June 4, 1939, p. 19.

1868. Spectator, 155 (December 6, 1935), 960.
[Tortilla Flat] (R).

1869. _____, 156 (May 8, 1936), 850.
[In Dubious Battle] (R).

1870. Spies, George Henry III. "J. S.'s In Dubious Battle and Robert Penn Warren's Night Rider: A Comparative Study," SQ, 4 (Spring), 1971), 48-55.

1871.   . "Van Wyck Brooks on J. S.: A Reminiscence," SQ, 4 (Fall, 1971), 106-107.

1872.   Spiller, Robert E. "J. S.," The Cycle of American
Literature: An Essay in Historical Criticism. New
York: Macmillan, 1955. pp. 289-91.

1873.   et al (eds.). "J. S.," Literary History of
the United States: History. 4 vols. New York:
Macmillan, 1963. Passim.

1874.   "Staging a Story," Times Literary Supplement,
August 18, 1951. p. 513.
        [Burning Bright] (R).

1875.   Stanford, Derek. "Mother McCarthy's Chickens (A
Review of S.'s Journal of a Novel. Hinemann,
1969)," Books and Bookman (London), 15 (1970),
14-15.

1876.   Stanton, Robert. "Allegory and Determinism in
S.'s Of Mice and Men," An Introduction to Fiction.
New York: Holt, Rinehart and Winston, 1965. pp.
83-8.

1877.   "S.," Always Something To Do In Salinas: The
World of Mankind, ed. Ted Patrick. New York:
The Golden Press, [n.d.]. p. 318.
        [Selected by the Writers, Photographers and
        Editors of Holiday].

1878.   "S. as a Columnist of Long Island's Newsday,"
Time, 86 (December 3, 1965), 68.

1879.   "S. Awarded Nobel Prize," San Jose Mercury.
October 26, 1962. pp. 1-2.

1880.   "S. Boom," Wilson Bulletin for Librarians, 13
(May, 1939), 640.

1880(a). S., C. Saturday Review of Literature, 10 (October
28, 1933), 224.
        [To a God Unknown] (R).

1881.   "S., California's Author, Dies," San Jose Mercury,
December 21, 1968. p. 1.

1882.   "S.: Critical Thorns and a Nobel Laurel," Newsweek,

60 (November 5, 1962), 65.

1883.   S., Elaine. "Letter from Abroad: Half a World from Home," McCall's, 94 (1967), 42, 137.

1884.   "S. Festival Readied," Spartan Daily (San Jose State College). November 23, 1970. p. 5.

1885.   "S. Film Backers Oust Young Originator," San Francisco Chronicle, January 6, 1960. p. 36.

1886.   "S. Got First Word on TV," New York Times, Western Edition. October 26, 1961. p. 7.

1887.   "S. Inflation," Time, 30 (October 11, 1937), 79.

1888.   "S. Interviewed," New York Times. September 18, 1958. 7:30.

1889.   Steinbeck, John. America and Americans, a Japanese edition, ed. K. Inoue and Y. Miyamoto; reviewed T. Hayashi, SN, I, ii (1968), 4 (R).

1890.   "S. Narrates The Gift of the Magi, a Screenplay by Walter Bullock," Facts on File, 12 (October 31-November 6, 1962), 355.

1891.   "S.," Newsweek, 60 (November 5, 1961), 65.

1892.   "S.," New York Herald Tribune. October 26, 1962. p. 41.

1893.   "S.," New York Times. October 26, 1961. Passim.

1894.   "S. Protests Barghoorn Arrest," Facts on File, 23 (November 14-20, 1963), 401.

1895.   "S. Receives Nobel Prize," San Jose Mercury. December 11, 1962. p. 3.

1896.   "S.'s Ashes Buried," San Jose Mercury. March 5, 1969. p. 61.

1897.   "S.'s Old Eddie Dies at 102," San Jose Mercury. March 18, 1963. p. 21.

1898.   "S.'s 'Paisanos' Near End of the Line," San

Jose Mercury-News. August 18, 1957. p. 14.

1899. "S.," The Penguin Companion to American Literature. New York: McGraw-Hill, 1971. pp. 240-1.

1900. "S.'s The Wayward Bus Was Listed As an Obscene
Book By the House Select Committee on Current
Pornographic Materials in Washington," Facts on
File, 12 (December 5-11, 1952), 397.

1901. "S. Up Front," Newsweek, 69 (January 30, 1967),
71.

1902. "S. Visits Roosevelt," New York Times. September 13, 1940. p. 10.

1903. "S.," Who's Who in America (1962-1963). Vol. 32.
Chicago: Marquis-Who's Who, 1963.

1904. "S. Wins Nobel Prize," Facts on File, 22 (November 1-7, 1962), 396.

1905. Stegner, Wallace. Boston Globe. March 11, 1942.
p. 19.
[The Moon Is Down, Novel]. (R).

1906. Stern, Milton R. and Gross, Seymour R. (eds.).
"S.," American Literature Survey. (Twentieth
Century). New York: Viking Portable Library,
1962. 4, 171-4.

1907. Stevens, George. "S.'s Uncovered Wagon,"
Saturday Review of Literature, 19 (April 15, 1939),
3-4.
[G. of W.] (R).

1908. Stovall, Floyd. "The Grapes of Wrath," American
Idealism. Norman: University of Oklahoma Press,
1943. pp. 159-66.

1909. Strachey, Julia. New Statesman, 24 (December 20,
1947), 496-7.
[The Wayward Bus] (R).

1910. Straumann, Heinrich. American Literature in the
20th Century. 3rd Rev. ed. New York: Harper
and Row, 1965. pp. 113-17, and Passim.

1911. _____. "S.," American Literature in the 20th
Century. New York: Hutchinson's University Li-
brary, 1951.
[Also by Watford, Hertsfordshire: The Mayflower
Press, 1951, pp. 107-11. The Moon Is Down].

1912. Strauss, Harold. "Realism in the Proletarian
Novel," Yale Review, 28 (Winter, 1939), 360-74.

1913. "Strife in California," Times Literary Supplement,
May 16, 1936, p. 417.
[In Dubious Battle] (R).

1914. Strong, L. A. G. Spectator, 187 (August 10, 1951),
196.
[Burning Bright] (R).

1915. Struve, Gleb. "S.," Soviet Russian Literature.
Norman: University of Oklahoma Press, 1951.
Passim.

1916. Stuckey, W. J. The Pulitzer Prize Novels: A
Critical Backward Look. Norman: University of
Oklahoma Press, 1966. pp. 118ff and Passim.

1917. Surgue, Thomas. New York Herald Tribune,
December 7, 1947. p. 4.
[The Pearl] (R).

1918. Swanberg, W. A. Dreiser. New York: Scribner's,
1965. p. 486.
[The story of S.'s abortive encounter with Dreiser
is reprinted here].

1919. "The Swedish Academy and The Nobel Prizes: Its
Official Statement Quoted," Contemporary Authors.
Detroit, Michigan: Gale Research, 1963. 2, 184.

1920. Swinton, Stan. Saturday Review, 41 (November 1,
1958), 18.
[Once There Was a War] (R).

1921. Tannehill, Ivan Ray. "Dusters and Black Blizzards,"
French (ed.), pp. 5-8.

1922. Tanner, Henry. "S. and E. Albee Speak Out in
Soviet for U. S. Professor," New York Times.

November 15, 1963. pp. 1, 5.

1923.   Tarr, E. Whitney. "S. on One Plane," Letter to
        the Editor, Saturday Review of Literature, 30
        (December 20, 1947), 20.

1924.   Taylor, F. J. "California's Grapes of Wrath;
        Joad Family Not Typical," Forum, 102 (November,
        1939), 232-8. Abridged in Reader's Digest, 35
        (November, 1939), 89-95. Discussion in Forum, 102
        (December, 1939), Supp. 7; 103 (January, 1940), 24-
        5.

1925.   _____. "California's G. of W.," Forum, 102
        (November, 1939), 232-8. Also in Donohue (ed.),
        pp. 8-19; Lisca (ed.), pp. 643-56.

1926.   Taylor, Horace Platt, Jr. "The Biological Natural-
        ism of J. S.," McNeese Review, 12 (Winter, 1960-
        1961), 81-97.

1927.   _____. "J. S.--The Quest," McNeese Review,
        10 (1965), 33-45.

1928.   Taylor, Walter Fuller. "The G. of W. Reconsidered,"
        Mississippi Quarterly, 12 (Summer, 1959), 136-44.
        Also in Donohue (ed.), 185-94; Lisca (ed.), pp. 757-
        68.

1929.   _____. "J. S.," The Story of American Letters.
        Chicago: Henry Regnery, 1956. pp. 457-60.

1930.   Tedlock, E. W., Jr. "A Pathos and a Power,"
        (Memorial Statement), SN, 2 (1969), 27-8.

1931.   Tenner, Robert L. "Fifteen Modern American Au-
        thors, ed. Jackson R. Bryer," SQ, 4 (Fall, 1971),
        113-15 (R).

1932.   Theatre Arts, 21 (October, 1937), 774-81.
        [Of Mice and Men, Play] (R).

1933.   _____. 22 (January, 1938), 13-16.
        [Of Mice and Men, Play] (R).

1934.   _____. 26 (May, 1942), 287.
        [The Moon Is Down, Play] (R).

1935.   . 34 (December, 1950), 16.
[Burning Bright, Novel] (R).

1936.   Thomas, Gilbert.   "A Visit to S.'s Eden Through
Monterey and Salinas," California (Scenic/Feature
Magazine), 45 (1970), 8-13.

1937.   "Thomas, Eulogized S.," San Jose Mercury.
December 24, 1968. p. 2.

1938.   Thompson, Eric.   "S.'s Oakies," Status, 2 (December, 1966), 42-5.
[G. of W.].

1939.   Thompson, Francis J.   "Travels with Charley in
Search of America," Florida Historical Quarterly,
41 (July, 1963), 59 (R).

1940.   Thompson, Ralph.   New York Times, February 27,
1937. p. 15.
[Of Mice and Men, Novel] (R).

1941.   . New York Times.   March 2, 1937.
p. 19.
[Of Mice and Men, Novel] (R).

1942.   . New York Times.   September 29, 1937.
p. 21.
[The Red Pony] (R).

1943.   . New York Times.   September 21, 1938.
p. 29.
[LV] (R).

1944.   . New York Times.   May 26, 1941. p. 17.
[The Forgotten Village] (R).

1945.   . Yale Review, 18 (Winter, 1939), 416,
476.
[LV] (R).

1946.   . Yale Review, 28 (Summer, 1939), viii.
[G. of W.] (R).

1947.   Thorp, Willard.   "S.," American Writing in the
Twentieth Century.   Cambridge, Massachusetts:
Harvard University Press, 1960.   pp. 130-2.

1948.   "Three New Plays Set, Moscow, Based on Works by
        Americans, J. S., J. Baldwin, and A. Mann,"
        New York Times, September 14, 1964. p. 41.

1949.   Thurber, James. New Republic, 106 (March 16,
        1942), 370.
        [The Moon Is Down, Novel] (R).

1950.   Time, 29 (March 1, 1937), 69.
        [Of Mice and Men, Novel] (R).

1951.   _____, 30 (October 11, 1937), 79.
        [The Red Pony] (R).

1952.   _____, 30 (December 6, 1937), 41.
        [Of Mice and Men, Novel] (R).

1953.   _____, 33 (April 17, 1939), 87.
        [G. of W.] (R).

1954.   _____, 35 (February 12, 1940), 70.
        [G. of W.] (R).

1955.   _____, 37 (June 2, 1941), 88.
        [The Forgotten Village] (R).

1956.   _____, 38 (December 22, 1941), 64.
        [Sea of Cortez] (R).

1957.   _____, 39 (March 9, 1942), 84.
        [The Moon Is Down, Novel] (R).

1958.   _____, 39 (April 30, 1942), 36.
        [The Moon Is Down, Play] (R).

1959.   _____, 39 (May 18, 1942), 84.
        [Tortilla Flat] (R).

1960.   _____, 39 (June 22, 1942), 88.
        [The Moon Is Down, Play] (R).

1961.   _____, 40 (September 22, 1942), 110.
        [East of Eden] (R).

1962.   _____, 45 (January 1, 1945), 62.
        [Cannery Row] (R).

1963.   _____, 49 (February 24, 1947), 118.

[The Wayward Bus] (R).

1964. _____, 50 (December 22, 1947), 90.
[The Pearl] (R).

1965. _____, 51 (January 26, 1948), 58.
[A Russian Journal] (R).

1966. _____, 51 (March 1, 1948), 84.
[The Pearl] (R).

1967. _____, 56 (October 30, 1950), 58.
[Burning Bright, Novel] (R).

1968. _____, 63 (June 14, 1954), 60.
[Sweet Thursday] (R).

1968(a) _____, 69 (April 15, 1957), 15.
[SRP] (R).

1969. _____, 77 (June 23, 1961), 70.
[The Winter of Our Discontent] (R).

1970. _____, 80 (August 10, 1962), 70.
[Travels with Charley] (R).

1971. Times (London), February 17, 1939. p. 9.
[The Long Valley] (R).

1972. _____, April 13, 1939. p. 10d.
[Of Mice and Men, Novel] (R).

1973. _____, September 8, 1939. p. 6.
[The Grapes of Wrath] (R).

1974. _____, June 9, 1942. p. 6.
[The Moon Is Down] (R).

1975. _____, June 9, 1943. p. 6c; June 10, 1943.
p. 6b.
[The Moon Is Down, Novel] (R).

1976. _____, May 11, 1944. p. 6e.
[The Forgotten Village] (R).

1977. _____, November 26, 1952. p. 10.
[East of Eden] (R).

1978.   _____, May 30, 1957. p. 13.
         [The Short Reign of Pippin IV] (R).

1979.   _____, June 29, 1961. p. 15.
         [The Winter of Our Discontent] (R).

1980.   _____, July 6, 1961. p. 10.
         [The Winter of Our Discontent] (R).

1981.   _____, "South African Ban," April 12, 1965.
         p. 10f.
         [Of Mice and Men, Novel] (R).

1982.   _____, November 10, 1966. p. 14.
         [America and Americans] (R).

1983.   TLS, June 15, 1933. p. 413.
         [The Pastures of Heaven] (R).

1984.   _____, April 11, 1935. p. 245.
         [To a God Unknown] (R).

1985.   _____, December 21, 1935. p. 877.
         [Tortilla Flat] (R).

1986.   _____, May 16, 1936. p. 417.
         [In Dubious Battle] (R).

1987.   _____, March 30, 1937. p. 214.
         [Cup of Gold] (R).

1988.   _____, October 2, 1937. p. 714.
         [Of Mice and Men] (R).

1989.   _____, February 4, 1939. p. 75.
         [The Long Valley] (R).

1990.   _____, (Spring Books Selection) March 25, 1939.
         p. xiv.
         [The Long Valley] (R).

1991.   _____, September 9, 1939. p. 525.
         [G. of W.] (R).

1992.   _____, June 20, 1942. p. 305.
         [The Moon Is Down, Novel] (R).

1993.   _____, November 3, 1945. p. 521.

[Cannery Row] (R).

1994. _____, November 29, 1947. p. 613.
[The Wayward Bus] (R).

1995. _____, December 5, 1952. p. 789.
[East of Eden] (R).

1996. _____, (Special Number: American Writing Today: Its Independence and Vigour), September 17,
1954. p. xciv, (A reprint of the review appearing
in the issue of September 9, 1939).
[The Grapes of Wrath] (R).

1997. _____, November 26, 1954. p. 753.
[Sweet Thursday] (R).

1998. _____, June 7, 1957. p. 345.
[SRP] (R).

1999. _____, "The Grapes of Wrath," American Writing Today: Its Independence and Vigour. New
York: New York University Press, 1957. pp.
398-9.

2000. _____, January 8, 1960. p. 15.
[Once There Was a War] (R).

2001. _____, July 7, 1961. p. 413.
[The Winter of Our Discontent] (R).

2002. _____, November 2, 1962. p. 843.
[Travels with Charley] (R).

2003. Toynbee, Philip. New Statesman, 23 (June 20,
1942), 408-409.
[The Moon Is Down, Novel] (R).

2004. _____. New Statesman, 30 (November 24, 1945),
356-7.
[Cannery Row] (R).

2005. Trilling, Lionel. "S.," The Liberal Imagination.
New York: Viking Press, 1950. Passim.

2006. Trimmer, Joseph F. "Warren French (ed.), The
Social Novel at the End of an Era," SN, 2 1969),
37-41. (R).

2007.   "A Trip to Israel and His Forthcoming Book,
         America and Americans," Time, 87 (February 11,
         1966), 41.

2008.   Tsuboi, Kiyohiko. "Hideo Inazawa's Sutainbekku
         Ron (Essays on S.) (In Japanese)," SQ, 3 (1970),
         33-5 (R).

2009.   Tsunematsu, Masao. "Ikari no Budo (The Grapes of
         Wrath) by J. S., tr. into Japanese by Rikuo
         Taniguchi," SQ, 3 (1970), 12-14 (R).

2010.   [Tsygankov, Veniamin.] "S. Play Praised," New
         York Times, November 15, 1963. p. 5.

2011.   Tuttleton, James W. "The Grapes of Wrath," in
         "S. in Russia: The Rhetoric of Praise and Blame,"
         MFS, 11 (Spring, 1965), Passim.

2012.   _____. "The Pearl," in "S. in Russia: The
         Rhetoric of Praise and Blame," MFS, 11 (Spring,
         1965), 77-89. Also in Donohue (ed.). pp. 245-56.

2013.   "TV Series Based on Travels with Charley Set;
         Steinbeck to Be Consultant," New York Times,
         April 22, 1963. p. 55.

2014.   Tyler, Parker. "The Grapes of Wrath," Magic
         and Myth of the Movies. New York: Henry Holt,
         1947. pp. 230-247, 274-8.

2015.   Uchida, Shigeharu. "Sentimental S. and His Tor-
         tilla Flat," KAL, 7 (1964), 8-12.

2016.   _____. "J. S.'s Non-Teleology and To a God
         Unknown," KAL, 6 (April, 1963), 13-17.

2017.   "U. S.: J. S. Says Youth Lack Aims and Suffers
         From War Fears and Anxiety in USSR," New York
         Times, October 19, 1963. p. 17.

2018.   Ueno, Naozo. "An Oriental View of The Old Man
         and the Sea," East-West Review, 2 (Spring-Summer,
         1965), 67-76.

2019.   Uzzell, Thomas H. "The Grapes of Wrath," The

Technique of the Novel. New York: Citadel Press, 1964. pp. 231 and Passim.

2020.   Van Doren, Carol Clinton. "The Grapes of Wrath," The American Novel, 1789-1939. New York: Macmillan, 1940. pp. 364-6.

2021.   _____. "Introduction" to The Grapes of Wrath. Cleveland: World Publishing, 1947.

2022.   _____. "S.," "Introduction" to The Grapes of Wrath. Cleveland: World Publishing, 1947.

2023.   _____. (ed.). "Revisions," American Novel, 1789-1939. New York: Macmillan, 1960. pp. 349-66.

2024.   Van Doren, Mark. Nation, 144 (March 6, 1937), 275.
         [Of Mice and Men, Novel] (R).

2025.   _____. Nation, 144 (April 18, 1942), 468.
         [Of Mice and Men, Novel] (R).

2026.   _____. "Wrong Number," The Private Reader. New York: Holt, 1942. pp. 255-7.
         [Of Mice and Men, Novel].

2027.   Van Gelder, Robert. "Interview with a Best-Selling Author J. S.," Cosmopolitan, 122 (April, 1947), 123-5. Reprint from Writers and Writing. New York: Scribner's, 1946.

2028.   Vaughan, James N. Commonweal, 30 (July 28, 1939), 341-2.
         [G. of W.] (R).

2029.   "Venice International Biennial J. S. Opens Exhibit of 65 Famous American Paintings," New York Times, June 11, 1952. p. 36.

2030.   Vernon, Grenville. Commonweal, 28 (June 3, 1938), 161.
         [Of Mice and Men, Play] (R).

2031.   Verschoyle, Derek. "Of Mice and Men by J. S. at

the Gate Theatre," Spectator, 162 (April 21, 1939),
668 (P.R.).

2032.   . "Of Mice and Men by J. S. at the
Apollo Theatre," Spectator, 162 (May 26, 1939), 901
(P.R.).

2033.   "Vestal High School, Vestal, New York has faculty
and students defy Harold C. May, the President of
the Board of Education and put S.'s The Grapes of
Wrath on sale despite the board action," New York
Times, March 28, 1965. p. 76.

2034.   "Victims of Mammon," TLS, September 9, 1939.
p. 525.
[The Grapes of Wrath] (R).

2035.   "Video V. Housework," Time, 52 (July 19, 1948), 65.

2036.   "Viewed As Nobel Literature Award Candidate,"
New York Times, November 8, 1945. p. 6.

2037.   "Viking Portable Library S. Selected by P. Covici,"
New York Times, August 22, 1943. 7:6.

2038.   "The Viking Press Buys Contract, Orders for The
Long Valley Earnings," Time, 32 (August 29, 1938),
47.

2039.   Virginia Quarterly Review, 37 (Autumn, 1961), cxii.
[The Winter of Our Discontent] (R).

2040.   Virginia Quarterly Review, 46 (Spring, 1970), 46.
[Journal of a Novel].

2041.   "Viva Zapata! Story of the Mexican Indian Leader
Emiliano Zapata, a screenplay by J. S.," Facts on
File, 12 (February 22-28, 1952), 67.

2042.   Vogel, Dan. "S.'s 'Flight': The Myth of Manhood,"
College English, 23 (December, 1961), pp. 225-6.
Reply by C. F. Chapin. College English, 23 (May,
1962), 676.

2043.   . "S.'s 'Flight': The Myth of Manhood,"
Fiction: Form and Experience by William M.
Jones. Lexington, Massachusetts: Heath, 1969.

pp. 376-8. Also in An Introduction to Short Fiction
and Criticism by Emil Hurtik and Robert Yarber.
Waltham, Massachusetts: Xerox College Publishing,
1971. pp. 392-4.

2044.   "Voices of Author's Recordings," Life, 35 (October
12, 1953), 132.

2045.   Wagenknecht, Edward Charles. "Two Kinds of
Novelist: S. and Marquand," Cavalcade of the American Novel, From the Birth of the Nation to the
Middle of the Twentieth Century. New York: Holt,
1952. pp. 438-48.

2046.   Walcutt, Charles C. "Cannery Row and In Dubious
Battle," American Literary Naturalism. Minneapolis: University of Minnesota Press, 1956. pp. 258-
70.

2047.   _____. "Later Trends in Form: S. Heming-
way, Dos Passos," American Literary Naturalism,
A Divided Stream. Minneapolis: University of
Minnesota Press, 1956. pp. 258-9. Also in
Donohue (ed.), pp. 162-5.

2048.   _____. "The Wayward Bus," American Literary
Naturalism, A Divided Stream. pp. 266-7.

2049.   Wallaston, Nicholas. Spectator, 209 (October 19,
1962), 604-605.
[Travels with Charley] (R).

2050.   Walter, Eda Lou. Nation, 147 (October 1, 1938),
331-2.
[LV] (R).

2051.   _____. New York Times Book Review, February
28, 1937. VII, 7:20.
[Of Mice and Men, Novel] (R).

2052.   _____. New York Times Book Review, October
10, 1937. 7:7.
[The Red Pony] (R).

2053.   "Wandering in S. Country," National Observer,
[n.v.] (February 16, 1970), 10.

2054.   Warfel, Harry Redcay. "J. S.," American Novelists
        of Today, New York: American Book Co., 1951.
        pp. 403-405.

2055.   Warren, Robert Penn. "A Fine Anthology of S.'s
        Writings," New York Times Book Review, August 22,
        1943. p. 6.
        [The Portable Steinbeck] (R).

2056.   _____. "Pure and Impure Poetry," Selected Es-
        says. New York: Random House, 1958. pp. 3-31.

2057.   Watson, Phil. "S.'s Whimsy," The Short Reign of
        Pippin IV. San Jose Mercury-News Magazine,
        April 21, 1957, p. 8 (R).

2058.   Watts, Richard, Jr. New Republic, 116 (March 10,
        1947), 37-8.
        [The Wayward Bus] (R).

2059.   _____. New Republic, 118 (April 19, 1948), 22-3.
        [A Russian Journal] (R).

2060.   "The Wayward Bus," Facts on File, 17 (June 27-
        July 3, 1963), 216.

2061.   Weales, Gerald. "S.," American Drama Since World
        War II. New York: Harcourt, Brace and World,
        1962. pp. 198-9.
        [Burning Bright, Play].

2062.   Weber, Daniel B. "Society and the American Novel,
        1920-1960," Diliman Review, 13 (October, 1965),
        366-79.

2063.   Webster, Harvey Curtis and Bernard Kolb. "Out of
        the New-Born Sun," Saturday Review, 35 (September
        20, 1952), 11-12.
        [East of Eden] (R).

2064.   Webster, Harvey Curtis. Saturday Review, 37 (June
        12, 1954), 11.
        [Sweet Thursday] (R).

2065.   "Weds G. Conger," New York Times, March 20, 1943.
        p. 23.

2066.   "Weds E. A. Scott," New York Times, December

29, 1950. p. 14.

2067. Weeks, Donald. Atlantic Monthly, 159 (April, 1937),
[n. p.: between 384-5].
[Of Mice and Men, Novel] (R).

2068. _____ . Atlantic Monthly, 169 (April, 1942),
[n. p.: between 398-9].
[The Moon Is Down, Novel] (R).

2069. _____ . "S. Against S.," Pacific Spectator, 1
(Autumn, 1947), 447-57.

2070. Weeks, Edward. Atlantic, 163 (April, 1939), 591;
(May, 1939), 734.
[G. of W.] (R).

2071. _____ . Atlantic, 179 (March, 1947), 126-8.
[The Wayward Bus] (R).

2072. _____ . Atlantic, 180 (December, 1947), 138-9.
[The Pearl] (R).

2073. _____ . Atlantic, 194 (August, 1954), 82.
[Sweet Thursday] (R).

2074. _____ . Atlantic, 200 (July, 1957), 83-4.
[SRP] (R).

2075. _____ . Atlantic, 208 (July, 1961), 122.
[The Winter of Our Discontent] (R).

2076. _____ . Atlantic, 210 (August, 1962), 138.
[Travels with Charley] (R).

2077. _____ . "Book Publishers, Readers Scored,"
New York Times, Western Edition. December 3,
1962. p. 10.

2078. _____ . "The Grapes of Wrath," Essays For Our
Time, ed. A. L. Boder and C. F. Wells. [n. p.,
n. d.], pp. 226-8.

2079. Weiss, Carol H. Commonweal, 53 (November 24,
1950), 178.
[Burning Bright, Play] (R).

2080. West, Anthony. "Books; California Moonshine,"

New Yorker, 28 (September 20, 1952), 121-2f.

2081.   . New Statesman, 18 (September 16, 1939),
         404-405.
         [The Grapes of Wrath] (R).

2082.   . New Yorker, 28 (September 20, 1952),
         111-13.
         [East of Eden] (R).

2083.   West, Roy B., Jr. "Chrysanthemums," Short Story
         in America 1900-1950. Chicago: Henry Regenery,
         1952. pp. 48-9.

2084.   Westwood, Horace. "The Grapes of Wrath," Unity,
         124 (February 5, 1940), 170-3.

2085.   Whicher, George F. "Proletarian Leanings,"
         The Literature of the American People, ed. Arthur
         Hobson Quinn.   New York: Appleton-Century
         Crofts, 1951. pp. 958-61.
         [The Grapes of Wrath].

2086.   Whipple, Leon. "Novels on Social Themes,"
         Survey Graphic, 28 (June, 1939), 401-402.

2087.   Whipple, Thomas K. "In Dubious Battle," Study
         Out The Land.   Berkeley: University of California
         Press, 1943. pp. 109-10.

2088.   . "S. Through a Glass, Though Brightly,"
         New Republic, 96 (October 12, 1938), 274-5.   Also
         in Study Out The Land.   Berkeley: University of
         California Press, 1945. pp. 104-11.

2089.   No entry.

2090.   Widmer, Kingsley. "J. S.: Examples of Senti-
         mental Rebellions," The Literary Rebel.   Carbon-
         dale: Southern Illinois University Press, 1965.
         pp. 114-29.

2091.   "Wife Gets Divorce," New York Times, March 13,
         1942. p. 12. (Carol Henning).

2092.   "Wife Gwyn Conger in Reno for Divorce; Dinner
         Partner Commits Suicide," Time, 52 (November 8,
         1948), 44.

2093.   Williams, Stanley T.   "J. S.," The Spanish Back-
        ground of American Literature. New Haven,
        Connecticut: Yale University Press, 1955. 1,
        Passim.

2094.   Williamson, S. T. New York Times Book Review,
        November 29, 1942. VI, 1: 30.
        [Bombs Away] (R).

2095.   Willingham, J. R. Christian Science Monitor.
        January 2, 1970. p. 11.
        [J. of a Novel].

2096.   _____ . "Journal of a Novel," Library Journal,
        95 (March, 1970), 899.

2097.   Wills, Arthur. "A Question of Manhood: S.'s
        'Flight'," Exercise Exchange, 12 (November, 1964),
        14-15.

2098.   Wilson, Edmund. "The Boys in the Back Room,"
        Classics and Commercials. New York: Farrar,
        Straus and Young, 1950. pp. 34-45.

2099.   _____ . "J. S.," The Boys in the Back Room,
        San Francisco: Colt Press, 1941. pp. 41-53.

2100.   _____ . "From Classics and Commercials,"
        Classics and Commercials. New York: Farrar,
        Straus and Young, 1950. pp. 35-45. Also in
        Donohue (ed.), pp. 151-8.

2101.   _____ . "The Californians: Storm and S.,"
        New Republic, 103 (December 9, 1940), 784-7.

2102.   _____ . "The Grapes of Wrath," Classics and
        Commercials. pp. 38-42.

2103.   _____ . "I Am S.'s Newest Novel and James
        Joyce's First," New Yorker, 20 (January 6, 1954),
        62.
        [Cannery Row] (R).

2104.   Wilson Library Bulletin, 35 (May, 1939), 104.
        [G. of W.] (R).

2105.   "Wins '62 Nobel Literature Prize," New York Times,

October 26, 1962.   pp. 1; 12; 30; December 9, 1962.
7:4; December 11, 1962.   p. 3.

2106.   Winter, Ella. _And Not to Yield, An Autobiography._
New York: Harcourt, Brace and World, 1963.
"S.," pp. 129, 212-13, 240.

2107.   Winterich, John T. _Writers in America: 1842-1967._
Jersey City: Davey, 1967. (Chapter on Steinbeck).

2108.   Wiskari, Werner. "Nobel Prize for Literature Is
Won by J. S.," _New York Times,_ Western Edition.
October 26, 1962.   pp. 1, 7.

2109.   _____. "Nobel Prizes Given to 7 in Ceremonies
in 2 Cities," _New York Times,_ Western Edition.
December 11, 1962.   pp. 1, 3.

2110.   Witham, W. Tasker. _The Adolescent in the American Novel, 1920-1960._ New York: Ungar, 1964.
pp. 2-3, 221-2.   _Passim._

2111.   _____. "J. S.," _Panorama of American Litera-
ture._ New York: Ungar, 1947. pp. 340-5.

2112.   Wollaston, Nicholas. _Spectator,_ 209 (October 19,
1962), 604-605.
[Travels with Charley] (R).

2113.   Woodress, James. "J. S.: Hostage to Fortune,"
South Atlantic Quarterly, 63 (Summer, 1964), 385-
97.   Also in Donohue (ed.).   pp. 278-90.

2114.   Wooster, Harold A. _Library Journal,_ 70 (January
1, 1945), 32.
[Cannery Row] (R).

2115.   "Workshop Slated in February on S.," _San Jose News._
November 26, 1970.   p. 18.

2116.   Worsley, T. C. _New Statesman,_ 20 (October 19,
1940), 396.
[Of Mice and Men] (R).

2117.   "Wrapped and Shellacked; Nobel Prize for Literature," _Time,_ 80 (November 2, 1962), 41-42.

2118.   Wright, Celeste Turner. "Ancient Analogues of an

Incident in J. S.," Western Folklore, 14 (January, 1955), 50-1. Also in Donohue (ed.), pp. 159-61.

2119. "Writing for Short-Wave Broadcast to Soldiers," Time, 39 (May 18, 1942), 54.

2120. "Wrote Story of Lifeboat," Time, 42 (January 31, 1944), 94.

2121. Wyatt, Bryant N. "Experimentation as Technique: The Protest Novels of J. S.," Discourse, 12 (1969), 143-53.

2122. Wyatt, Euphemia Van Rensselaer. Catholic World, 146 (January, 1938), 468-9.
[Of Mice and Men, Novel] (R).

2123. _____. Catholic World, 146 (January, 1938), 468.
[Of Mice and Men, Play] (R).

2124. _____. Catholic World, 155 (May, 1942), 213-14.
[The Moon Is Down, Play] (R).

2125. _____. Catholic World, 171 (December, 1950), 228.
[Burning Bright, Play] (R).

2126. _____. Catholic World, 172 (December, 1950), 228.
[Burning Bright, Novel] (R).

2127. Yale Review, 22 (Winter, 1933), 22.
[PH] (R).

2128. _____, 31 (Spring, 1942), 8.
[The Moon Is Down, Novel] (R).

2129. _____, 42 (Autumn, 1962), 8.
[East of Eden] (R).

2130. Yano, Shigeharu. "The Imagery in The Winter of Our Discontent," Reitaku University Quarterly, 12 (1971), 116-39.

2131. _____. "The Pearl as a Prelude to East of

Eden, " Reitaku University Quarterly, 10 (1970), 27-52.

2132. _____. "Psychological Description in The Way-ward Bus," Reitaku University Quarterly, 13 (March, 1972), 1-19.

2133. _____. "Right and Wrong in The Moon Is Down," Reitaku University Quarterly, 2 (1971), 15-32.

2134. Yoshida, Hiroshige. "Gender of Animation in J. S.'s The Grapes of Wrath," Anglica, 2 (October, 1956), 106-22.

2135. Young, Stanley. New York Times Book Review, September 25, 1938. p. 7. [LV] (R).

2136. Young, Stark. New Republic, 93 (December 15, 1937), 170-1. [Of Mice and Men, Novel] (R).

2137. _____. New Republic, 93 (December 15, 1937), 170. [Of Mice and Men, Play] (R).

2138. _____. New Republic. 106 (May 11, 1942), 638. [The Moon Is Down, Novel] (R).

2139. _____. New Republic, 106 (May 11, 1942), 638. [The Moon Is Down, Play] (R).

2140. Zolotow, Sam. New York Times, October 27, 1950. p. 24. [Burning Bright, Play] (R).

H. BIBLIOGRAPHIES: A LIST OF STEINBECK BIBLIOGRA-PHIES AND BIBLIOGRAPHICAL ARTICLES (2141-2184)

2141. Beebe, Maurice and Jackson R. Bryer. "Criticism of J. S.: A Selected Checklist," MFS, 11 (Spring, 1965), 90-103.

2142. Beyer, Preston. "Collecting J. Steinbeckiana," SQ, 2 (1969), 56-9.

2143.   . "The Joad Newsletter," SQ, 4 (Fall, 1971), 105-106.

2144. Blanck, Jacob (ed.). "American First Editions," Publishers' Weekly, 131 (April 17, 1937), 1701. ["Checklist of J. S.'s Works" by Lawrence C. Powell].

2145. Burnett, Whit (ed.). "S. Bibliography," The World's Best: 105 Greatest Living Authors, New York: Dial Press, 1950. p. 1155.

2146. Davis, Robert Murray (ed.). Steinbeck: A Collection of Critical Essays. Englewood Cliffs, N.J.: Prentice-Hall, 1972. pp. 179-83.

2147. DeMott, Robert. "A Miscellany of Bibliographical Notes," SQ, 3 (1970), 41-3.

2148. Dickinson, A. T., Jr. American Historical Fiction. New York: Scarecrow Press, 1958. "S.," pp. 11, 20-1, 84, 147, 210, 232, 234. (1963 ed., pp. 96, 204).

2149. Donohue, Agnes McNeill (ed.). A Casebook on The Grapes of Wrath. New York: McGraw-Hill, 1968. pp. 296-9.

2150. Ethridge, James M. (ed.). Contemporary Authors: A Bio-Bibliographical Guide to Current Authors and Their Works. Detroit: Gale Research, 1963. "S.," pp. 2, 184.

2151. Fontenrose, Joseph. John Steinbeck: An Introduction and Interpretation. New York: Barnes and Noble, 1963. pp. 142-4.
[American Authors and Critics Series, No. 8].

2152. French, Warren G. (ed.). A Companion to The Grapes of Wrath. New York: Viking Press, 1960. pp. 229-35.

2153.   . John Steinbeck. New York: Twayne, 1961. pp. 175-81.

2154. Gannett, Lewis. John Steinbeck: Personal and Bibliographical Notes, A Pamphlet. New York: Viking Press, 1939.

2155.   Gerstenberger, Donna, and Hendrick, George. The
        American Novel 1789-1959: A Checklist of Twentieth
        Century Criticism. Denver: Allan Swallow, 1961.
        "J. S. ," pp. 225-30.

2156.   Hayashi, Tetsumaro. "A Brief Survey of John
        Steinbeck Bibliographies," KAL, 9 (1966), 54-61.

2157.   _____. "J. S.: A Checklist of Movie Reviews,"
        Serif, 7 (1970), 18-22.

2158.   _____. John Steinbeck: A Concise Bibliography
        (1930-1965), Metuchen, N.J.: Scarecrow Press,
        1967.

2159.   _____ (ed.). John Steinbeck: A Guide to the
        Doctoral Dissertations (A Collection of Dissertation
        Abstracts, 1946-69). Steinbeck Society, Ball State
        University, 1971 (Steinbeck Monograph Series, No.
        1). 32 pp.

2160.   _____ and Donald L. Siefker. The Special Stein-
        beck Collection of the Ball State University Library.
        Muncie, Indiana: John Steinbeck Society, Ball State
        University, 1972.

2161.   Hill, Clarence Gohdes (ed). Russian Studies of
        American Literature, A Bibliography. University of
        North Carolina Press, 1969.

2162.   Hoffman, Hester R. (ed.). The Reader's Advisor
        and Bookman's Manual. 9th ed. New York:
        Bowker, 1960. "S.," pp. 993-4.

2163.   Humanities Research Center of the University of
        Texas. John Steinbeck: An Exhibition of American
        and Foreign Editions. Austin, Texas: The Center,
        1963.

2164.   Jackson, Joseph Henry. "A List of Books By and
        Essays About J. S.," We Moderns, Catalogue Issued.
        New York: Gotham Book Mart, 1920-1940. pp. 24,
        66-7.

2165.   Johnson, Merle. American First Editions. 4th rev.
        ed. Revised and edited by Jacob N. Blanck. New
        York: R. R. Bowker, 1942. Reprinted from

Publishers' Weekly, 131 (April 17, 1937), 1701. [Checklist by Lawrence Clark Powell].

2166. _____. Merle Johnson's First Editions, Rev. and enlarged by Jacob Blanck. Waltham, Massachusetts: Mark Press, 1965. pp. 472-3.

2167. Leary, Lewis Gaston. Articles on American Literature 1900-1950. Durham, N.C.: Duke University Press, 1954. pp. 278-9.

2168. Lisca, Peter (ed.). John Steinbeck: The Grapes of Wrath, Text and Criticism. New York: Viking, 1972. pp. 869-81.

2169. _____. The Wide World of John Steinbeck. New Brunswick: Rutgers University Press, 1958. "A Working Checklist of Steinbeck's Published Work," pp. 310-14.

2170. Millett, Fred B. Contemporary American Authors. New York: Harcourt, Brace, 1950. pp. 596-7.

2171. Moore, Harry Thornton. The Novels of John Steinbeck: A First Critical Study. Chicago: Normandie House, 1939. "Bibliographical Checklist of First Editions," pp. 97-101.

2172. Powell, Lawrence Clark. "American First Editions," Publishers' Weekly, 131 (April 17, 1937), 1701.

2173. _____. "On Collecting J. S.," The Book Collector's Packet, ed. Irving Haas, 2 (July, 1938), Chicago: Black Cat Press, 1938. pp. 11-12.

2174. _____. "Toward a Bibliography of J. S.," Colophon, 3 (Autumn, 1938), 558-68. See also Johnson, Merle.

2175. Pratt, John Clark. John Steinbeck, A Critical Essay. Grand Rapids, Michigan: William B. Eerdmans, 1970. pp. 46-8.

2176. Quinn, Arthur Hobson, et al (eds.). The Literature of the American People. New York: Appleton-Century-Crofts, 1951. p. 1102.

2177. Simmonds, Roy S. "J. S.: Works Published in the

British Magazine Argosy," SQ, 4 (Fall, 1971), 101-105.

2178. _____. "The Typescript of S.'s America and Americans," SQ, 4 (Fall, 1971), 120-1.

2179. Singleton, R. H. (ed.). Two and Twenty, A Collection of Short Stories. New York: St. Martin's Press, 1962. p. 239. "The Great Mountains," pp. 236-8 contain bio-bibliographical information.

2180. Spiller, Robert E., et al (eds.). Literary History of the United States: Bibliography. New York: Macmillan, 1963. "J. S.," pp. 192-3, 730-1.

2181. Steele, Joan. "J. S.: A Checklist of Biographical, Critical, and Bibliographical Material," Bulletin of Bibliography and Magazine Notes, 24 (May-August, 1965), 149-52, 162-3.

2182. Tedlock, E. W., Jr., and C. V. Wicker (eds.). SHC, "A Checklist of Steinbeck's Books," p. 310.

2183. Wagenknecht, Edward Charles. Cavalcade of the American Novel. New York: Henry Holt, 1942. pp. 554-5.

2184. Watt, Frank William. John Steinbeck. (Evergreen Pilot E. P. 13). New York: Grove Press, 1962. pp. 115-17.

APPENDIX A

A LIST OF STANDARD REFERENCE GUIDES CONSULTED

Abstracts of English Studies.

American Drama Criticism, ed. Helen H. Palmer and Jane Anne Dyson. Hamden, Connecticut: Shoe String Press, 1967.

American Literary Scholarship. An Annual.

American Literary Manuscripts, comp. Joseph Jones, et al. Austin: University of Texas Press, 1960.

American Literature (Bibliography).

Annual Bibliography of English Language and Literature, ed. Marjory Rigby, et al. Cambridge: England: Modern Humanities Research Association.

Bibliographic Index.

Biography Index.

Book Review Digest.

Book Review Index.

Books in Print.

British Humanities Index.

British Museum General Catalogue of Printed Books.

Canadian Index to Periodicals and Documentary Films.

Contemporary Authors. Detroit: Gale Research, 1963.

Cumulative Book Index.

Cumulative Dramatic Index, 1909-49.

Current Biography.

Dissertation Abstracts.

Dissertation Abstracts International, (DAI).

Dissertations in American Literature, 1891-1955 with Supplement, 1956-61 by James Woodress. Durham, North Carolina: Duke University Press, 1962.

Education Index.

Essay and General Literature Index.

Filmed Books and Plays, 1955-57. London: Grafton, 1958.

A Guide to Critical Reviews (Part One: American Drama from O'Neill to Albee) by James M. Salem. New York: Scarecrow, 1966.

Index to Little Magazines, 1953-63.

International Index to Periodicals (now called Humanities and Social Science Index).

International Motion Picture Almanac.

The Library of Congress Catalog of Printed Cards.

A Library of Literary Criticism: Modern American Literature.

Literary and Library Prizes.

MLA Bibliography.

Modern Drama (Bibliography).

Modern Drama: A Checklist of Critical Literature of 20th Century Plays.

Modern Fiction Studies (Bibliography).

The National Union Catalog.

New York Times Film Reviews, 1913-1968. New York: New York Times and Arno Press, 1970 [Vol. VI].

New York Times Index.

The Reader's Adviser.

Reader's Guide to Periodical Literature.

Short Story Index.

Steinbeck Quarterly (Annual Index).

Subject Guide to Books in Print.

Twentieth Century Authors, with Supplements.

Twentieth Century Literature (Bibliography).

APPENDIX B

A LIST OF ANNUALS, NEWSPAPERS
AND PERIODICALS INDEXED

AB Bookman's Weekly
America (National Catholic
   Weekly Review)
Americana (The American
   Motors Magazine)
American Book Collector
American Dialect
American Literature
American Mercury
American Quarterly
American Scholar
American Studies Research
   Center Newsletter (India)
American West
Anglica (Japan)
Antioch Review
Aoyama Gakuin University
   Studies in British and
   American Literature
   (Japan)
Appalachian State Teachers
   College Faculty Publications
   (Formerly ASTC Bulletin)
Argosy (New York)
Asian Student (San Francisco)
Atlantic Monthly
Ausonia
Australian Quarterly
   (Australia)
Author and Journalist
Avon

Ball State University Forum

(See Forum)
Banathali Patrika
Beacon Study in Language and
   Literature (Kemmei Junior
   College, Japan)
Black and White
Book Collector's Packet
Booklist (and Subscription
   Books Bulletin) (Formerly
   ALA Booklist)
Booklover's Answer
Bookman (London, England)
Bookmark (New York State
   Library)
Book-of-the-Month-Club News
Books Abroad (An Interna-
   tional Library Quarterly)
Books and Bookmen
Book Week; For Libraries
   and Schools
Boston Globe
Boston Transcript
Brief (Phi Delta Phi)
British and American Litera-
   ture (Kansei Gakuin Uni-
   versity, Japan)

California
California State Poetry
   Quarterly
California Teachers' Asso-
   ciation Journal (CTA
   Journal)

Canadian Forum (Canada)
Catholic World
CEA Critic
Chicago Daily Tribune
Chicago Jewish Forum
Chicago Sun Book Week
Chicago Sunday Tribune
    Magazine of Books
Choice
Christian Century
Christian Herald
Christian Scholar
Christian Science Monitor
Chu-Shikoku American
    Literature Society Bul-
    letin (Japan)
College English
College Language Association
    Journal (CLAJ)
Collier's
Colophon (A Quarterly for
    Bookman)
Colorado Quarterly
Columbia Literary Columns
Commentary
Commonweal
Comparative Literature
Coronet
Cosmopolitan
Cresset (A Review of
    Literature)
Current Biography
Current History

Daily Express (England)
Daily Mail (England)
Daily Sketch
Daily Telegraph Magazine
    (London, England)
Dayton Daily News
Delphian Quarterly
Diliman Review
Discourse
Duquesne Review

East-West Review (Japan)
English and American Litera-

ture Studies (Aoyama
    Gakuin University, Japan)
Editor and Publisher
English Journal
English Language and
    Literature Studies
    (Kyushu University,
    Japan)
English Record
Esquire
Essays and Studies in British
    and American Literature
    (Tokyo Women's Christian
    College, Japan)
Etudes Anglaises (France)
Evening Standard
Exercise Exchange, A
    Quarterly for the Inter-
    change of Classroom Ideas
    among Teachers of Com-
    position and Literature
Explicator
Extension, The National
    Catholic Monthly

Facts on File
Films and Filming
Florida Historical Quarterly
Ford Times
Fortnightly (England)
Fortune
Forum (Ball State University)
Forum (University of Houston)
Forum (Formerly Forum and
    Century)

Gekkan Pen (Monthly Pen)
    (Japan)
Genre
Good Housekeeping

Harper's Magazine
Hartford Studies in
    Literature
Harvard Law Review (HLR)
Hokkaido Educational Uni-
    versity Quarterly
    (Japan)

The Hokkaido University
   Essays in Foreign Lan-
   guages and Literature
   (Japan)
Holiday
Hollywood Tribune
House and Garden
Hudson Review
Huntington Library
   Quarterly (HLQ)

Illustrated London News
   (England)
Indian Journal of American
   Studies
Indian P(oetry), E(ssays),
   N(ovels) (Indian PEN)
   (India)
Iowa English Yearbook

Journal of Aesthetics and
   Art Criticism
Journal of American
   Medical Association
Journal of English and
   Germanic Philology
   (JEGP)
Journal of Narrative
   Technique

Kansai Gakuin Times (Japan)
Kentucky Romance Quarterly
Kenyon Review
Knight
Komazawa University Quar-
   terly (Japan)
Korea University Journal
   (Korea)
Kyushu American Literature
   (KAL) (Japan)
Kyushu Institute of Tech-
   nology Report (Japan)

Ladies' Home Journal
Library Journal
Life
Life and Letters Today
   (England)

Lilliput
Listener (England)
Literary Criterion
Literary Digest
London Magazine (England)
London Mercury (England)
Los Angeles Examiner
Los Angeles Times West
   Magazine
Lovat Dickson's Magazine
Lumina (Okayama University,
   Japan)

McCall's
McNeese Review
Manchester Guardian
   (England)
Massachusetts Review
Mississippi Quarterly
Modern Fiction Studies (MFS)
Modern Language
Modern Monthly
Modern Quarterly (England)
Modern Review (India)
Monterey Beacon
Monterey Peninsula
Monthly Film Bulletin
Monthly Record

Nation
National Education Associa-
   tion Journal (NEA
   Journal)
National Observer
National Parent Teacher
National Review
Negro History Bulletin
Die Neueren Sprachen
   (Germany)
New Leader
New Masses
New Republic
News Chronicle
New Statesman (and Nation);
   an Independent Political
   and Literary Review
   (England)
Newsweek

New Yorker
New York Evening Post
(Later New York Post)
New York Herald Tribune
Books
New York Nichibei
New York Times (Book
Review)
New York Times Magazine
North American Review

Occident
Opera News

Pacific Discovery
Pacific Historical Review
Pacific Spectator; A Journal
of Interpretation
Pacific Weekly
Parade: Sunday Newspaper
Magazine
Paris Review
Peninsula Living
Perspectives (U.S.A.)
Quarterly of Literature
and the Arts)
Photography
PMLA (Publications of the
Modern Language Associa-
tion of America)
Prairie Schooner
Princeton Seminary Bulletin
Princeton University Library
Chronicle
Proceedings of the American
Academy of Arts and
Letters
Proceedings of the Utah
Academy of Sciences,
Arts, and Letters
Progressive Weekly
Psychoanalytic Study of
The Child (England)
Publishers' Weekly
Punch (England)

Ramparts

Reader's Digest
Reading and Collecting
Reitaku University Kiyo
(Japan)
Religion in Life
Renascence (A Critical
Journal of Letters)
Reporter
Reports of Studies (Otani
Women's Junior College,
Japan)
Revues des Langues Vivantes
(Brussels, Belgium)
Rocky Mountain Review

Sacramento Union Family
Weekly
St. Louis Post Dispatch (Sun-
day Pictures)
San Francisco Chronicle
San Francisco Evening News
San Francisco Examiner
San Francisco News
San Francisco Sunday
Chronicle ("This World"
Magazine)
San Francisco Sunday
Examiner and Chronicle
San Jose Mercury-News
San Jose News
Saturday Night (Canada)
Saturday Review (S.R.)
(Formerly Saturday Review
of Literature)
Scholastic
Science and Society
Science Digest
Sewanee Review
Shore Review
Sight and Sound
Sociology and Social
Research
South Atlantic Quarterly
South Dakota Review
Southern Review
Southwest Review
Soviet Review

SPAN (India)
Spartan Daily
Spectator (England)
Stage (England)
Stanford Lit
Stanford Spectator
Status
Steinbeck Newsletter (SN)
 (See Steinbeck Quarterly)
Steinbeck Quarterly (SQ)
 (formerly Steinbeck
 Newsletter)
Stetson Studies in the
 Humanities
Strand Magazine
Studies in American
 Literature (Japan)
Studies in Short Fiction
Study of Current English
 (Tokyo, Japan)
Style
Sunday Citizen
Sunday Times
Sunset Magazine
Survey Graphic

Taira Technical Junior
 College Reports of Studies
 (Japan)
Teacher's College Journal
Theatre Arts
Time
Time and Tide; Independent
 Weekly (England)
Times (London) Literary
 Supplement (TLS)
 England)
The Times (London) Weekly
 Review (England)
Today
Today's Health
Transatlantic Review (an Inter-
 national Literary Review)
True
Twentieth Century Literature:
 A Scholarly and Critical
 Journal (TCL)

Unity, Fellowship and
 Character in Religion
University of Houston Forum
 (See Forum.)
The University of Kansas
 City Review (UKCR)
University of Missouri
 Studies

Virginia Quarterly Review
 (A National Journal of
 Literature and Discussion)
Visvabharati Quarterly
 (India)
Vlaamse Gids
Vogue

Way--Catholic Viewpoints
 (U.S.A.)
Weekend Telegraph (England)
Western American Literature
 (WAL)
Western Folklore
Western Review (A Literary
 Quarterly)
Wilson Library Bulletin
 (formerly Wilson Bulletin
 for Librarians)
Wings; The Literary Guild
 Review
Wisconsin Studies in Con-
 temporary Literature
Woman's Home Companion
Writer's Yearbook

Yale Review

GENERAL INDEX (AUTHOR, SUBJECT, AND TITLE)

Aaron, Daniel 668
Abels, Cyrilly 669
Abramson, Ben 670-671
Adams, James Donald 133, 177, 234, 320, 342, 672-674
Adams, Scott 675
Adey, Alvin 676
ADAPTATIONS 290-295
Adrian, Daryl 677
Agee, James 565, 679
Albee, Edward 1693, 1922
Aldiss, Brian (ed.) 59
Aldridge, John W. 1077
Alexander, Charlotte 395
Alexander, Stanley Gerald 381, 419, 681-682
Allen, Fred 129
Allen, Walter 683-686
American Academy of Arts and Letters 357
Anderson, Hilton 691-692
Anderson, Sherwood 1572
Anderson, Wallace L. (ed.) 1503
Angoff, Allan (ed.) 693
Angoff, Charles 694
Anstey, Edgar 493, 545, 558, 640
ANTHOLOGIZED WORKS 352-356
Antico, John 695
Apseloff, Stanford S. 696
Armitage, Merle 697
Arno, Peter 49
Arrowsmith, J. E. S. 698

ARTICLES ABOUT STEINBECK 668-2140
Asselineau, Roger 700
Astro, Richard 380, 387, 420, 703-711, 992, 1234, 1425, 1530
Atkinson, Brooks 713-717
Atkinson, Oriana 718
Atkinson, Ted 719-720
Atticus 97
AUDIO-VISUAL MATERIAL 442-445

Bach, Bert C. 22
Baker, Carlos 726-737
Baker, Denys Val (ed.) 1758
Baker, Howard 738-739
Baker, Nelson M. 740
Baldwin, James 1948
Ball State University Library 358
Bancroft Library, University of California 372
Barbour, Brian M. 741-742, 1460
Barnes, Douglas R. (ed.) 55
Barney, Virginia 743
Barron, Louis 744
Barry, Iris 745
Barry, John D. 407
Baudelaire 1785
Beach, Joseph Warren 393, 746-750
Beck, Warren 1474

Covici, Pascal, Jr. 388,
947-948, 950-951
Cowley, Malcolm 382, 952-
956
Cox, Martha Heasley 957
Coyle, William (ed.) 329
Crandell, R. F. 958
Crane, Milton (ed.) 37
CRITICISM (BOOKS) 380-
394
CRITICISM (DOCTORAL DIS-
SERTATIONS) 419-438
CRITICISM, IN PERIODICALS
& BOOKS 668-2140
CRITICISM (MONOGRAPHS,
BOOKLETS, AND
PAMPHLETS) 395-418
Crockett, H. Kelly 382, 960-
961
Cummins, P. D. 962
Cunliffe, Marcus 963
Cuppy, Will 964
Current-Garcia, Eugene
(ed.) 69

Daiches, David 966
Davis, Elmer 968-969
Davis, Robert Murray (ed.)
381, 776, 893, 1058,
1072, 1145, 1154, 1412,
1416, 2146
Davis, Thurston N. 1215
Dawson, Margaret C.
970-971
Degnan, J. P. 380
Delisle, Arnold F. 973
DeMott, Benjamin, 974
DeMott, Robert 380, 975-
976, 2147
Dent, Alan 645, 656, 977
DeRoos, Robert 978
De Schweinitz, George
382, 979
DeVolld, Walter L. 982-983
DeVoto, Bernard 984-987
Dickinson, Asa Don 989
Dickinson, A. T., Jr.
2148

Didion, J. 990
Dietrich, R. F. 991
Ditsky, John 380, 387,
423, 439, 922-994
DOCTORAL DISSERTATIONS
419, 438
Dodds, John W. 996
Dodson, Kenneth 262
Dohanos, Stevan 307, 351
Dolbier, Maurice 997
Dolch, Martin 43, 1257
Donohue, Agnes McNeill (ed.)
270, 382, 806, 809, 871,
874, 880, 891, 929, 953,
960, 979, 998, 1001, 1013,
1022, 1071, 1125, 1189,
1192, 1209, 1287, 1426,
1463, 1468, 1507, 1539,
1575, 1619, 1707, 1831,
1832, 1837, 1925, 1928,
2012, 2047, 2100, 2113,
2118, 2149
Dos Passos, John 438,
1846, 2047
Dougherty, Charles T.
382, 1001
Doughty, Howard H., Jr.
1002
Downs, Robert B. (ed.)
1002(a)
Dreiser, Theodore 242,
1003, 1918
Duchene, Anne 1006
Duffus, R. C. 1007-1008
Duffy, Charles 1009
Duhamel, P. Albert 1010
Dunaway, Philip 325, 1011
Dunn, Thomas F. 382,
960, 1012-1013
Dunning, Stephen 1570
Durant, Ariel (ed.) 1014
Durant, Will (ed.) 1014
Durgnat, Raymond 526
Dusenbury, Winifred L.
1015
Dvorak, Jermila 1016

210

211

Hawthorne, Nathaniel 998
Hayashi, Tetsumaro 380,
386-387, 408-409, 742,
914, 992, 1217-1232,
1234, 1425, 1530, 1566,
1889, 2156-2160
Hayman, Lee Richard 440,
1233
Hedgpeth, Joel W. 380,
1234-1235
Hedley, George 1236
Hefner, Hugh M. (ed.) 59
Heiney, Donald W. 1237,
1237(a), 1238
Hemenway, Robert 1239
Hemingway, Ernest 437-
438, 760, 867, 939,
1354, 1434, 1572, 1697,
1738, 1822, 2047
Henderson, Caroline A. (ed.)
384, 1240
Hendrick, George 2155
Henning, Carol 995, 2091
Hersey, John 1241
Herzberg, Max J. (ed.)
1242
Hester, Sister Mary 1243,
1842
Hickey, Neil 1244
Hicks, Granville 1245-1247
Higashiyama, Masayoshi
1248
Highland, Frederick C. 410
Hildebrand, William H.
1249
Hill, Clarence Gohdes (ed.)
2161
Hinkel, Edgar J. 1250
Hirose, Hidekazu 1251,
1251(a)
Hitchcock, Alfred 526-528
Hitler, Adolf 1137
Hobson, L. Z. 1252
Hodgart, Matthew 1253
Hoellering, Franz 505
Hoffman, Frederick J.
1254-1255
Hoffman, Hester R. (ed.)

2162
Hogan, William 1256
Holman, C. Hugh 1259,
1652
Horton, Rod W. 1458
Houghton, Donald E. 690,
1260
Houghton Library, Harvard
University 361
Houlihan, T. 1261
Houston, Penelope 470
Howard, Leon 1262
Hughes, Riley 1263-1265
Huie, William Bradford
1266
Humanities Research Center
(University of Texas at
Austin) 2163
Humphries, Rolfe 30
Hunter, Anne 1267
Hunter, J. Paul 388, 1268-
1269
Hurtik, Emil 32, 2043
Hutchens, John K. 1271-
1272
Huxley, A. 738
Hyman, Stanley Edgar 393,
1273-1277, 1277(a)

Inazawa, Hideo 2008
Indiana University Library
362
Inglis, R. B. (ed). 32
Inoue, Atsuko 1279
Inoue, Kenji 1279
Isaacs, Edith J. R. 1283-
1285
Isaacs, Hermine Rich 495-
579
Isherwood, Christopher 382,
1286-1287
Ishi, Ichiro (ed.) 1564

Jack, Peter Monro 1290
Jackson, Frank Henry 1291
Jackson, Joseph Henry 50,
264, 355, 384, 388, 411,
1292-1309, 1652, 2164

213

224

Witham, W. Tasker 2110-2111
Wolfe, Thomas 844
Wollaston, Nicholas 2113
Woodress, James 382, 1112
Woods, Ralph L. 24
Woodward, Robert H. (ed.) 311, 322, 1249
Wooster, Harold A. 2114
Wooten, William Patrick 519
Worsley, T. C. 2116
Wright, Austin 1385
Wright, Basil 521, 600
Wright, Celeste Turner 382, 2118
Wyatt, Bryant N. 2121
Wyatt, Euphemia Van Rensselaer 2122-2126
Wylder, Robert C. 32

Yale University Library 379
Yano, Shigeharu 2130-2133
Yarber, Robert 32, 2043
Yoshida, Hiroshige 2134
Young, Leo Vernon 438
Young, Stanley 2135
Young, Stark 2136-2139

Zola, Emile 1343
Zolotow, Sam 2140